Building Higher Education Cooperation with the EU

Global Perspectives on Higher Education

Series Editors

Philip G. Altbach
(*Center for International Higher Education, Boston College, USA*)
Hans de Wit
(*Center for International Higher Education, Boston College, USA*)
Rebecca Schendel
(*Center for International Higher Education, Boston College, USA*)

This series is co-published with the Center for International Higher Education at Boston College.

VOLUME 49

The titles published in this series are listed at *brill.com/gphe*

Building Higher Education Cooperation with the EU

Challenges and Opportunities from Four Continents

Edited by

Elizabeth Balbachevsky, Yuzhuo Cai,
Heather Eggins and Svetlana Shenderova

BRILL
SENSE

LEIDEN | BOSTON

All chapters in this book have undergone peer review.

The Library of Congress Cataloging-in-Publication Data is available online at http://catalog.loc.gov

Typeface for the Latin, Greek, and Cyrillic scripts: "Brill". See and download: brill.com/brill-typeface.

ISSN 2214-0859
ISBN 978-90-04-44540-6 (paperback)
ISBN 978-90-04-44541-3 (hardback)
ISBN 978-90-04-44542-0 (e-book)

Copyright 2021 by Koninklijke Brill NV, Leiden, The Netherlands.
Koninklijke Brill NV incorporates the imprints Brill, Brill Hes & De Graaf, Brill Nijhoff, Brill Rodopi, Brill Sense, Hotei Publishing, mentis Verlag, Verlag Ferdinand Schöningh and Wilhelm Fink Verlag.
All rights reserved. No part of this publication may be reproduced, translated, stored in a retrieval system, or transmitted in any form or by any means, electronic, mechanical, photocopying, recording or otherwise, without prior written permission from the publisher. Requests for re-use and/or translations must be addressed to Koninklijke Brill NV via brill.com or copyright.com.

This book is printed on acid-free paper and produced in a sustainable manner.

Contents

Foreword IX
   Ulrich Teichler
Acknowledgements XIII
List of Acronyms XIV
List of Figures and Tables XIX
Notes of Contributors XX

PART 1
Introduction

1 Higher Education Cooperation between the EU and Countries in Four Continents: From the Perspective of the Internationalisation of Higher Education 3
   Elizabeth Balbachevsky, Yuzhuo Cai, Heather Eggins and Svetlana Shenderova

PART 2
Higher Education Cooperation and Internationalisation: Global and European Overview

2 Higher Education and Research Policies: The Current Global Agenda and Implications for International Cooperation 15
   Merle Jacob and Mary-Louise Kearney

3 Internationalisation in EU Higher Education: Between National Concerns, EU Internal Policy and Global Ambitions 35
   Nadine Burquel and Laura Ballesteros

PART 3
The Context of Higher Education Cooperation and Internationalisation in Countries of the Four Continents

4 Brazil-EU Cooperation in Higher Education 53
   Creso M. Sá and Magdalena Martinez

5 China's Policies and Practices with Respect to Higher Education Cooperation with the EU   68
    Yuzhuo Cai and Gaoming Zheng

6 Russia-EU Internationalisation of Higher Education: Cooperation vs Competition?   86
    Svetlana Shenderova

7 The Policy Context of EU-South Africa Higher Education Cooperation: An Overview of Policies and Practices   107
    Patrício V. Langa and Charl Wolhuter

PART 4
Case Studies: How Higher Education Institutions of the EU and Countries from the Four Continents Collaborate

8 EU-Brazil Cooperation: The Science without Borders Programme Experience   129
    Cintia Denise Granja and Ana Maria Carneiro

9 Higher Education Internationalisation and Student Integration: A Case Study of Chinese Students' Social and Academic Integration in Finland   146
    Hanwei Li

10 Seeds of Success in Russian-Dutch Collaboration: The Case of a Higher Education Capacity-Building Project   163
    Olga Ustyuzhantseva, Olga Zvonareva, Klasien Horstman and Evgenia Popova

11 South Africa: The Role of Cross-Continental Research Initiatives: Case Studies of the EU and Others   182
    Patrício V. Langa and Charl Wolhuter

PART 5
Conclusion

12   Opportunities and Challenges in Higher Education Cooperation between the EU and Four Continents: Towards a Typology of the Internationalisation of Higher Education   199
   Elizabeth Balbachevsky, Yuzhuo Cai, Heather Eggins and Svetlana Shenderova

Index   215

Foreword

Experts agree that higher education has been challenged again and again in recent decades to examine its basic concepts and practices. The enormous expansion of higher education has provoked a search for more diverse profiles of institutions, study programmes and research priorities. The growing relevance of systematic knowledge for many spheres in life, often referred to by the term "knowledge society", is widely interpreted as an incentive for higher education to strive for a better balance between efforts to raise quality according to internal academic criteria and making an impact which is clearly visible to society at large. Last, but not least, awareness has grown in recent decades that higher education in each country is affected increasingly by international cultural, social, economic and technological developments. It therefore has to find ways of enhancing knowledge and understanding of these international challenges and of shaping international cooperation in higher education.

Traditionally, higher education has been more international in some respects than most other sectors of society. Knowledge in many disciplines is universal and crosses borders freely. It is customary all over the world to search for improvements in our fundamental knowledge base, and the intellectual climate in higher education institutions is often more cosmopolitan than anywhere else. On the other hand, organisational matters of higher education, such as funding, study programmes and degrees, academic careers, etc. continue to be formed according to national conventions and regulations. This paradoxical situation of an extraordinarily strong international leaning and a system that has been developed within a country has always created substantial difficulties for participants in the higher education system to shape the internationality of higher education in a consistent and convincing way.

Obviously, higher education has become increasingly international in recent decades, and efforts have been intensified to ensure that this fact is recognised at all levels. But institutions of higher education and scholars have always faced problems of shaping their international activities consistently according to their potential and their goals. The international political scene as well as the dominant foreign policies of their respective countries tend to have a powerful influence, which might open doors but also imply constraints.

Institutions of higher education and scholars also face difficulties in opting for policies of internationalisation and pursuing international activities in tune with their potential and their strategic views. This is because concurrent general higher education policies are often dogmatic and inconsistent. For example, globalisation trends are often proclaimed in higher education policy discourses with the obvious intention of declaring certain developments in certain countries as most modern and irreversible and to push others to follow suit. Also, managerial and "ranking" fads in higher education are advocated internationally as best practice which should be followed in order to open the door for internationalisation of higher education. However, these often turn out to be irrelevant or even counterproductive in reality. Furthermore, the "knowledge society" paradigm is often interpreted as calling for a complete utilitarian subordination of international activities in higher education under currently dominant economic policy rationales. Moreover, internationality of higher education is frequently interpreted as merely vertical; economically and academically less advanced countries and institutions are strongly urged to imitate higher education in the more advanced ones, and international mobility should be primarily upwards with the aim of adapting to the best.

Fortunately, however, such kinds of pressures, which limit the chances of higher education institutions and scholars of making appropriate decisions in terms of international cooperation and other international activities, are not as dominant as their proponents wish and their critics fear. There is clear evidence that the conditions for institutions of higher education and for scholars in Europe are far more complex and all together more flexible. For example, the ERASMUS programme, which was established in 1987 in order to promote intra-European short-term mobility and triggered many other cross-border activities in Europe, made the higher education institutions, departments and scholars involved aware that curricula have to be opened conceptually to accept knowledge emphasised in other countries as equally valuable to knowledge emphasised at home in order to provide a real chance for students to "learn from comparison". Also, the acceptance by most Europe countries since the late 1990s of the so-called "Bologna Process" showed an enormous willingness to change study conditions and provisions at home in order to facilitate international student mobility. In addition, such acceptance led to other ways of cooperation between higher education institutions and scholars both within Europe and between Europe and other countries of the world. Both initiatives indicate a widespread awareness in Europe that international cooperation is most fruitful if the cooperating partners reflect and call into question their own national higher education traditions in this process of cooperation.

Moreover, thorough analyses undertaken in the early years of the 21st century and again about a decade later have shown that the internationalisation policies of the governmental agencies in charge of higher education as well as the internationalisation strategies of higher education vary substantially between the European countries (see de Wit et al., 2015; Huisman & van der Wende, 2004, 2005). This suggests that the door is quite open in many European countries for the institutions and for individual scholars to opt for internationalisation strategies which they consider meaningful and creative as well as being in tune with their specific aims and objectives.

All in all, we note that there is an abundance of documents analysing international policies and activities in the higher education systems of economically advanced countries. Internationalisation seems to be nowadays the single most popular theme in the public discourse on higher education. The emphasis in these analyses on the internationalisation of higher education in developing countries has grown substantially in recent years. This book is distinctive in providing a wealth of information on the international dimension of higher education in select countries other than the economically most advanced ones. It is also unique in examining the actual international cooperation between the various drivers of these emerging countries located on different continents and of the economically advanced countries in Europe. Special attention is paid to relatively large countries such as Brazil, China, Russia and South Africa.

It should be pointed out that most of the editors and most of the authors of this book have had a dual biographic relationship to the thematic area of analysis: they have been involved in higher education policy and practice and thus in professional work of shaping the daily life in higher education, and they have been active in research on higher education. This obviously has contributed to a good understanding of the conditions under which internationalisation policies and strategies in higher education are developed as well as to a comprehensive view of the complexity of the conditions under which international cooperation of higher education operates and tries to find the most fruitful modes of survival and success.

The range of authors and the range of analysis is too wide to allow a concise comprehensive summary in this preface of the findings presented in this book. But altogether, it suggests that it is justified to look with cautious optimism at the potential for international cooperation between these four countries from four continents and the European countries by institutions and scholars. On the one hand, there are enormous constraints due to widespread international misunderstandings; these arise from the foreign and economic policies of the individual countries not in tune with the aim of international cooperation in higher education. Current fads in higher education policy and management aimed at steering higher education in ways which are not the most conducive for creative international cooperation can also be very unhelpful. On the other hand, there are many interesting examples of international cooperation between the countries which are addressed in this book. It is hoped that this will contribute to a creative increase in the quality and relevance of higher education to the modern world and to improved international understanding.

References

de Wit, H., Hunter, F., Howard, L.& Egron-Polak, E. (Eds.). *Internationalisation of Higher Education: Study* (pp. 273–280). European Union. https://www.europarl.europa.eu/RegData/etudes/STUD/2015/540370/IPOL_STU(2015)540370_EN.pdf

Huisman, J., & van der Wende, M. (2004). *On cooperation and competition. National and European policies for the internationalisation of higher education.* Lemmens.

Huisman, J., & van der Wende, M. (2005). *On cooperation and competition II. Institutional responses to internationalisation, Europeanisation and globalisation.* Lemmens.

Ulrich Teichler
Former Director, International Centre for Higher Education Research (INCHER-Kassel), University of Kassel, Kassel (Germany)

Acknowledgements

The editors wish to acknowledge the support of their families and friends, with particular help from Jack Simmons and Jean Mangan for their work on the editing. It has been a truly collaborative project which has provided stimulating insights.

Acronyms

AAACSB	Association to Advance Collegiate Schools of Business
AAAS	American Association for the Advancement of Science
ABS	Australian Bureau of Statistics
ACP	African, Caribbean and Pacific
ACUP	Catalan Association of Public Universities (Catalonia, Spain)
ADB	Asian Development Bank
ADBI	Asian Development Bank Institute
AfDB	African Development Bank
AIP	American Institute of Physics
AMBA	Association of MBAs (Master of Business Administration degree)
APIKS	Academic Profession in Knowledge Society (survey)
APRU	Association of Pacific Rm Universities
ARC	European Research Council
ARES	Belgian Academy of Higher Education and Research
ARWU	Academic Ranking of World Universities (also known as the Shanghai Rankings)
ASEAN	Association of South East Asian Nations
AU	African Union
BERD	Bureau for Expenditure on Research and Development (Singapore)
BIAC	Business Advisory Committee (OECD)
BRAFITEC	Brazil-France Program for technology and Engineering
BRICS	Brazil, Russia, India, China, and South Africa
CAP	Changing Academic Profession
CAPES	Foundation Coordination for the Improvement of Higher Education Personnel, Quality Assurance agency of the Brazilian Federal Ministry of Education
CAPES-PrInt	Programme for Institutional Internationalization of the Higher Education Institutions and Research Institutions of Brazil
CCISP	Portuguese Polytechnics Coordinating Council
CERI OECD	Centre for Educational Research and Innovation, Organization for Economic Cooperation and Development
CESA 16–25	Continental Education Strategy for Africa 2016–2025 (African Union)
CFM	EU-China Co-funding Mechanisms for Research and Innovation
CHE	Council of Higher Education
CIA	Central Intelligence Agency
CIFRE-Brasil	Industrial Partnership for learning through research Brazil-France
CNPq	National Council for Scientific and Technological Development

ACRONYMS

CNRS	French National Centre for Scientific Research
COFECUB	Programme for international cooperation between CAPES and the French Committee for evaluation of the higher education and science cooperation with Brazil
COLUMBUS	Network of Latin American and European Universities for training and cooperation
CONACYT	National Council for Science and Technology (Mexico)
CONICYT	National Commission for Scientific and Technological Research (Chile)
COVID-19	Coronavirus disease 2019
CRASP	Conference of Rectors of Academic Schools in Poland
CRUP	Council of Rectors of Portuguese Universities
CSC	China Scholarship Council
CsF	Science Without Borders Programme (SwB)
DAAD	German Academic Exchange Service
DHET	Department of Higher Education and Training
DMAG	Arab Maghreb Union
DST	Department of Science and Technology
DZS	Centre for International Cooperation in Education (Czech Republic)
EACEA	Education, Audiovisual and Culture Executive Agency
EC	European Commission
ECTS	European Credit Transfer System
Education 2020	Guidelines on National Mid- and Long-Term Educational Reform and Development Planning (2010–2020)
EEA	European Economic Area
EHEA	European Higher Education Area
EIT	European Institute of Technology
ENQA	European Association for Quality Assurance in Higher Education
EQAR	European Register for Higher Education
EQUIS	European Quality Improvement System (for accreditation of business and management schools)
ERA	European Research Area
ERASMUS	European Union Student Exchange Programme launched in 1987
ERASMUS+	EU's programme to support education, training, youth and sport in Europe
ESIG	Ecole Superieure Internationale de Gestion (Business School in Casablanca and Rabat, Morocco)
ESSEC	Ecole Superieure des Sciences Economiques et Commerciales (Paris Business School founded in 1907 with campuses in Singapore and Rabat, Morocco)
EU	European Union
Eurydice	network of 43 national units based in all 38 countries of the Erasmus+ programme

FAPESP	São Paulo Research Foundation
FNDCT	National Fund for the Development of Science and Technology
FONDAP	Fund for Research Centres in Priority Areas (Chile)
FONDECYT	National Fund for Scientific and Technological Development (Chile)
FP	Framework Programme
FP7	seventh framework programme for research
FTE	full-time equivalency
GUNI	Global University for Innovation
HAQAA	Harmonising, Quality Assurance and Accreditation
HE	Higher Education
HEA	Higher Education Authority (Ireland)
HEI(s)	Higher Education Institution(s)
HEPCE	EU-China Higher Education Platform for Cooperation and Exchange
HER	Higher Education and Research
HES	Higher Education Systems
HPLD	(EU-Africa) High-Level Policy Dialogue ICT: Information, Communication and Technological
HPPD	EU-China High-level-People-to-People Dialogue
HRC	Hungarian Rectors' Conference
IADB	Inter American Development Bank
ICT	Information and Communication Technology
IDB	Invest Investment agency of the Inter American Development Bank
IESEG	School of Business Management of the Catholic University of Lille, France
IGO	Inter Governmental Organization
INRIA	The French national institute for computer science and applied mathematics
INSERM	French Health Institute
IoHE	internationalisation of higher education
IRD	French Research Institute for Development
ITN	Innovative Training Network
IVET	Initial Vocational Education and Training
KCUE	Korean Council for University Education (Republic of Korea)
KE	Knowledge Economy
KFU	Kazan Federal University
KICS	Knowledge and Innovation Communities
KPI(s)	key performance indicator(s)
KS	Knowledge Society
LAC	Latin America and the Caribbean
LERU	League of European Research Universities
MCTI	Ministry of Science, Technology and Innovation
MEC	Ministry of Education (Brazil)

MEXT	Ministry of Education, Culture, Sport, Science and Technology (Japan)
MinEd	Ministry of Education
MITACS	Mathematics of Information Technology and Complex Systems Platform (Canada)
MNCS	Mean Normalised Citation Score
MoE	Ministry of Education in China
MOST	Ministry of Sciences and Technology in China
MSCA	Marie Skłodowska Curie Actions
MSU	Lomonosov Moscow State University
NCPS	National Contact Points
NIED	National Institute for Educational Development (Republic of Korea)
NISTEP	National Institute of Science and Technology Policy (Japan)
NMP	New Management Philosophy
NSFC	National Natural Science Foundation of China
NUFFIC	Dutch Organisation for Internationalisation in Education
OBOR	Policy: "One Belt One Road" Policy or "New Silk Road" Policy
OeAD GmbH	Austria Service Centre for European and international mobility and cooperation programmes in the fields of education, science and research
OECD	Organization for Economic Cooperation and Development
OMC	Open Method of Coordination
PISA OECD	Programme for International Student Assessment
PROAFRICA	Research Support Program for Collaboration with African Countries
PROSUL	Research Support Program for Collaboration with South America Countries
QF-EHEA	Qualification Framework for European Higher Education Area
QS	Quacquarelli Symonds (Education Consulting firm specialised in university rankings)
RBC	Royal Bank of Canada
R&D	Research and Development
R&I	Research and Innovation
Regulation SFCRS	Regulations on Sino-Foreign Cooperation in Running Schools
RF	Russian Federation
RF Government	Government of the Russian Federation
RIKEN	Japan's largest scientific research institution founded in 1917
RMB	Ren Min Bi (Currency: Chinese yuan)
RUS	Research Universities
SA	South Africa
SADC	Southern African Development Community
SDG	Sustainable Development Goals
SMES	small- and medium-sized enterprises
SPbSU	Saint-Petersburg State University
STEM	Science, Technology, Engineering and Mathematics

STI	Science Technology and Innovation
SwB	Science without Borders
TDCA	Trade, Development and Cooperation Agreements
TEKS OECD	Tertiary Education in the Knowledge Society
THE	Times Higher Education
TRANSMIC	Transnational Migration, Citizenship and the Circulation of Rights and Responsibilities
TUAC OECD	Trade Union Advisory Committee
TVET	Technical and Vocational Education and Training
UAS	University of Applied Sciences
UASR	University Alliance of the New Silk Road
UHR	Swedish Council for Higher Education
UK	United Kingdom
UNDP	United Nations Development Programme
UNESCO	United National Educational, Cultural and Scientific Organization
UNICAMP	State University of Campinas
Universitas 21 (U21)	Network of research-intensive universities
UNU	United Nations University
USA	United States of America
USSR	Union of Soviet Socialist Republics
VET	Vocational Education and Training
VLUHR	The Flemish Council of Universities and Colleges
WB	World Bank
WCHE UNESCO	World Conference on Higher Education
WCS UNESCO	World Conference for Science
WTO	World Trade Organization
WUR(s)	world university rankings

Figures and Tables

Figures

8.1 Destination countries of UNICAMP SwB grants, 2011–2015 (based on data from CsF, 2016).   138
8.2 Evolution of partnerships between UNICAMP and international institutions, 2008–2018 (based on data from UNICAMP, 2019).   139
12.1 Policy logics of internationalisation of higher education: The EU and four countries.   203

Tables

5.1 Compatibility of the EU's and China's expectations for the internationalisation of higher education.   75
8.1 SwB European Union partners.   135
12.1 Typology for the internationalisation of higher education: political economy drivers.   202
12.2 Compatibility of policy logics of the internationalisation of higher education between the EU and the four countries.   209

Notes of Contributors

Editors

Elizabeth Balbachevsky
is Associate Professor at the Department of Political Science at the University of São Paulo (USP), Brazil, Director of USP's Center for Public Policy Research (NUPPs/USP), and Fellow at the Laboratory of Studies in Higher Education, State University of Campinas. From 2016 up to 2017 she was Head of the International Affairs Office at the Department of Higher Education, Ministry of Education, Brazil. She is the Regional Editor for Latin America for the *Encyclopedia of International Higher Education Systems and Institutions* (Springer, 2020).

Yuzhuo Cai
is a Senior Lecturer and Adjunct Professor at the Higher Education Group (HEG), Faculty of Management and Business, Tampere University, Finland. He has been with the HEG for 18 years and was the Acting Professor there from August 2013 to July 2014. He is the Director of Sino-Finnish Education Research Centre, a board member of the Triple Helix Association and the Associate Editor of the *Triple Helix Journal*. His main teaching and research areas are higher education policy and management, organisation theory, internationalisation of higher education, innovation studies and comparative education, with over 100 scholarly publications in these fields.

Heather Eggins
is Visiting Professor and Senior Research Fellow at Staffordshire University, UK, and Fellow Commoner at Lucy Cavendish College, University of Cambridge. Her areas of higher education research include policy and strategy, access and equity, quality assurance and enhancement, and globalisation. She was a Fulbright New Century Scholar, Director of the Society for Research into Higher Education, and a consultant to UNESCO. Recent publications include the edited book *The Changing Roles of Women in Higher Education* (Springer, 2017) and a chapter on the challenges of Brexit for UK higher education, in *Universities as Political Institutions* (L. Weimer and T. Nokkala, eds., Brill | Sense, 2020).

Svetlana Shenderova
is a Researcher of EDUneighbours study of Finnish-Russian double degree implementation, hosted by Tampere University, Finland. She has worked for more than 30 years in research, administration, consulting and expertise in

the fields of higher education policies, internationalisation, university governance and degree programme management focusing on transaction costs of EU-Russia internationalisation. She has worked in academia as an associate professor being involved in teaching, research and consulting projects in nine Russian universities. Svetlana holds a D.Econ.Sc. (St. Petersburg State University of Economics and Finance, 2012), and PhD in Political Economy (St. Petersburg State University, 1997).

Authors

Laura Ballesteros
is a consultant specialising in research on higher education and vocational education and training. Her areas of expertise include internationalisation, quality assurance, adult education and skill development. She has more than 10 years of experience in the field having participated in projects funded by the EU, OECD, and World Bank, among others. She has a background in International Relations and earned a Master of Philosophy in Higher Education as an Erasmus Mundus scholar with an in-service training at the European Commission. She is a current member of the Board of Trustees of the Universidad del Noroccidente de Latinoamérica.

Nadine Burquel
is Director of BCS, a strategy consultancy specialising in higher education. As international expert she has some 30 years' experience in EU higher education policies and programmes, internationalisation, governance and leadership, quality assurance, entrepreneurship and innovation. She has worked extensively in Europe, South East Asia, the Middle East, Africa, Russia, and with universities in Australia, the US, Canada and Latin America. In the HUMANE network of heads of administration in universities, she is director of three highly successful leadership programmes for senior managers of professional services. Until recently she was EFMD director of business school services.

Ana Maria Carneiro
is a researcher at the Centre for Public Policy Studies (NEPP) at UNICAMP, Brazil, where she conducts studies regarding access and success in Higher Education, student engagement, undergraduate and graduate student experience, evaluation of higher education and science and technology programmes. She is the Coordinator of the Laboratory for Studies in Higher Education (LEES) and also a Collaborator Professor at the Graduate Program in Science & Tech-

nology Policy. Since 2018, she has been the advisor for Institutional Evaluation at the Office of Vice-President where she coordinates the current cycle of institutional evaluation in close collaboration with strategic planning.

Cintia Denise Granja
is a PhD Fellow at the United Nations University (UNU-MERIT), in the Programme on Innovation, Economics and Governance for Development. She holds a bachelor degree in Economics and a master in Science and Technology Policy from the University of Campinas (UNICAMP), Brazil.

Klasien Horstman
is Professor of Philosophy of Public Health at Maastricht University, in The Netherlands. Drawing from philosophy, sociology, and science and technology studies she studies the dynamics of science, politics and society in diverse public health practices: (mental) health promotion, health promotion at the workplace, community health, vaccination, and antimicrobial resistance prevention. As she is interested in participatory approaches to public health, she developed an urban health living lab in disadvantaged neighbourhoods in Maastricht (www.universiteitmetdebuurt.nl). She was coordinator of BIHSENA and is director of the Maastricht-Tomsk Participatory Public Health Center (https://www.makinghealthpublic.org/). For more information about her work, see www.klasienhorstman.nl

Merle Jacob
is Professor of Research Policy at Lund University and UNESCO Chair in Research Management and Innovation Systems. Professor Jacob's main research interest is in the governance of science. Her current project is focused on research funding instruments and their impact on research scholarship.

Mary-Louise Kearney
is an Honorary Research Fellow of Auckland University, New Zealand. After Director posts at UNESCO, she established Kearney Consulting collaborating with the OECD/IMHE Programme for university management and the Sida/Sweden IHERD Programme for higher education, research and innovation. Other appointments include Senior Research Fellow of Oxford University's Education Department, a Vice-President of the Society for Research into Higher Education, and Special Issues co-editor for the SRHE Journal, *Studies in Higher Education*. A consulting editor for Cambridge Scholars Publishing, she has authored numerous publications on Higher Education policy and practice.

NOTES OF CONTRIBUTORS   XXIII

Patrício V. Langa
is an Associate Professor of Sociology & Higher Education Studies at the University of the Western Cape (UWC), South Africa and Eduardo Mondlane University (UEM), Mozambique. He is a visiting Professor and Research Fellow at the Royal Institute of Technology, Sweden, Danube University Krems, Austria, and Universidade Autonoma de Lisboa, Portugal. He is also the Adviser of the UEM Rector for Strategic Planning. Professor Langa served as the National Executive Director of the HE Quality Council (CNAQ), Mozambique. He is the founding President of the Mozambican Sociological Association (AMS). His research interests and publications are in the intersection between Sociology and Comparative Higher Education, Policy and Innovation Studies.

Hanwei Li
is a research associate at Manchester China Institute, University of Manchester. She holds a PhD in education from Tampere University and a PhD in Sociology from Bielefeld University. She was a Marie Curie PhD researcher working on a European Commission funded project-Transnational Migration, Citizenship and the Circulation of Rights and Responsibilities (TRANSMIC). Her research interests include Asia-Europe student mobility, academic integration, sociocultural integration, internationalisation of higher education transnationalism, investment migration and citizenship.

Magdalena Martinez
is a PhD candidate, the Centre for the Study of Canadian and International Higher Education, and Coordinator of the Higher Education Program at OISE.

Evgeniya Popova
is Associate Professor of Department of Political Science and research fellow at Centre for Policy Analysis and Studies of Technologies at the Tomsk State University, Russia. She completed her graduate studies at the European University at St. Petersburg and defended her dissertation in political science (Moscow, Moscow State Institute of International Relations). Based on science and technology studies and political science she studies Russian innovation policy, entrepreneurial strategies in Russian high-tech industries, and interaction of infrastructure and everyday life in Russian cities.

Creso M. Sá
is Professor of Higher Education at the Ontario Institute for Studies in Education (OISE), University of Toronto. He is Director of the Centre for the Study of

Canadian and International Higher Education, and Coordinator of the Higher Education Program at OISE.

Ulrich Teichler

is Professor Emeritus at the International Centre for Higher Education Research Kassel (INCHER), Universität Kassel. His research interests are in Qualitative Social Research and Quantitative Social Research. Major themes of his research on higher education were higher education and the world of work, higher education systems in comparative perspective, the internationality of higher research and the academic profession. After having been active in research projects for more than 40 years, he continues to be involved in advisory activities for institutions, projects and doctoral candidates

Olga Ustyuzhantseva

is a Director of the Centre for Policy Analysis and Studies of Technologies at the Tomsk State University, Russia. In 2014, she earned her PhD in history by researching the development of science, technology, and innovation in India. For the last five years, she has studied the grassroots innovation phenomenon based on the cases of India and Russia. Her current research interests are in innovation development and innovation policy, and the changes in innovation systems due to the growth of the participative activity of society.

Charl Wolhuter

studied at the University of Johannesburg, the University of Pretoria, the University of South Africa and the University of Stellenbosch, South Africa. He obtained a doctorate in Comparative Education at the University of Stellenbosch. He was a junior lecturer in History of Education and Comparative Education at the University of Pretoria and a senior lecturer in History of Education and Comparative Education at the University of Zululand. Currently he is Comparative and International Education Professor at the Potchefstroom Campus of the North-West University, South Africa. He has held Visiting Professorships at i.a. Brock University, Canada; the University of Queensland, Australia, the University of Modena and Reggio Emilio, Italy, and The Education University of Hong Kong. He is the author of various books and articles on History of Education and Comparative Education.

Gaoming Zheng

holds a doctoral degree in higher education research and management from Tampere University, Finland. Her research interest of higher education, covers internationalisation, doctoral education, quality assurance, academic profession, institutional logics. Since 2015 she has been writing and presenting on issues related to international cooperation in higher education, with a focus on Europe-China collaboration. Her doctoral dissertation titled with Quality and Quality Assurance of Europe-China Joint Doctoral Education: An Institutional Logics Perspective was recently published by Tampere University Press.

Olga Zvonareva
is Assistant Professor of Health, Ethics, and Society at Maastricht University in the Netherlands, as well as an Associate Professor at the National Research Tomsk State University and the Siberian State Medical University in Russia. Situated on the intersection of science and technology studies, global health, and bioethics, her research focuses on biomedical knowledge production and public engagement in health. Olga is the coeditor (with Evgeniya Popova and Klasien Horstman) of *Health, Technologies,* and *Politics in Post-Soviet Settings: Navigating Uncertainties,* and the author of *Pharmapolitics in Russia: Making Drugs and Rebuilding the Nation.*

PART 1

Introduction

∴

CHAPTER 1

Higher Education Cooperation between the EU and Countries in Four Continents: From the Perspective of the Internationalisation of Higher Education

Elizabeth Balbachevsky, Yuzhuo Cai, Heather Eggins and Svetlana Shenderova

Abstract

This chapter presents the main issues addressed by this book when analysing the experiences of cooperation between European Union and Brazil, China, Russia and South Africa. These four countries represent four continents, respectively South America, Asia, Europe and Africa. We chose them as important players in political and economic aspects in the EU's international relations. These countries are also a major student source for the European higher education market; in recent years all of them have become keen to welcome students from the EU member states and to enhance their internationalisation activities in partnership with European higher education institutions.

The internationalisation of higher education receives support from different sides of society. Depending on the perspectives of participants or stakeholders, internationalisation of higher education may mean different things. In fact, one can argue that a successful initiative for university internationalisation answers the expectations of both the university's internal and external stakeholders. However, it is not unusual that efforts to build a successful international partnership go into disarray. One of the challenges to effective internationalisation is the lack of real understanding of the partners' perspective. Awareness of the differences in the rules shaping higher education around the world and of the diversity of goals and expectations each partner brings to the cooperation are the central issues that must be considered when building successful cooperation in higher education. Partners should be aware that higher education is a key factor, historically linked with the state building process and thus an integral part of any country's identity. The complexity of the higher education system in any country should not be underestimated. By systematically studying the policies for the internationalisation of higher education in both the EU and some of its major partners in other continents and reviewing some concrete experiences, this book will further the understanding of the many challenges that stand in the way of building successful international cooperation in the higher education field.

Keywords

Brazil – China – Russia – South Africa – policies for internationalisation of higher education – academic international partnership – source of success of the internationalisation of higher education – sources of failure of the internationalisation of higher education

1 Introduction

In recent years, the European Union (EU) has made rapid development in higher education cooperation with countries outside the EU, facilitated by various programmes. International higher education cooperation is intertwined with the EU's strategy concerning international relations, e.g. on the economic and political dimensions. Indeed, higher education's link to other agendas of the EU has been reinforced by the Lisbon Agenda in 2000 and the Europe 2020 Strategy in 2010, which aimed to develop Europe as a more competitive knowledge economy and to attract global talent (Burquel & Ballesteros, Chapter 3 of this book).

Referring to the practice of the EU's Internationalisation of higher education, however, Brandenburg et al. (2019) argue that 'instead of considering internationalisation as one tool to support social engagement and responsibility – locally, nationally and globally – it is seen as a concept that draws resources, focus and infrastructure away from social engagement'. Accordingly, they call for 'the internationalisation of higher education for society'. A similar observation is made by Cai, Ferrer, and Lastra (2019) in the context of the EU's international cooperation in science, technology and innovation, stating that 'transnational university cooperation … is primarily concerned with the teaching and research missions of universities or with the mobility of knowledge from the human perspective', and not aligning with societal priorities.

The present book is a timely response to the call for scholarly and practical efforts to explore the 'underused potential' (Brandenburg et al., 2019) or 'hidden links' (Cai et al., 2019) for the internationalisation of higher education, by examining higher education cooperation between the EU and some representative third countries. Although the focus of the book is on higher education cooperation itself, the book analyses and discusses the EU's higher education cooperation with the third countries, highlighting its challenges and opportunities associated with the internationalisation of higher education.

The four countries under consideration are Brazil, China, Russia, and South Africa, representing four continents, respectively South America, Asia, Europe and Africa. We chose them as important players from the point of view of the political and economic aspects of the EU's international relations. These countries, listed together in alphabetical order, are a major student source for the European higher education market; in recent years all of them have become keen to welcome students from the EU member states and to enhance their internationalisation activities in partnership with European higher education institutions.

In particular, they have extensive higher education systems based on well-developed secondary education on the related continents and a long history of cooperation with their partners in Western Europe. The oldest universities there were established under the influence of European ideas and since then they have had continuing links with European universities. It is hoped that the lessons drawn from this book may help other countries in understanding the nature of higher education cooperation with the EU, and also support the EU's strategies on higher education cooperation with other countries.

Alongside the growing opportunities to expand and deepen cooperation in higher education between each of the four countries and the EU, there are also challenges to be overcome, largely due to the lack of understanding of each other's higher education systems, traditions, strategic goals, and various stakeholders' interests concerning the internationalisation of higher education. While some available scholarly literature may provide useful empirical insights on the EU's higher education cooperation with a single third country, such as China (Cai, 2019), and Russia (Deriglazova & Mäkinen, 2019), it is rare to see studies comparing and generalising the experience of the EU's higher education cooperation with multiple countries, and using a consistent analytical framework.

The edited book we are offering aims to fill the gaps by providing collected studies on higher education cooperation between the EU and the four countries from various perspectives. Following the discussions on the experience of each chosen country in cooperation with the EU or with higher education partners in the EU member states, we try, in the Conclusion, to categorise and discuss the tendencies, challenges, and opportunities. There, we also make recommendations on what and how the EU and these four countries, along with their stakeholders involved in higher education cooperation, can learn from each other and even make joint efforts in advancing the globalised knowledge society after the Corona crisis.

Specifically, we explore the following questions: what are the main rationales guiding the EU, its national governments, agencies, higher education institutions, academics, and students in these four countries to collaborate internationally? What is the role of the EU in the strategies of internationalisation in the chosen countries? What do governments, institutions, stakeholders and individuals expect to gain from collaboration? And how can the discourse of higher education cooperation and internationalisation be seen from the broad perspective of international relations/strategic partnerships between the EU and the four countries?

Apart from the Introduction and the Conclusion, the book is structured in three parts as follows. The following themes are considered in the volume:
- Part 2 provides a global and European overview of higher education cooperation and internationalisation;
- Part 3 highlights the national contexts of higher education cooperation and internationalisation with the EU in the chosen countries of the four continents;
- Part 4 reviews and discusses the lessons drawn from the case studies in terms of the experience at the institutional level. For each chosen country there is a case study focusing on examples of collaboration with the EU's higher education institutions during the implementation of internationalisation policies.

We hope that our book will be helpful for those in the policy and academic communities concerned with the internationalisation of higher education and its activities implemented in cooperation. We address researchers and students of higher education studies; higher education policy-makers and civil servants; university leaders and administrators engaged in international cooperation; academics involved in internationalisation activities; students whose aim is to gain an international study experience, and their parents; and all the other readers interested to know more of higher education cooperation.

2   The Internationalisation of Higher Education

When it comes to the internationalisation of higher education, one most commonly cited definition is by de Wit, Hunter, and Coelen (2015) who define the internationalisation of higher educations as 'the intentional process of integrating an international, intercultural, or global dimension into the purpose, functions, and delivery of post-secondary education, in order to enhance the quality of education and research for all students and staff and to make a meaningful contribution to society' (de Wit et al., 2015, p. 281). This definition is based on Knight and de Wit (1995) and several rounds of refinement afterwards, but adding an emphasis on the relevance of the internationalisation of higher education for society. At the same time, it should be noted that international cooperation is just one aspect of the Internationalisation of higher education, but not the whole (Brandenburg & de Wit, 2011).

While such a definition of the internationalisation of higher education is comprehensive and becoming popular, it has been noted by Yang (2014) that the definition based on Knight and de Wit (1995) 'is only based on and thus suitable for Western experience'. As the four countries collaborating with the EU are out of the Western context, our book also extends de Wit et al.'s (2015) definition in two ways. First, we conceptualise the internationalisation of higher education to the level of operationalisation aligned with empirical studies. Second, we propose a typology of internationalisation based on comparison of the experiences of the four countries' cooperation with the EU. These are presented in the Conclusion.

Through international cooperation in higher education, two or more academic entities establish connections and develop concrete collaborative initiatives. Among the most important cooperative activities that support the internationalisation of higher education are those of academic staff mobility, student mobility, degree and credit mobility, internationalisation of curricula, and collaborative degree programmes including joint and double degrees.

The internationalisation of higher education receives support from different sides of society. Depending on the perspectives of participants or stakeholders, the internationalisation of higher education may mean different things. In fact, one can argue that a successful initiative for university internationalisation answers the expectations of both the university's internal and external stakeholders. However, it is not unusual that efforts to build a successful international partnership fall into disarray. One of the challenges to effective internationalisation that we shall be examining in this book is the lack of real understanding of the partners' perspective. Awareness of the differences in the rules shaping higher education around the world and of the diversity of goals and expectations each partner brings to the cooperation are the central issues that must be taken into consideration when building successful cooperation in higher education. Partners should be aware that higher education is a key factor historically linked with the process of state building and thus is an integral part of any country's identity (Ordorika & Pusser, 2007). The complexity of the higher education system in any country should not be underestimated. By systematically studying the policies for the internationalisation of higher education in both the EU and some of its major partners in other continents and reviewing some concrete experiences, this book will further the understanding of the many challenges that stand in the way of building successful international cooperation in the higher education field.

From their inception in the 1980s, policies supporting the internationalisation of higher education focused mostly on expanding academic and student mobility. The central rationale behind the programmes for university internationalisation has been the exposure of local academic and student communities to diverse experience in approaches to research and to those enshrined in curriculum design and learning practices, brought about by the links with other academic communities abroad. For the students, this international experience has been supposed to support the development of the skills necessary for facing the challenges posed by globalisation and the competencies leading to the appreciation of the opportunities created by the diversity present in a closely interconnected world.

For society as a whole, a successful policy supporting the internationalisation of higher education creates opportunities for sharing technological assets present in other countries and preparing the country's national system to face the challenges posed by trends and developments taking place in other countries. In this sense, some authors point out that, to some extent, the internationalisation of higher education is a national response to globalisation (Eggins, 2003) (Shenderova provides an overview of this approach in Chapter 6 of this book).

In the eyes of the academics, a successful policy for university internationalisation creates vast opportunities for expanding and reinforcing their links with the international networks of specialists, who share the disciplinary identity and develop cross-disciplinary research agenda (Balbachevsky & Kohtamäki, 2020).

Furthermore, the global challenge posed by the 2020 pandemic caused by the global spread of the Corona virus raises societies' awareness of the centrality of academic research cooperation as a public good. The global research networks linking academics from different continents forged in past years are now a strategic tool which can enable our societies to face and answer the global challenges.

3 Policies for the Internationalisation of Higher Education in Europe

In recent years, European initiatives have achieved significant progress in developing the internationalisation of higher education based on higher education cooperation with countries on other continents. These initiatives were facilitated by several supranational programmes and opened up relevant policy dialogues with higher education institutions and authorities from outside the EU. In this book, we analyse some experiences in internationalisation between the higher education systems of the EU and the chosen countries. In doing this, in Part 2, Chapters 2 and 3 provide the reader with the main framework of the policy context shaping the driver for the internationalisation of higher education in the EU.

In Chapter 2, Mary-Louise Kearney and Merle Jacob articulate a comprehensive review of the policy agenda pursued by the key international organisations in the field of the internationalisation of higher education and other international actors. The chapter also discusses how these organisations support or hinder the development of real patterns of cooperation that could help countries and societies deal with some of the most pressing issues faced by the world, linked to environmental or developmental challenges. In Chapter 3, Nadine Burquel and Laura Ballesteros provide an in-depth overview of the evolving patterns of contemporary EU policies supporting the internationalisation of higher education, with a special emphasis on the policies targeting the partnership between the EU and emerging countries, underlining how these policies have helped to shape the patterns of cooperation between them.

There is a large literature discussing differences in the strategies and goals of internationalisation, as implemented by higher education institutions from different countries in Europe and how the country's policy framework helps to shape these differences (e.g. Huisman & van der Wende, 2005; Graf, 2009; Powell, Graf, Bernhard, Coutrot, & Kieffer, 2012; Curaj, Matei, Pricopie, Salmi, & Scott, 2015).

However, all the processes of internationalisation of higher education involve two or more partners: at least two countries or two institutions from different cultures, and institutional environments. The movement of senders and receivers between countries is well researched: what is less explored by the literature is how the features of domestic higher education systems, domestic rules, cultural practices of their interplay and expectations of both partners shape the design and the extent of success of any collaboration.

4 The Internationalisation of Higher Education with the EU: Policy Perspectives of Building Cooperation from Four Continents

From the point of view of countries outside the EU, their approach to the internationalisation of higher education with the EU carries its own particular challenges both at policy and at institutional level (Shenderova, 2018). For successful international cooperation, it is necessary that both partners are aware of the other's expectations and values, as well as a deep understanding of how the local rules and regulations condition the ways cooperation will unfold. A clear understanding of how the partner's higher education system works could also help to build trust, allowing for the exploration of different collaborative approaches. These dynamics are necessary ones to forge long-lasting partnerships.

Thus, Part 3 explores the differences in the external institutional environments outside higher education institutions in the chosen countries in four continents. In particular, the authors study the policy frameworks, motivations and obstacles for higher education cooperation where the internationalisation of higher education is implemented between the EU and the chosen countries.

In Chapter 4, Creso Sá and Magdalena Martinez review the experience of Brazil-EU cooperation in higher education, basing the discussion on the context of relevant stakeholders, and on long-term patterns of higher education institutions' engagement in internationalisation. The chapter also addresses some relevant recent developments experienced by the Brazilian policy for higher education, exploring the opportunities and challenges these new policies posed to cooperation with the EU. In Chapter 5, Yuzhuo Cai and Gaoming Zheng review China's experience on collaborating with Europe and analyse how the new developments in higher education policies in China shape the design and goals of the country's internationalisation of higher education with the EU. In Chapter 6 Svetlana Shenderova explores rationale, evolution, challenges and opportunities in higher education cooperation between Russia and the EU. The policy measures to support the internationalisation of higher education are investigated in the context of coexistence between the EU and Russia within the European Higher Education Area and their growing competition on the world stage. Finally, Chapter 7 addresses the experience of South Africa, analysing how the new post-apartheid agenda has opened opportunities and framed the country's expectations while deepening the cooperation with the EU and its member states.

5 Cooperation with EU Higher Education Institutions at the Institutional Level: Case Studies

This book also provides a collection of case studies exploring particular examples of cooperation with the EU at the institutional level. Part 4 is dedicated to presenting and exploring particular cases of collaboration with EU partners carried out in higher education institutions in the chosen countries. This section also highlights the challenges and opportunities made available to higher education institutions as a result of collaboration. In Chapter 8 Cintia Granja and Ana Carneiro present and review how the Brazilian programme *Science Without Borders* impacted on the implementation of the internationalisation of higher education with the EU in the country. The authors compare the objectives of the programme announced by the Federal Government, the results achieved and the challenges faced by the higher education institutions whose students participated in the programme. In Chapter 9 Hanwei Li gives an overview of the experience of Chinese students when they integrate into the Finnish internal university environment. In Chapter 10, Olga Ustyuzhantseva, Olga Zvonareva, Klasien Hortsman and Evgenya Popova study the experience of a partnership between Dutch, Bulgarian, Polish, Russian, and Ukrainian higher education institutions in building a double degree programme. The authors investigate the administrative barriers for internationalisation which emerged in establishing a double degree partnership within an external institutional environment, including Russian legislation and the constraints brought about by the differences between the internal institutional environments of the EU and non-EU partners. Chapter 11 examines the significance of the patterns of research collaboration between the EU and South African research institutions and universities. It illustrates the value of such collaboration for South African scholars and institutions in terms of the provision of regional and international frameworks and platforms to enhance strategic cooperation, and integration at both economic, geo-political, research and cultural levels.

The volume thus offers to readers a series of policy chapters which are interleaved with case studies of each country: the insights gained open up a new understanding of the complexity of the notion of internationalisation of higher education, particularly in its manifestation within the countries from four continents interacting with the European Union.

References

Balbachevsky, E., & Kohtamäki, V. (2020). University, science and the new (and old) academic roles: Inner sources of institutional resilience. *Sociologias, 22*(54), 64–86. http://doi.org/10.1590/15174522-99512

Brandenburg, U., de Wit, H., Jones, E., & Leask, B. (2019, April 20). Internationalisation in higher education for society. *University World News – The Global Window of Higher Education*. https://www.universityworldnews.com/post.php?story=20190414195843914

Cai, Y. (2019). China-Europe higher education cooperation: Opportunities and challenges. *Frontiers of Education in China, 14*(2), 167–179. doi:10.1007/s11516-019-0009-5

Cai, Y., Ferrer, B. R., & Lastra, J. L. M. (2019). Building university-industry co-innovation networks in transnational innovation ecosystems: Towards a transdisciplinary approach of integrating social sciences and artificial intelligence. *Sustainability*, *11*(17), 1–23. doi:10.3390/su11174633

Curaj, A., Matei, L., Pricopie, R., Salmi, J., & Scott, P. (2015). *The European higher education area between critical reflections and future policies*. Springer. https://doi.org/10.1007/978-3-319-20877-0

de Wit, H., Hunter, F., & Coelen, R. (2015). Internationalisation of higher education in Europe: Future directions. In H. de Wit, F. Hunter, L. Howard, & E. Egron-Polak (Eds.), *Internationalisation of higher education* (pp. 273–280). European Union.

Deriglazova, L., & Mäkinen, S. (2019). Still looking for a partnership? EU-Russia cooperation in the field of higher education. *Journal of Contemporary European Studies*, *27*(2), 184–195. doi:10.1080/14782804.2019.1593113

Eggins, H. (Ed.). (2003). *Globalization and reform in higher education*. Open University Press.

Graf, L. (2009). Applying the varieties of capitalism approach to higher education: Comparing the internationalisation of German and British universities. *European Journal of Education*, *44*(4), 569–585.

Huisman, J., & Van der Wende, M. (Eds.). (2005). *On cooperation and competition. National and European policies for the internationalisation of higher education*. Lemmens.

Knight, J., & de Wit, H. (1995). Strategies for internationalization of higher education: Historical and conceptual perspectives. In H. de Wit (Ed.), *Strategies for internationalization: A comparative study of Australia, Canada, Europe and the United States of America* (pp. 5–32). EAIE.

Ordorika, I., & Pusser, B. (2007). La máxima casa de estudios: Universidad Nacional Autónoma de México as a state-building university. In P. G. Altbach & J. Balan (Eds.), *World class worldwide: Transforming research universities in Asia and Latin America*. The Johns Hopkins University Press.

Powell, J. J. W., Graf, L., Bernhard, N., Coutrot, L., & Kieffer, A. (2012). The shifting relationship between vocational and higher education in France and Germany: Towards convergence? *European Journal of Education*, *47*(3), 405–423.

Shenderova, S. (2018). Permanent uncertainty as normality? Finnish-Russian double degrees in the post-Crimea world. *Journal of Higher Education Policy and Management*, *40*(6), 611–628. https://doi.org/10.1080/1360080X.2018.1529134

Yang, R. (2014). China's strategy for the internationalization of higher education: An overview. *Frontiers of Education in China*, *9*(2), 151–162. doi:10.1007/bf03397011

PART 2

Higher Education Cooperation and Internationalisation: Global and European Overview

∵

CHAPTER 2

Higher Education and Research Policies: The Current Global Agenda and Implications for International Cooperation

Merle Jacob and Mary-Louise Kearney

Abstract

International collaboration is clearly a key priority in higher education and research (HER) policy and practice. The competition for students and excellent research and teaching staff is now a global one and this is reflected in the increasing salience of phenomena such as the Shanghai and Times Higher Education Rankings for monitoring the performance of HER institutions. This chapter takes its point of departure in the fact of international collaboration and seeks to interrogate and understand the factors that stimulate international collaboration. The chapter focuses on two critical drivers of international academic collaboration: globalisation and the governance initiatives initiated by international governmental organisations (IGOs).

The chapter draws on literature review and an analysis of major global and regional policy priorities to demonstrate the ever-expanding influence of global trends over national HER policy priorities and academia. Numerous IGOs reiterate the importance of knowledge to achieve further progress. Creativity, critical thinking and complex problem-solving capacity are deemed vital. All are intrinsic components of HER policies so support for these domains will surely increase. Academic cooperation, through its partnership with governments and other stakeholders and its renewed role and modalities, emerges as a crucial force to help attain these goals.

The authors contend that international collaboration is an important and persistent feature in an attraction narrative which is intended to position higher education as an entry ticket to a global lifestyle. Reasoning from this perspective, student and scholarly mobility are critical facilitators of globalisation while at the same time being subject to globalising forces. While previous analyses have tended to focus on universities as being objects of globalisation, this chapter extends this.

Keywords

globalisation – knowledge society/economy – HER policy priorities – strategic partnerships – academic cooperation – diverse socio-economic contexts

1   **Introduction**

The purpose of this introductory chapter is to preface the contributions with an outline of the dominant forces that are shaping international collaboration with the European Union in higher education and research (HER). International academic cooperation was initially defined as student exchange and was, up until the latter part of the 20th century, an optional experience. Today, international academic cooperation has expanded well beyond the boundaries of a few student exchange programmes to include a range of activities that are now classified as internationalisation. Given that the focus of this volume is cooperation with EU institutions, we will take our point of departure in the definition of internationalisation that circulates in EU's HER policies.

Following Knight we define internationalisation as the process of integrating an international, intercultural or global dimension into the purpose, functions or delivery of post-secondary education. (Knight, 2003, p. 2) HER internationalisation within the EU refers to at least three categories of activities: (i) mobility of students, administrative staff, teachers and researchers; (ii) interorganisational collaboration (e.g. joint/accredited degrees, shared course modules, networked institutions, overseas campuses) and (iii) open and transparent recruitment routines. ERASMUS+, Marie Curie Sklodowska and Bologna are among the initiatives that embody these imperatives. Apart from Bologna, the EU flagship initiatives of HER internationalisation are increasingly inclusive of other regions. For instance, both ERASMUS+ and MC Sklodowska include a component that is open to mobility to and from non-EU member states. Likewise, the European Research Council accepts research applications from applicants regardless of nationality. Internationalisation from the perspective of the EU is clearly not a European affair but a global one and, seen from this perspective, the individual narratives that the chapters in this book present are part of a dialogue that ought to be relevant well beyond the research community in higher education.

For EU member states and their citizens, the HER internationalisation initiatives initiated by the EU represent a clear message but a minority moment in the everyday reality of HER. ERASMUS+ accounts for approximately 5% of the student mobility in the EU region and the Framework programme research budget also accounts for less than 10% of the research funding in the region. Given that EU Commission-supported initiatives represent such a small percentage of the total volume of international collaboration conducted within HER, it is clear that the drivers of this activity are either inherent to the sector itself or that they represent such a pressing force that they cannot be easily ignored. The latter two issues are important considerations given that HER policies are traditionally anchored in national ambitions. HER policy documents and academic literature converge on the observation that the last three decades have been game changing for HER because the balance between national and global drivers of HER collaboration policies has shifted in favour of the global (Cerdeira Bento et al., 2020; Paradeise & Thoenig, 2015).

This chapter aims to outline two key triggers of HER policies on international collaboration that stand out as of particular import for this volume: (i) the role of HER in the globalisation discourse and (ii) the impact of soft power measures emanating from international governmental organisations such as the OECD and UNESCO. The extent to which each or both of these factors plays a role in the different regional contexts will differ. The contributions in the rest of this volume however confirm these as significant imperatives for HER policies on collaboration. The rest of this chapter is structured in the following way. This brief introduction will be followed by a synthetic discussion of the theme of this book, i.e. international academic cooperation alternatively known as internationalisation. Following this we will focus on some of the imperatives for international collaboration emanating from the HER sector itself. The fourth section will provide a brief overview of the role of intergovernmental organisations in promoting international collaboration in HER. The fifth section will provide some concluding remarks.

2   International Collaboration, Globalisation and Higher Education and Research (HER)

A perusal of trade publications, newspapers and the like would reveal that internationalisation is not limited to HER: the business, policy and not for profit sectors are all focusing on this issue either as a way of signalling legitimacy or distinction. It is in part because of this pervasiveness that it is instructive to focus on internationalisation in the HER context. We maintain that the focus on the HER sector will allow us to unmask aspects of internationalisation which are not always visible to the average observer. Additionally, given the fact that HER policies are framed and even experienced as primarily national, the import of internationalisation and ultimately globalisation is sometimes difficult to grasp. Although there is no consensus on this issue, we argue that most HER scholars would concede that internationalisation should be distinguished from globalisation. We further contend that the last two decades witnessed the evolution of a new and qualitatively different phase of internationalisation in HER. This is the emergence of internationalisation as a key performance indicator for individual academics and higher education institutions (HEI). The latter development is perhaps the most important reason for maintaining a definitional distinction between internationalisation and globalisation.

Student and scholarly mobility are perhaps the two most well-known and important defining features of international collaboration across HEIs. These two features are also the most significant markers of internationalisation because it is through these two that HER alternatively facilitates globalisation and is itself globalised. Many authors in HER research have adopted the practice of using globalisation and/or New Public Management (NPM) as explanatory factors without always necessarily making it clear what aspects of these two phenomena may be the explanatory variable (see for example Henry et al., 2001; Cowen, 2000; Currie, 2004; Zajda & Rust, 2020). This is not a habit that is limited to HER research but it is a particularly unfortunate turn for HER because it obscures the ways in which practices that emerge in the sector are contributing to some of the developments that are attributed to NPM and globalisation. This is despite the availability of a whole range of HER scholarship that provides more nuanced analyses (see for example Gérard & Uebelmesser, 2015).

Pinpointing specific changes in the HER sector and attributing these changes to particular drivers is a complex issue. This complexity increases several fold if one chooses the institution as the level of analysis. Reasoning from the institutional perspective reveals a number of key challenges. One is the diversity of the HER sector and that although global pressures affect all HEIs, situatedness does determine how the HEI would respond to these pressures. Another is that HEIs are not monolithic organisations but are multicultural with each culture providing its own set of imperatives which in turn act as a filter through which global and national pressures are perceived. For instance, the same HEI may at once be engaged in research collaborations with other HEIs and with local national actors about teaching. Some of the collaborations may overlap through staff members but the interest(s) connected with the activity may differ and, in some cases, even conflict. A further complicating factor is that staff agency in initiating and organising collaborative activities in teaching and research differs across HEIs. Many European universities have strong traditions of staff autonomy particularly in research. This implies that at any given moment, the university itself may not have a full overview of collaborative activities. This has consequences for the degree of credence that may be given to documents such as university strategies for internationalisation.

Another way in which HEIs constantly straddle multiple universes is via the discourses (practices, expectations and regulations) in which they are embedded. For instance, scholars, students and degrees are all outputs of HEIs. The latter two are in some respects seen as plug and play devices, in that they are supposed to be adaptable regardless of context. This is a prerequisite for and at the same time makes international collaboration possible. While all HEIs operate with this expectation, some HEIs treat these products as commodities while others regard them as public goods. This more than any other factor drives the way in which internationalisation pressures have been interpreted by HEIs. Further, one may contend that the commodity/public good provider may be a potential analytical frame for differentiating among HEIs as being driven by or drivers of globalisation.

3   HEIs and Globalisation

Globalisation has become a defining frame for how we understand the interventions and requirements for an interconnected world in a way that trade, telecommunications, international relations and even the Bretton Woods institutions did not achieve. Given that our brief is education, it is fitting to take our point of departure in UNESCO's[1] definition of globalisation as an 'unprecedented acceleration and intensification in the global flows of capital, labour, and information'. This definition, although vague, has the merit of being distinct from internationalisation, which is merely one of the many characteristics of globalisation. What the UNESCO definition hides however is the fact that globalisation has both agency and structure. Capital, labour and information do not flow of their own accord. This flow is facilitated by individual choices, institutions, organisations and the preferences and opportunities they create and obscure. Higher education and research are two activities that contribute to individual agency and ultimately to the structures that promote and mediate capital, labour and information flows. This function is not an artefact of globalisation, it predates globalisation. It also explains why HER is a frontier site in globalisation. Further, technological developments such as information and communication technology (ICT) have enhanced the capacity of HER to promote and mediate the flow of capital and labour. Thus, while universities have always used 'global' or 'international' as part of their blurb, the scale of this activity is now unprecedented in relation to the past. For instance, the OECD reported that 3.7 million students were enrolled in tertiary education outside their home country in 2009 (OECD, 2011). This is an appreciable increase from the 0.8 million in 1975. These figures, impressive as they may appear, do not account for all forms of student mobility.

Higher education is one of the acknowledged means by which the European Union exercises soft power to promote integration of the European Union labour market. The Erasmus and Bologna programmes are the primary tools used to achieve this objective (Teichler, 2012). An indication of the importance of the programme is that the 2014–2020 budget for the ERASMUS+ programme is €14.7 billion. A cursory perusal of the publicity for the ERASMUS+ programme provides insight and introduction to the debatable problem of the student mobility variable in internationalisation. According to the Erasmus impact study, mobility enhances employability, Erasmus+ alumni are more likely to engage in other forms of international mobility later on in life and more than 30% of them marry someone from another nationality (EU, 2017). Parey and Waldinger (2010) and Oosterbeek and Webbink (2009) among others converge on the finding that individual labour market mobility is enhanced by previous mobility. Erasmus+ and other types of student mobility programmes are therefore portals to a global lifestyle for the individual and a channel for net inflow of knowledge for the recipient nation/firm. The mobility narrative is a compelling part of internationalisation on many levels but its attractiveness is perhaps enhanced because it reinforces already existing expectations of higher education such as enhanced employability and social mobility.

Mobility is however just one component of internationalisation and ultimately globalisation. In order for mobility to work, an infrastructure of supporting arrangements has to be in place in the networks of universities that receive these students. This includes accreditation regimes like EQUIS,[2] AACSB[3] and AMBA,[4] for business schools and generally comparable grading arrangements, course structures, calendars and curricula. International academic collaboration is a key component of this infrastructure. Higher education institutions need to collaborate to facilitate student and staff exchanges represented by ERASMUS, staff need to collaborate across institutions to perform accreditation, etc. Thus, while internationalisation itself may be seen as a requirement that is emanating from outside the HEI context, the collaborative moves HEIs make to facilitate or comply with these requirements are driven from within. The growing prevalence of university networks such as the League of European Research Universities (LERU) and Universitas 21 provide further evidence of the way HEIs are reshaping the sector themselves and creating market differentiation.

The increased importance of global ranking tables of HEIS is perhaps the single most telling sign of differentiation in the HEI sector. For years, *Times Higher Education, Macleans*[5] and *US News*[6] provided rankings of their respective national universities. These rankings were intended to provide parents with some idea of how to evaluate colleges and universities. This was a pragmatic exercise premised on an early recognition of higher education as a commodity. The ranking business exploded however when the Shanghai ranking was created in response to China's need to improve its national university system and to assess which foreign universities should be prioritised for Chinese students going abroad. Shanghai changed the rankings game in two important ways: (i) it intensified competition between universities that were already in the business of selling higher education and (ii) it enrolled even public universities in the global competition for students.

A glance at the 2019 ARWU (Shanghai) Rankings[7] of the best universities for excellence in teaching and research shows that 8 of the first 10 places are occupied by American universities. The remaining 2 slots are filled by British institutions. A list for the same purpose proposed by Quacquarelli Symonds (QS)[8] gives a slightly different result but HEIs in the USA and the UK still dominate. However, a third selection, again proposed by QS, lists the 10 best student cities assessed according to 6 indicators (*affordability, student mix, quality of student life, access to top universities, employer activity and student preferred choice*). Top cities are: London, Tokyo, Melbourne, Munich, Berlin, Montreal, Paris, Zurich, Sydney, Seoul (QS Rankings, 2019).

Ranking the cities as well as the universities is consistent with the narrative of mobility as a portal to another lifestyle and it integrates student life with parallel discourses about urban development. It also provides insight into the importance of HEI collaboration in the facilitation of globalisation. Despite the positive terms in which internationalisation and particularly mobility is framed, there is an emerging critique of this view and several have observed that internationalisation in HER is surprisingly monocultural (Marginson, 2016; Knight, 2011). Knight (2011) observed for instance that while an international student body is universally touted as positive, the reality is different. She argues that foreign students exist in a separate sphere from their local counterparts and in the best of cases interact only with other foreign students. While this might be a description that does not fit all cases, it is common enough to be easily recognisable. Globalisation promotes and is facilitated by the internationalisation of higher education but ironically enough, the more internationalisation is embraced, the less it seems that campuses are able to provide truly international experiences.

If one changes focus to pose the question of who benefits from student mobility, the picture is more nuanced. According to a study commissioned by the European Union, the ERASMUS programme performs similarly to other mobility programmes. Other studies have shown that student propensity to engage in mobility in higher education is largely determined by family background, and experience of mobility prior to university education. EU (2017) claims that student mobility is the most significant indicator of internationalisation for higher education institutions.

If higher education is seen as global, it is perhaps in research that the forces of globalisation are easiest to trace and pinpoint. Research collaboration is also a space where the agenda of internationalisation, excellence and quality converges in a different way from how it plays out in higher education. The researcher is addressed in this narrative not as a teacher sometimes and researcher at other times but as a researcher. Research excellence is therefore distinct from its teaching counterpart and research collaboration is more often an issue that is the province of the group or individual rather than the institution. Researchers may therefore choose to be global citizens or local ones in a way that teachers may not. The HEI-researcher interface in the discourse about internationalisation and collaboration occurs primarily through recruitment, publication/patenting and funding.

Mobility is an indicator of individual excellence. This implies that in order to get tenure, or even an entry level position, the average researcher must engage in some type of mobility. Likewise, universities must demonstrate commitment to excellence by showing that staff recruitment policies emphasise internationalisation via advocating diversity, gender equality and mobility. These requirements are treated as universally applicable to all disciplines. The focus on internationalisation in recruitment within European Union countries has not been seen as a universal good. On one hand, the transparency that comes with the new guidelines for recruitment is welcome as the research community has long held that recruitment, particularly in some of the top institutions, is subject to cronyism and a tendency to favour 'those trained here'. On the other hand, the focus on international recruitment has facilitated a flourishing global market for academic labour which, critics argue, favours the resource rich organisations in Europe. Further, the holy trinity of mobility, diversity and gender equality do not always cohere when translated to the everyday reality of the individual career. Some careers, particularly of those with high care burdens, are unable to avail themselves as easily of mobility. Unlike student mobility, researcher mobility is heterogeneous in that international mobility is only one aspect; researchers can also be mobile by transiting to another sector e.g. secondment to a firm, civil society or public sector organisation. A third option would be to move to another university in the same country. While all three types of mobility are acknowledged, international mobility still appears to be the most desirable and most closely linked with excellence. In other words, in an age where researchers can communicate and collaborate at a distance, physical relocation has become an item of merit in the individual cv. This is distinct from the trend in higher education which embraces ICT to provide e-learning and virtual classrooms.

4 IGOs and International Collaboration in HER

In summary, international collaboration with EU HEIs is therefore a process that HEIs are driven to for a variety of reasons that emanate from the changing modes of knowledge production and dissemination as well as the changing missions. The EU and its member states have regarded internationalisation as a sector priority for decades but this discourse is not completely driven by the EU and its HEIs. In the next section, we would like to turn our attention to the other significant group of actors who, individually and together, form a second source of the push for international collaboration in the HER sector: this is the intergovernmental organisations at the international and regional levels (IGOs).

Intergovernmental organisations form a diverse and often difficult to grasp group but, for the sake of brevity, we will divide this group into two main categories, the international and the regional. This is a rather crude designation in so far as all these organisations are strictly speaking international. However, some of them have a global remit (e.g. World Bank, World Trade Organisation) while others are regional. Amongst the main players in HER policies, are the World Bank, UNESCO, the UNDP and the OECD. In addition, those such as the African Development Bank, the Asian Development Bank and the InterAmerican Development Bank play critical roles in influencing HER agendas in Asia, African and Latin America. These organisations influence HER policies mainly through a number of soft power mechanisms which together form an advisory framework for cooperative action across different contexts and on varying scales. Considerations of space do not allow us to do an exhaustive coverage of the IGO initiatives nor does it allow us to cover all IGOs. We have decided to focus on a giving insight into a few of the lead actors. On the global level we focus on UNESCO, the OECD and the World Bank because these three have a specific education mandate. We are however mindful of the fact that the World Trade Organisation for instance is of increasing importance for the HER sector particularly for marketised higher education.

5   The United Nations Organisation for Education, Science and Culture (UNESCO) and International Collaboration

UNESCO led the initial worldwide reflection on the future of HER policies via a dual strategy comprising both world conferences and an exercise of continuous reflection involving policy-makers, the academy and social stakeholders. The first event, entitled *Higher Education in the 21st Century: Vision and Action*, was convened in Paris (1998) and was complemented by the World Conference on Science (*Science for the 21st Century*) held in Budapest in 1999. Both examined the challenges for these respective but closely interlinked domains in the 21st century. Both conferences were based on wide-ranging regional debates in Africa, Arab States, Asia. Europe and Latin America. For higher education, these regional dialogues aimed to forge a global pact to promote quality, relevance and international cooperation. The broad agenda tackled issues such as defining quality in relation to context, facilitating equitable access to advanced study and enhancing networking and collaboration amongst the academy worldwide. These ambitious goals would rely on strong public funding, partnership with the private sector and judicious use of the potential of information and communication technologies. In parallel, the UNESCO World Science Conference stimulated debate between the scientific community and society at large. The former group, through its expertise in the many areas of science, can help resolve the societal challenges affecting the lives of the latter group in multiple areas including health, agriculture, transport, communications, the environment and climate change. Both conferences, rooted in UN ideology, mounted a robust defence of academic freedom and scientific enquiry to encourage cooperation and social responsibility among scholars.

The follow-up to these events was a decade-long process involving both regular reflection and reporting along with stocktaking conferences to gauge progress and discuss new trends. From 1999 onwards, regular reporting on higher education change was undertaken by the Global University Network for Innovation (GUNI), a partnership between UNESCO and the Catalan Association of Public Universities (ACUP) with support from the United Nations University (UNU). GUNI produces an annual report entitled *Higher Education in the World* covering domains such as *The Financing of Universities* (2006), *Accreditation for Quality Assurance: What's at Stake?* (2007), *Higher Education's Commitment to Sustainability: from understanding to action* (2011) and *Towards a Socially Responsible University: balancing the global with the local* (2017). In tandem, monitoring progress in scientific action and research was reviewed at biennial World Science Fora on topics such as *Harnessing Science to Society*, (2002) *Investing in Knowledge. Investing in the Future* (2007) and *Science for Global Sustainable Development* (2013). This action was complemented by *The World Science Report* which is published by UNESCO every five years. In 2009, UNESCO convened global follow-up conferences: *The New Dynamics of Higher Education and Research for Societal Change and Development* gauged progress towards the 1998 goals and identified new forces affecting the global pact for cooperation amongst governments, HEIs and social stakeholders and the *Budapest +10 Conference on Science* covered similar ground in that particular field.

The principal report for the 2009 Higher Education conference merits particular attention. Entitled *Trends in Global Higher Education: Tracking an Academic Revolution* (Altbach et al., 2009), this documented the vastly changed context for the higher education sector which was resulting from globalisation policies. The authors concluded that an academic revolution had occurred, comparable in impact to the Humboldian change in university organisation in 19th century Germany. Four critical motors were identified: massified enrolments (many of which are now offered by private provision), the reality of globalisation (a more economic model than internationalisation), addressing the consequences of the Knowledge Society and Economy and the impact of ICT. In short, this report described a new world marked by financial precariousness in terms of public support but often attracting generous private funding. Resulting problems included steeper tuition fees for students and an academy with more restricted tenure and rising contract teaching.

The report further noted that in 2009, 72% of university research was still financed by governments in OECD countries, though this was shifting from block grants to project-specific funding. Increased partnership with the private sector (the so-called Triple Helix linking governments, universities and industry) was strongly encouraged and the academy had become a major stakeholder in the growing and lucrative field of intellectual property. Already this had impacted on institutional management and organisation with the advent of university science parks and research management offices. Furthermore, the world's top research universities, notably the Super Research Universities famed for their scientific excellence and for attracting the best academics and students, were mainly located in the wealthiest nations. Certain middle level economies such as Brazil, China, India and South Africa were striving to ensure access to this world of advanced R+D and innovation but low income countries with limited public budgets were virtually excluded. Thus, such unequal access to advanced knowledge was considered a dangerous problem for global development, necessitating urgent action by governments and donors to prevent an ever-widening gulf. The report concluded that, while institutions of post-secondary learning would continue to thrive, their mission and operating strategies had undergone irrevocable redefinition to meet the new socio-economic world order. This reshaping of the academy would also affect its future approaches to international cooperation.

6 The Organization for Economic Cooperation and Development (OECD)

The OECD has now grown from 24 countries in 1957 to 37 members in 2020. Using evidence-based research as its principal tool, the OECD has been able to nudge countries to adopt innovative policy-making measures for over six decades.

The OECD's 1998 Report *Redefining Tertiary Education* constituted an early landmark analysis of post-secondary education because it provided data on the changing situation in the HER sector in 10 countries. *Redefining Tertiary Education* showed that demand for post-secondary learning and training was increasing at the same time as student profiles were undergoing radical change. The prognosis was that further differentiation of HEIs might occur with universities becoming the primary institutions for academic research and research-based teaching. Other types of employment-specific training would be undertaken in a range of institutions, while advanced research would continue to be done in highly specialised locations. Tertiary Education emerged as the term to describe this new landscape, necessitating diversified institutions and provision, both public and private, to satisfy the steady growth in demand. A decade later, the OECD report, *Tertiary Education for the Knowledge Society* confirmed the principle and practice of tertiary education based on case studies from 24 countries with another 14 special reports and contributions from multiple partners including other IGOs, NGOs, foundations and the OECD Committees which liaise with business and industry and with trade unions respectively. This document (often referred to as TEKS) constituted an operational blueprint for countries to design their post-secondary education systems with due consideration for their specific context and resources. Internationalisation was one of the thematic issues singled out for particular attention. The proposals for achieving internationalisation included national strategies for quality assurance and to strengthen the international comparability of internationalisation strategies amongst countries.

To complement this policy initiative, the OECD specialised institute CERI (Centre for Educational Research and Innovation) undertook a global research-based reflection entitled *University Futures* to analyse important subjects (e.g. technology, demographic change, globalisation, market and quasi-market forces, the future of university research and labour market needs). This also addressed primarily economic issues arising from increased internationalisation, such as returns on cross-border provision, international academic mobility, teaching and research delivery costs and returns on investment in access and quality assurance. These issues are now central to the economic performance of certain OECD member countries. For example, the Australian Bureau of Statistics (ABS)[9] reported that the country had 398,563 international students in higher education who injected some U$32 billion into the national economy. Similarly, Universities UK reported that tuition fees paid by overseas students accounted for 14% of universities' incomes in 2018 (the UK being the second most popular destination for foreign students with Business Studies as the preferred field of study).

7 The World Bank and International Collaboration in HER

The World Bank is a major player among international governmental organisations, particularly for low and middle income countries. The Bank is both a funder and a source of policy expertise in HER. The Bank collects and publishes data on *inter alia* enrolment levels, public investment in tertiary education, the percentage of a population with tertiary qualifications, the R+D percentage of GNP, academic research citations and intellectual property indicators such as patents, trademarks, licenses and royalties. This data is for many countries an important source for national policy-making and bench-marking.

The World Bank has published landmark reports on higher and tertiary education to chart the progression to the knowledge society such as *Constructing Knowledge Societies. New Challenges for Tertiary Education* (2002), *The Challenges of Establishing World-Class Universities* (2009) and *What Matters Most for Tertiary Education Systems* (2016). The World Bank's influence on HER comes primarily through its collaboration with the regional IGOs such as the African Development Bank and its policy support.

8 Regional IGOs, HER Policies and International Academic Collaboration

Regional IGOs are perhaps the frontline organisations for countries in the low to middle income category. Regional IGOs function also as a collaborative partner for organisations such as UNESCO and the World Bank. In the rest of this section, we will use the African Development Bank (AfDB), the Asian

Development Bank (ADB) and the Inter-American Development Bank (IADB) to highlight the role of regional IGOs in facilitating international collaboration.

The African Development Bank (AfDB) collaborates closely with the African Union (AU) which is charged with defining major sectoral policies for development in the region. The AU's *Continental Education Strategy for Africa 2016–2026* (known as CESA 16–25) deals with a range of HER topics including university leadership and management, academic networking, graduate education, quality assurance, R+D +Innovation, promoting the STEM disciplines, public-private financing partnerships, access to HER for women and strengthening ICT capacity.

Since 2000, demand for Tertiary Education in Sub-Saharan Africa has doubled from 4% to 9%. According to a report in *The Economist* (17 August 2019), African students overseas doubled between 1997 and 2017 to some 374,000. International collaboration has been an important mechanism for meeting this increased demand. The European Union is however competing with universities globally as a potential collaborative partner. The pattern of collaboration exemplifies a new model for international collaboration, i.e. the overseas campus or a domestic HEI, which is accredited by a prestigious foreign partner. The AfDB invested US$13 million in the first American campus in the region jointly set up in 2012 by Carnegie Mellon University in partnership with the University of Rwanda and focused on IT and engineering capacity. The Toulouse Business School is a paradigmatic example of international collaboration with the African region. Others include the Centrale Superelec, EIGI Business School in Casablanca and ESSEC in Rabat.

The demand for internationally recognised academic qualifications is a significant driver for international collaboration and apart from overseas campuses; internationally accredited institutions such as Rwanda's Kepler College exemplify another strategy to achieve this end.

In Latin America and the Caribbean, IGO action in the HER sector is sharply contrasted. *The Inter-American Development Bank* (IDB),[10] founded in 1959, helps to shape development policies by providing loans and funding technical assistance projects to boost socio-economic modernisation and competitiveness amongst 48 member countries. The region of 639 million people has traditionally been led by Brazil, Mexico,[11] Colombia and Argentina which also boast the best universities according to the QS rankings due to their robust academic heritage and the influence of the Catholic church. After 30 years of military regimes (1960–1990) involving 11 countries, democracy and economic renovation stimulated rapid change in the region. In 2012, the IDB was already cooperating with the OECD's PISA programme to benchmark student achievement and by 2018, the institution had created *IDB Invest* to deal with private sector investment including SMEs. Development projects have focused on areas where advanced education and research capacity were required inter alia, US$70 million for TVET (Technical and Vocational Training) in the Dominican Republic; US$75 million to modernise university teaching, quality and relevance in Peru; US$8 million for digital skills in Uruguay; US$600 million for energy reform in Mexico; and US$34 million for water management in Haiti. This direction continued in 2019 when some 150 loans related to human capital and education were approved.

Concurrent with this action, the OECD's relations with the region have quickly consolidated as countries have stabilised politically and embraced free-market economic policies in line with global trends. At the present time, Mexico, Chile and Colombia are OECD members with Costa Rica in initial accession talks. Brazil is a key member of the OECD Development Centre which has also designed tailor-made programmes for Argentina and Peru and cooperates with numerous LAC states including the Dominican Republic, El Salvador, Panama, Paraguay and Uruguay for data collection and adherence to OECD reporting mechanisms.

In the HER sphere, action has also thrived as witnessed by the global diversity of academic cooperation arrangements. As examples, Science Po (the International Relations School of the University of Paris) has some 50 agreements with Latin American counterparts including 6 dual degree programmes and ISEG (the Business School of Lille's Catholic University) has 48 academic partnerships in the region under the Erasmus+ Programme; Montreal University offers joint doctoral programmes with Brazilian institutions. Edinburgh University has agreements with the top 10 THE (Times Educational Supplement) Latin American universities as well as a Regional Centre in Chile to manage joint public and private research and innovation opportunities in health, energy and business. Melbourne University's 12 partnerships and Auckland University's 3 agreements attest to increased linkages between Australasia and Latin America both for international study and advanced research cooperation in strategic fields for Pacific Rim development issues; the Columbus Association, set up in 1987, links some 50 universities in Europe and Latin America for capacity-building and innovation exchanges.

Scientific research is a robust area with the Academy of Science of Cuba (1961) and of Argentina (1869) as regional pioneers. Others proliferated with Brazil (1916), Venezuela (1917), Colombia (1933), Mexico (1959), Bolivia (1960) and more recently, Honduras (1985) and Uruguay(2009). Also, two regional coordinating bodies exist: the LAC Academy of Sciences set up in 1982 in Venezuela and sponsored by the Vatican's Pontifical Academy of Sciences and the Caribbean Academy of Sciences established in Trinidad and Tobago in

1988 with 200 members. The original intention of these bodies was to recognise and network excellent scientists primarily as an academic exercise. Now, the role of the "modern academy" is wider with particular responsibilities in terms of national development and international connections. As a result of the NMP strategies, national authorities have now understood the importance of research management capacity in universities and related R+D+I bodies to address the challenges of this competitive space including funding opportunities. Obviously public investment in R+D is a primary issue and indicates socio-economic development. Brazil leads the LAC region ranking 11th in the world and investing 1.17% in R+D followed by Mexico in 27th place with 0.941% and Colombia (47) with 0.24%. These contrast with Ecuador (69) 0.12%, Costa Rica (73) 0.47%, Bolivia (83) 0.25% and Paraguay (89) 0.13%. The leading economies usually locate their research management entities in relevant ministries (e.g. Chile's CONICYT, FONDECYT and FONDAP[12] are in the Ministry of Education; Mexico's CONICYT and Brazil's CAPES Foundation[13] which manages programmes such as Science Without Borders with its counterpart, CNPq, are in the Ministry of Science and Technology). However, even well-managed systems will flounder if national economic performance adversely affects resources. In 2019, the American Association for the Advancement of Science (AAAS)[14] reproached Argentina for its austerity measures citing reduced career openings for PhDs in sciences and engineering.

9 The Asian Development Bank (ADB)

Asia's rapid rise in the global economy in recent decades is well documented. With a population of 4.5 billion already, Asia controls US$31 billion of the world's GNP ahead of North America (US$24 billion) and Europe (US$21 billion). Asia is a success story with increasingly skilled and mobile populations. As an IGO, the Asia Development Bank (ADB) founded in 1966 has grown from 31 to 49 members (19 of which come from other regions including the USA, UK, Armenia, Georgia and Niue) and the ADB Institute ranks amongst the world's top 25 think tanks. The ADB invests in priority capacity-building for more vulnerable nations (strengthening employment skills for Mongolia's Tourism sector and innovative Higher Education strategies in Sri Lanka in 2019), as well as region-wide projects such promoting Brain Networking amongst the ASEAN Economic Community (ADB, 2017) as an important component of knowledge societies.

Asian academic cooperation plays a crucial role in development activities but has specific features not found elsewhere. Firstly, many nations invested early in modernising their universities to become key entities in the approaching knowledge society. As Asian governments anticipated the economic benefits of globalisation, their universities addressed development challenges. Secondly, the key motor of this action was China's carefully planned academic modernisation. The global proliferation of Confucius Institutes[15] has spearheaded cooperation with a view to Chinese academic supremacy before 2100. From 1975 to 2000, China steadily built powerful academic capacity involving post-graduate study (often in STEM disciplines) for selected cohorts both at the leading research universities (generally in the USA and the UK) and also in Canada, Australia and New Zealand. Thirdly, international undergraduate study has increased exponentially with young Chinese often choosing market-related skills in fields such as finance and business, computer science and media as well as English proficiency and remaining abroad after graduation to join local workforces. Consequently, international HER is a booming and lucrative domain at all levels and for all fields and the ARWU (Shanghai) Rankings with their emphasis on STEM-related excellence have gained special geo-political influence. China has also accelerated investment in its own universities. The American Institute of Physics reported that Chinese PhD graduates in S+E fields rose from 8,000 in 2000 to 34,000 in 2014. In 2016, China led the world in S+E publications with 18.6% of the global share (AIP Science Policy News, 31 January 2018).

The economic purposes of academic cooperation across the Asia /Pacific region is evidenced by the commercial character of activities Numerous universities have established branch campuses in Asia for local delivery or Liaison Offices to recruit international students and negotiate strategic R+D+I partnerships. Universities are expected to be entrepreneurial and competitive, especially those in the top 100 of the Shanghai Rankings. Their contribution to country GNPs are closely monitored by national data agencies both public and private. Examples include the Australian Bureau of Statistics, Education New Zealand,[16] Singapore's BERD,[17] Japan's MEXT,[18] NISTEP[19] and RIKEN,[20] the NIIED agency in the Korean Ministry of Education[21] and Council for University Education (KCUE),[22] RBC Economic Research (conducted by the Royal Bank of Canada[23]) and the Association of Pacific Rim Universities (APRU)[24] located in Hong Kong.

10   Conclusions

In summary, international academic collaboration with the EU is a small but growing part of a larger cross section of activity. Internationalisation is clearly a strategic priority for HEIs. Actors such as intergovernmental organisations play an important role in promoting internationalisation but a great deal of the impetus comes from within the HEI sector. Drivers such as the emergence of a global competition for students and scholars as well as the increased emphasis on institutional competitiveness imposed by regimes such as global rankings, international accreditation and other benchmarking exercises push HEIs to prioritise the internationalisation of their educational offerings. On the research side, internationalisation, like publication, is a performance indicator for scholars and determines the individual scholar's suitability for recruitment. Likewise, the level of internationalisation of the HEI also enhances or detracts from its attractiveness as a prospective employer.

Our analysis shows that far from being merely impelled by globalisation, HER is one of the activities that facilitates globalisation. This is achieved through the inscription of mobility as an imperative for employability for both scholars and students. Mobility in its turn demands infrastructures of standardisation such as accredited degrees, modular educational offerings, etc. The mobile student and scholar do not exist in a vacuum. Living conditions in the cities that compete for students and scholars are important contextual factors in enhancing what the HEIs that inhabit these cities offer. It should come as no surprise therefore that the synergies between urban development and internationalised HEIs is a rapidly expanding part of the urban studies discourse.

HER has traditionally been international but has simultaneously been mired in the national psyche. The current era is loosening this link between the national and the HEI as HER itself becomes more tightly integrated into a global culture and set of practices and norms. What does this imply for the future of an activity that has often been funded by the public purse and motivated by its potential contribution to growth and national development? Who are the potential winners and losers of international collaboration in HER? Is there a particular EU profile that may be forged and if so what would this profile look like?

Notes

1 The United Nations Organisation for Education, Science and Culture (UNESCO), The future we want: the role of culture in Sustainable Development, see http://www.unesco.org/new/en/culture/themes/culture-and-development/the-future-we-want-the-role-of-culture/globalization-and-culture/
2 European Quality Improvement System (EQUIS), see www.efmdglobal.org
3 Association to Advance Collegiate Schools of Business (AACSB), see www.aacsb.edu
4 Association of MBAS (AMBA), see www.associationofmbas.com

5 *Macleans Magazine*, Canada, see www.macleans.ca
6 US News College Rankings, see www.usnews.com
7 Academic Ranking of World Universities (ARWU), see www.shanghairanking.com
8 Quacquarelli Symonds, United Kingdom, see www.qs.com
9 Australian Bureau of Statistics, Government of Australia, see www.abs.gov.au/AUSSTATS
10 Inter-American Development Bank. IDB Invest, see www.idbinvest.org
11 Mexican Council for Science and Technology, CONACYT, www.conacyt.gob.mx
12 Chile Ministry of Education: CONICYT, FONDACYT, FONDAP, see www.gob.cl/ministry-of-education
13 CAPES, Brazil, see www.capes.gov.br
14 American Association for the Advancement of Science (AAAS), see www.aaas.org
15 The Confucious Institute, see www.harban.org
16 Education New Zealand, see www.enz.govt.nz/keystatistics
17 Business Expenditure on R+D (BERD), Singapore, see www.data.gov.sg
18 The Ministry of Education, Culture, Sports, Science and Technology (MEXT), Japan, see www.mext.go.jp
19 The National Institute for Science and Technology Policy (NISTEP), Japan, see www.nistep.go.jp
20 Basic and Applied Scientific Research Institute (RIKEN), Japan, see www.riken.go.jp
21 The National Institute for International Education (NIIED), Republic of Korea, see www.niied.go.kr
22 The Korean Council for University Education (KCUE), Seoul, Republic of Korea (http://english.kcue.or.kr).
23 Royal Bank of Canada, RBC Economic Research, see www.rbc.com/economics
24 Association of Asia Pacific Rim Universities (APRU), see www.apru.org

References

African Union. (n.d.). *Agenda 2063: The Africa we want*. www.au.int/agenda 2063

African Union. Continental Education Strategy for Africa 2016–2026. CESA 15-25. www. edu-au.org/strategies

Altbach, P. G., Reisberg, L., & Rumbley, L. E. (2009). *Trends in global higher education, tracking a global academic revolution: A report for the UNESCO 2009 World Conference on Higher Education*. UNESCO.

Altbach, P. G., & Knight, J. (2007). The internationalization of higher education: Motivations and realities. *Journal of Studies in International Education, 2007*(11), 290–305.

American Institute of Physics. (2018). *AIP science policy news*. www.aip.org

Batalova, J., Shymonyak, A., & Sugiyarto, G. (2017). *Firing up regional brain networks, the promise of brain circulation in the ASEAN economic community*. Asian Development Bank, Manila.

Cerdeira Bento, J. P., Martínez-Roget, F., Pereira, E. T., & Rodríguez, X. A. (Eds.). (2020). *Academic tourism: Perspectives on international mobility in Europe*. Springer.

Cowen, R. (2000). The market-framed university: The new ethics of the game. In J. Cairns, R. Gardner, & D. Lawton (Eds.), *Values and the curriculum* (pp. 93–105). Woburn Press.

Currie, J. (2004). The neo-liberal paradigm and higher education: A critique. In J. K. Odin & P. T. Manicas (Eds.), *Globalization and higher education* (pp. 42–62). University of Hawaii Press.

European Union (EU). (2017). *The Erasmus impact study: Effects of mobility on the skills and employability of students and the internationalisation of higher education institutions*. Study DG Education, Youth, Sport and Culture. http://www.unesco.org/new/en/culture/themes/culture-and-development/the-future-we-want-the-role-of-culture/globalization-and-culture/

Gérard, M., & Uebelmesser, S. (Eds.). (2015). *The mobility of students and the highly skilled* (pp. 83–104). The MIT Press.

Henry, M., Lingard, B., Rizvi, F., & Taylor, S. (2001). *The OECD, globalisation and education policy*. Pergamon.

Knight, J. (2003). Updated internationalization definition. *International Higher Education, 33*, 2–3.

Knight, J. (2011). Five myths about internationalization. *International Higher Education, 62*, 14–15.

Marginson, S. (2016). High participation systems of higher education. *The Journal of Higher Education, 87*(2), 243–271.

Marginson, S., & Van derWende, M. (2009). The new global landscape of nations and institutions. In *Higher education in 2030* (Vol. 2, pp. 17–57). OECD Publishing.

Marmolejo, F. (2016). *What matters most for tertiary education: A framework paper.* SABER Working Paper, No. 11. World Bank. https://openknowledge.worldbank.org/handle/10986/26516

Oosterbeek, H., & Webbink, D. (2009). Does studying abroad induce a brain drain? *Economica, 1*, 1–29.

Paradeise, C., & Thoenig, J. C. (2015). *In search of academic quality*. Palgrave Macmillan.

Parey, M., & Waldinger, F. (2010). Studying abroad and the effect on international labor market mobility: Evidence from the introduction of Erasmus. *The Economic Journal, 1*, 1–29.

Sehoole, C., & Knight, J. (Eds.). (2013). *Internationalisation of African higher education: Towards achieving the MDGs*. Springer. https://doi.org/10.1007/978-94-6209-311-9

Teichler, U. (2012). International mobility and the Bologna process. *Research in Comparative and International Education, 7*(1), 34–49.

CHAPTER 3

Internationalisation in EU Higher Education: Between National Concerns, EU Internal Policy and Global Ambitions

Nadine Burquel and Laura Ballesteros

Abstract

The chapter will provide a brief overview of European higher education internationalisation from a historical perspective. Its focus is on EU level policies and instruments, contextual developments and the inter-governmental process that resulted in the on-going construction of the European Higher Education and Research Area.

Intergovernmental agreements between Member States materialised in the Bologna Process in 1999 (with which the European Commission was ultimately associated), and subsequently the European Higher Education Area (EHEA) in 2010. The purpose of the Bologna Process was to enhance the competitiveness of European higher education through the transparency and comparability of education systems. Currently the EHEA includes 48 countries, thus going well beyond the 28 EU Member States.

From the early 2000s, EU education started to emerge as a policy linked to other EU policy agendas – the Lisbon Agenda (in 2000) and the Europe 2020 Strategy (in 2010) to make Europe a more competitive economy in the world able to attract global talents to the European continent. The international dimension of education policy was supported through the Erasmus Mundus programme launched in 2004. Later in 2013 the EU issued its "European higher education in the world" strategy (European Commission, 2013), and launched a number of education policy dialogues with key countries and regions such as all individual BRICS countries.

More recently as a response to Europe's growing social and democratic challenges, higher education institutions have been called upon to be more inclusive, to engage more actively and be better connected to the needs of their communities. The 2017 Renewed EU Agenda for Higher Education (European Commission, 2017) seeks to address this social dimension while at the same time addressing the economic challenges of the times ahead.

Keywords

EU policy – globalisation – modernisation – transnational education – international mobility

1 Different Times, Different Responses

The European Union is currently being tested in many different ways, not least by the challenges of the UK Brexit, one among several examples of some inward-looking and populist views in the EU. These protectionist views are at the opposite of the very essence of the European construction and endeavour for an open and democratic society built on peace. There is the perception of a disconnection between the local, the European, and the global agenda, which also affects higher education.

In the current turbulent times, the tremendous achievements of the EU as a unique model developed on the European continent since the fifties, and European higher education in particular, should not be forgotten. Even if higher education policies are decided by every Member State in accordance with the EU subsidiarity principle, and not by the EU itself, the supporting and coordinating role that the EU has been playing has led to major structural transformations in higher education. EU objectives have been taken forward in action programmes and non-binding forms of cooperation to share best practice, achieve common goals and periodic monitoring. The various forms are grouped under the Open Method of Coordination (the OMC), which was first proposed by the Heads of State (the 'European Council') in the Lisbon Declaration in March 2000 (European Council, 2000).

Higher education systems and individual institutions have seen significant transformations, as a result of intra-European and cross-border cooperation, first at the grassroot levels through academic and student mobility. These have been instrumental for the initiation of major curriculum reforms and the development of new forms of teaching and learning, through double or joint degree programmes, as well as other forms of blended learning, either through partnerships with industry, or as virtual delivery, which both emerged at a later stage.

From the late nineties governments in the Member States started to get more involved in education as intra-European cooperation was seen for its potential to achieve structural reforms and the modernisation of higher education systems in Europe. It is therefore no surprise that four countries came together in 1998, followed by others at a later stage, with the European Commission coming on board as a formal actor, to discuss ways in which mobility could be facilitated across the European Union for the purposes of education, through better understanding, transparency and comparability of national higher education systems, which led to the Bologna Process.

The intergovernmental nature of the Bologna Process reflects the sensitivity and importance of education in general for the preservation of States' interest, identity and economic prosperity. Preserving the rich and diverse culture of higher education systems while ensuring an acceptable degree of compatibility and comparability has been one of the key issues accompanying the Process of integration of European Higher Education. Protecting institutional autonomy and academic freedom has been vital in this. The London Communiqué (2007) reflects this concern by highlighting the importance of "institutional autonomy, academic freedom, equal opportunities and democratic principles" (p. 1). The internationalisation drive promoted by the Bologna Process and the required trust-building and compatibility mechanisms[1] gave the Ministers of higher education an additional tool to gain support for higher education modernisation reform efforts at home.

The European Commission has always played a pioneering and foresight role in higher education, to stimulate innovative approaches to education through the cross-cultural dialogue between individual Member States and universities. At the same time EU policy has had to adapt to major challenges such as the 2008 economic crisis which led to new policy to stimulate the development within education programmes of skills highly relevant for the (global) labour market, or education policy addressing issues of global competitiveness yet at the same having a local impact in the Member States, responding more explicitly to social and democratic challenges. New challenges related to the digital revolution, a growth of inequalities, a shrinking of the middle class, an ageing population in Europe, youth unemployment, and a skill mismatch have led to the rise of populism, emerging economic protectionism and growing tensions in Europe which have also called for new responses by higher education to demonstrate societal relevance.

2 An Intra-European Mobility Scheme – The Launch and Growth of the Erasmus Programme

The Erasmus programme began in 1987 in 11 countries. From the first Erasmus exchanges to the current credit and degree mobility that has expanded to include 33 countries,[2] more than 4,400,000 students (European Commission, 2018a) have benefited from the Erasmus programme in a period of just over 30 years.

However, if one compares the Erasmus mobility to the total student body for the 28 Member States, the percentage of EU-funded mobile students is 3.7% of young people (European Commission, 2018a). In 2016 bachelor students with mobility under Erasmus+ accounted for 55% of all credit mobility while 44% did so under a national mobility programme or out of their own initiative (Eurostat, 2019). Such mobility was very rare pre-Bologna as the question of recognition hampered the opportunities to study abroad.

The launch of the Erasmus programme saw the emergence of the first European networks of universities (such as the Utrecht, Unica and Coimbra networks) that grew out of Erasmus academic and student mobility, and over the years contributed to the European-wide "stakeholders' conversation" and advocacy on EU policy in higher education and research.

Through its Erasmus+ and Horizon 2020 programmes the European Commission supports international mobility of students, academics and staff, as well as institutional collaboration. Erasmus+ is the most widely available mobility programme in the EHEA. At least a third of the €16.3 billion budget is earmarked for higher education and 2 million staff and students are expected to benefit in the 2014–2020 period (European Parliament, 2019). In 2017 alone the programme supported 800,000 international placements including higher education and vocational training students and staff, youth and youth workers. Half of these placements were granted to higher education students and staff (ICEF, 2019).

More than half of all credit mobility in the EU takes place under Erasmus+ or other EU programmes; 312,300 higher education students and 62,500 staff benefited from a mobility period under Erasmus+ in 2017 (European Commission, 2018a). The most popular destinations for student and staff mobility under Erasmus+ are Spain, Germany, the UK, Italy, and France. The top sending countries are Spain, Germany, France, Italy and Poland (European Commission, 2018b). Roughly a third of students from abroad studying higher education in Europe come from Asia, making it the highest sending region of mobile students to the EHEA (Eurostat, 2019).

Germany, France, Ukraine and Italy have the highest numbers of outward degree mobile students.[3] The overwhelming majority of students (about 80%) choose to stay within the EHEA. Those who decide to go outside the EHEA for their entire degree are mostly students from the UK, France, Germany, Russia, Italy and Spain. Together these top six countries account for almost two-thirds of this type of outward flow (European Commission/EACEA/Eurydice, 2018a).

The most popular destinations for degree mobile students are the UK, France and Germany. Together they account for a third of inward degree mobility from EHEA countries and over half of students coming from outside the EHEA. Russia, Austria and the Netherlands also receive a considerable amount of inward degree mobile students (European Commission/EACEA/Eurydice, 2018a).

In 2013, the Ministers of Higher Education agreed on a target that by 2020 at least 20% of graduating students should have had an experience abroad. Even though some countries have achieved this target, according to the latest Bologna Implementation Report (2018) it is not yet possible to estimate whether the target will be met collectively.

Despite these numbers there is a still limited amount of student mobility at the level of the entire EHEA student population, which accounts for less than 4%. According to the latest Bologna Implementation Report, the main obstacles to mobility are financial issues, organisation of programmes, language skills, recognition issues and information provision. Mobility funding seems to be the most significant barrier to mobility, and to help tackle the issue, the portability of grants and loans is now high on the agenda. In addition, the European Commission introduced in 2015 the Erasmus+ Master Degree Loans (European Commission/EACEA/Eurydice, 2018b). These low-interest rate loans are meant to help cover tuition and living expenses. No collateral is required as the loans are guaranteed by the EU and offer favourable pay-back terms whereby graduates benefit from a grace period of up to two years after graduation before repayment. Students can receive a loan of up to €12,000 for a one-year Master programme and €18,000 for a two-year programme. Currently this scheme is only available for residents of Spain, Italy, Croatia, Romania and Turkey, but this list is expected to grow (European Union, 2019b).

Thirty years ago, the focus was clearly on student mobility, possibly for credit acquisition. Yet at the end of the nineties, reactions emerged calling for more attention to those students who for their own reasons could not spend a period abroad. The question was raised whether the intercultural experience gained during student exchanges could not somehow be replicated for non-mobile students. This led to the concept and support for forms of "internationalisation at home". The rationale behind the concept was that graduates would work in an increasingly interconnected and globalised world as professionals and citizens, and that the curriculum had to prepare them better for a labour market that was looking for global professionals with the right social behaviours to act as responsible citizens, have the capacity to solve complex problems and communicate effectively in increasingly multicultural local and global contexts.

Although the content of Erasmus has varied over the years, there have always been three main groups of action, i.e. grants for student mobility, grants to "internationalise" university staff (short study visits and teaching exchange visits), as well as grants to support the "Europeanisation" of higher education more generally (for example with large university thematic networks that focused on curricula updates in particular disciplines, and support to develop different forms of transparency instruments or qualifications systems). The programme has now major brand recognition and has underpinned the Bologna Process, as well as most other transnational activities in higher education in Europe.

3 Beyond Mobility: Reforming Higher Education in Europe and Engaging Globally

The early EU intervention in higher education under Erasmus developed further into structural reforms with the Bologna Process. Launched with the Bologna Declaration in 1999 as an overall architecture and framework to increase transparency in higher education, it now includes 48 States which compose the European Higher Education Area (EHEA).

The Process was originally an intergovernmental intervention of only four Member States (France, Germany, Italy and the UK). With the Sorbonne Declaration in 1998 they called on other European countries to join forces in addressing a number of issues regarding their higher education systems. The underlying driver was clearly to create a distinctive high quality European higher education through international activities. Signatory countries of the Bologna Declaration were invited to achieve a series of practical objectives, originally with little supervision. The Bologna Process quickly became highly successful as it enabled countries to make progress with their own reforms in higher education. The mechanism of external pressure assisted national higher education reform efforts by stimulating support at home. The Commission had been intentionally excluded by the founding countries: however, by the Ministerial meeting in Prague in 2001 it became clear that some additional support was needed for the Process, and the Commission became an influential player (Bologna Process, 2001).

Six key areas were covered under the original Declaration, i.e. the adoption of a system of easily readable degrees (including with the proposed Diploma Supplement), the end of the long first degree that existed in many European countries in favour of "two main cycles, undergraduate and graduate" (Bologna Process Committee, 1999, p. 3), the adoption of a credit system (i.e. the *European Credit Transfer System* first developed under the *Erasmus Programme*), the promotion of mobility (students, academics and support staff), the development of European cooperation in quality assurance, and the promotion of the European dimension in Higher Education (in curricular development, inter-institutional cooperation and integrated study programmes). Further action lines have been added over the years, i.e. employability, social policy, qualifications frameworks, fair recognition of degrees, equal access, alignment with national lifelong learning policies, flexible learning paths, global dimension, and more recently learning and teaching relevance and quality, to name a few. Doctoral education was formally introduced as the third cycle of the Process in 2003 (Bologna Process, 2003).

Since its inception, the Bologna Process has always had international ambitions that go beyond Europe. Strengthening worldwide recognition, attractiveness, and competitiveness of Higher Education Systems (HES) (Bologna Process Committee, 1999) was always stated as part of the objectives, which could be achieved by promoting Europe as a study destination. Another aim was to foster the recognition of European degrees across the globe, with robust quality assurance systems seen as critical for external credibility. It was also seen as a way to support social, economic and political developments in countries outside Europe, and to position the EU as a global player.

The key driver was to position Europe as a global reference point for quality in higher education which has driven the development of joint and double degree programmes as a distinctive European added value. Support for student/scholar mobility was provided as a means to attract talent to Europe, enable them to gain valuable experiences and better prepare them to live in a multicultural knowledge-based society.

The launch of Erasmus Mundus in 2003 linked the concern for quality and the rise of international cooperation in higher education, driven by international actors, technological change, globalisation and competition, as well as institutions and scholars' eagerness to explore new opportunities. It opened up new forms of teaching and learning and developments of partnerships.

The 2005 Ministerial Summit formally introduced "The Global Dimension of the Bologna Process" when the Bologna Follow-up Group (BFUG) was mandated to explore and develop an external dimension strategy to increase mobility and cooperation with non-EU countries (Bologna Process, 2005). As a result, "A Strategy for the External Dimension of the Bologna Process" was introduced in 2007.

The influence of the Bologna Process in other parts of the world depends on interests and perceptions. Countries that seek EU membership are eager to comply with the reforms, while countries interested in EU funding opportunities through programmes such as Erasmus+ are inclined to adopt the recommendations. On the other hand, there are some that view the Bologna recommendations as a new form of colonialism and are less eager to participate. Furthermore, the concern of another set of countries with the Bologna

Process is limited to how it affects the global trade in Higher Education and mobility of international students such as in Canada or in New Zealand (Klemenčič, 2019).

The positioning of the EU as a global player through the desire for intercultural dialogue and understanding between people within Europe has long underpinned interventions in education and training as a vehicle for peace and stability. The EU five priorities in the field of higher education international cooperation are focused on promoting EU education and training as a centre of excellence, supporting modernisation efforts of partner countries, promoting mutual understanding and shared values, supporting internationalisation efforts, and improving quality of education and training through peer learning and exchange of best practice.

The geopolitical realities of globalisation and the roles played by governments in that process have always been understood. Therefore, the European Commission initiated Policy dialogues that take place through different types of fora, such as seminars, conferences and studies, bringing together experts and senior officials from the EU and the specific country or region. Currently, the EU is engaged in policy dialogue activities with Africa, Brazil, China, India, Mexico, South Africa, South Korea, USA, as well as the Southern Mediterranean, Western Balkans and Eastern regions. These activities are meant to deepen cooperation, increase quality of education in Europe and partner countries through the exchange of best practice, and support partner countries in their higher education reform efforts (European Union, 2019e).

As a whole, implementation of the Bologna Process is still very uneven across the 48 signatory countries (European Commission/EACEA/Eurydice, 2018a), between the early adopters and the latecomers. Implementation is voluntary and there are no punitive measures for non-compliance. Recent histories, path dependencies, different levels of support, and the fact that different countries have joined the Process at different times has led to uneven implementation.

However, the framework exists and has facilitated major exchanges and cooperation in many different ways. Member States of the EHEA are committed to implementing the structural reforms necessary to achieve the agreed objectives. It is a successful example of a process which at first appeared independent of the EU, but which builds heavily on the Erasmus programme, and the related financial incentives provided to assist signatory countries to bring diverse systems together, and to independently support the academic experimentation that was necessary, and as a result make it academically acceptable.

Beyond the support for the Bologna Process, in 2006 the Commission also launched the Modernisation Agenda to support three essential objectives for universities: greater autonomy, funding reform (leading both to additional financial autonomy and greater funding source diversification), and curricular reform (to adapt teaching methods and content to the needs of the labour market) (European Commission, 2006a). Internationalisation has also always been a high priority underpinning the Modernisation Agenda.

4 Higher Education and Research – European and Global Competitiveness

For the first time the 2000 'Lisbon Strategy' brought the Commission into the area of education policy as it was believed that education and training had to improve to support economic growth and competitiveness. The Commission and individual Member States started a conversation which led to the adoption of benchmarks, good practices and mutual learning exercises between individual Member States, for all levels of education and training through the Open Method of Coordination (OMC).

The European Semester was launched in 2010 to enable EU Member States to coordinate their economic policies and coordinate efforts towards the EU 2020 targets. The European Semester includes a monitoring of education and training policies and reforms and is one of the instruments under the European and Training 2020 Framework that was adopted in May 2009 to disseminate best practices in education policy and advance educational policy reforms at national and regional levels. Based on the lifelong learning approach, the Framework has focused on educational outcomes, from early childhood to adult vocational and higher education. It has four objectives to make lifelong learning and mobility a reality, improve the quality and efficiency of education and training, promote equity, and social cohesion and active citizenship. Out of its seven benchmarks, two focus directly on higher education, i.e. that at least 40% of people aged 30–34 should have completed some form of higher education, and at least 20% of higher education graduates should have spent some time studying abroad (Council of the European Union, 2009). In addition to the European Semester, other tools include Working Groups, Peer Learning Groups and counselling, an annual Education and Training Monitor, and stakeholders' consultations (with among others a European Education Summit).

In 2010 the European Council had also just reviewed the state of competitiveness of the Union in response to the phenomenon of globalisation, and set out objectives for what it wanted to achieve by 2020. As a 10-year plan the Europe 2020 Strategy was proposed by the European Commission for the advancement of EU's economy as a 'smart, sustainable, inclusive growth', with greater coordination of national and European policy (European Commission, 2010). It gave the Commission a mandate to stimulate Member States to achieve sectoral targets, including education.

In addition to competitiveness issues, labour market trends also forced the EU to pay more attention to education and training. It was clear that demographic shrinkages would start in Europe and would have a serious effect on the overall workforce size in some countries. In a global economy, attracting talented graduates for a well-qualified workforce was seen as critical to meet local labour market needs, all the more reason to attract talented people to Europe. Employment and competitiveness issues thus also underpinned at least in part the Commission's support for higher education and research, that were considered as key to grow the knowledge economy.

In research, the idea of a European Research Area (ERA) was put forward by the European Commission in 2000, with its Communication "Towards a European Research Area" (European Commission, 2006b). The aim of the ERA was to enable researchers to move freely and work with excellent networks of research institutions, and to share knowledge effectively for social, business and policy purposes. It was also to open European, national and regional research programmes to support the best research in Europe, and to develop strong links with partners around the world for Europe to benefit from worldwide knowledge and expertise. There were two additional underlying aims: to attract the best talents to research careers in Europe, and to encourage Member States to spend 3% of their GDP on research, which was seen as a minimum for a competitive knowledge-based economy and society.

Achieving the ERA has been an ongoing process: however it is a good example of the way the Commission and Member States have joined forces to achieve goals that are political in nature, but would have been difficult to achieve by legislation alone. The practical implementation has taken place through the Research Framework Programmes and will be continued in the next 2020–2027 Research and Innovation Framework Programme, i.e. the Horizon Europe Programme, that will have a budget of 93 billion euros (European Union, 2019d).

Many initiatives have emerged to support the development of the ERA through collaboration and coordination of national and EU-wide strategies in innovation and research. These initiatives include public-private partnerships, joint programmes, platforms, and networks. One such initiative strongly supported by the EC are the Knowledge and Innovation Communities (KICS) of the European Institute of Technology (EIT) (ERA-LEARN, 2018). Created in 2008, the aim of the EIT is to strengthen the innovation capacity of the EU as an independent body bringing innovators and entrepreneurs in Europe together into the KICS. Dedicated to finding solutions for specific pressing global issues (e.g. climate change, sustainable energy, health, food innovation) these communities offer genuinely innovative education programmes in partnership with leading companies and higher education institutions, with an innovation and entrepreneurial focus. So far more than 50 innovation hubs have been created across Europe, over 2,000 new ventures launched (with 1.5 billion euros of venture capital raised) and 900 products and services created; some 2,300 students have graduates and more than 6,000 jobs have been created. The EIT is a key component of the EU Horizon 2020 Framework Programme for research and innovation (European Institute of Innovation and Technology, 2019).

In higher education the principle of the European Higher Education Area (EHEA) was first mentioned in the Sorbonne declaration of 1998, and the Bologna Process took it a step further by setting out specific objectives to establish an EHEA "within the first decade of the third millennium" (Bologna Process Committee, 1999, p. 3), centred around the areas mentioned earlier, i.e. a two-cycle system of easily readable and comparable degrees, a European Credit Transfer System (ECTS), mobility recognition, European cooperation in quality assurance, and promoting the European dimension in higher education (i.e. curriculum, institutional cooperation, integrated programmes and mobility schemes). Ministers of Education agreed to coordinate their policies to reach these goals and have been meeting periodically ever since to assess progress and decide new steps to be taken.

Formally launched in 2010, the EHEA has come a long way since its inception, and significant progress has been made to meeting the initial goals, with the emergence of new institutional players, guidelines, frameworks, and topics of interest: The European Association for Quality Assurance in Higher Education (ENQA) and the European Register for Higher Education (EQAR) have played a key role in quality assurance; a three-tier degree system,[4] an overarching qualifications framework (QF-EHEA), and the Diploma supplement are used to ensure comparability and transparency; the ECTS users' guide and the European Standards and Guidelines for quality assurance and qualifications framework serve as guiding documents; and student centred learning is now more established, as teaching and learning has begun to gain momentum. Most notably the EHEA has emerged as a unique intergovernmental forum that also includes representatives from HEIs, faculty and students (Bergan & Deca, 2018).

5 New Responses – A Renewed Agenda for Higher Education

As new trends and challenges emerge, policies are refocused to address these. Skill gaps continue to persist, the nature of work is becoming increasingly complex, requiring creative, flexible, innovative and entrepreneurial graduates and mindsets to produce new solutions and position the EU as a key player in the global economy (European Commission, 2017).

The 2017 Renewed EU Agenda for Higher Education is seeking to address the new challenges that the EU has been facing in the last few years. Framed in the context of a broader strategy to strengthen the European Pillar of Social Rights and to support young people, it recognises the importance of higher education in promoting a fair, inclusive, open and prosperous democratic society.

The Agenda identifies four action priorities: addressing skills mismatches and promoting excellence in skill development; encouraging inclusive higher education systems that are better connected to their immediate communities' needs; boosting the higher education contribution to innovation; and improving efficiency and effectiveness in higher education systems. To stimulate progress in these areas the European Commission together with the OECD is reviewing the incentives and reward structures for higher education systems, supporting evidence-based policy-making, ensuring financial resources are available,[5] and promoting international mobility and cooperation to increase quality (European Commission, 2017).

In the future, the EHEA is foreseen as a part of a European Education Area (EEA) envisioned for 2025. The EEA will encompass the entire education and training system. It aims to foster a strong sense of European identity, where speaking three languages is the norm, and spending time abroad for education or work purposes is standard (European Union, 2019a).

Under the framework of the EEA, three key actions relate to higher education: the development of a European digital student card, automatic diploma recognition, and the creation of a Network of European Universities (European Union, 2019a).

The European Universities Initiative is one of the most exciting developments shaping the future of the EHEA and the ERA, meant to bring forward the European universities of the future. Early in 2019, the first European Universities were selected, i.e. seventeen consortia out of a total of fifty-four submitted applications.[6] These networks consist of bottom-up transnational alliances of universities, many of which already have a long historical collaboration. Alliances are required to include all types of higher education institutions and cover a wide geographical scope. They are meant to promote European values and 'revolutionise' European higher education. The initiative aims to support long-term strategies (20 to 30 years) and a deeper integration of these networks. Learning pathways should allow students to build their own learning programme and be genuinely mobile within the network. Strategies should adopt an interdisciplinary problem-based approach to contribute to solving

Europe's most significant challenges. The initiative is now in its pilot phase, testing different models, and will be fully rolled-out as part of the next Erasmus programme in 2021–2027. A total of 20 European Universities are envisioned by 2024 (European Union, 2019c).

6 Conclusion

Internationalisation in EU higher education is a fascinating construction of more than 30 years of EU education programmes and policy interventions, between the EU, its Member States and other parts of the world, bringing together all stakeholders, in bottom up and top down initiatives.

Major progress has been made to facilitate intra-European mobility in higher education through a more transparent European higher education that has been developing under the Bologna Process and all its associated tools. These have also facilitated links to other parts of the world, supporting the EU ambition to be a global player in higher education.

Academic and student exchange have led to study programme curricular transformations and novel forms of cross border and cross sector delivery modes for education, first piloted through EU-funded initiatives, then streamlined in a growing number of higher education institutions. Different forms of internationalisation have also contributed to major structural reforms at institutional and system level, in Member States and beyond in the European Higher Education Area.

In and outside the EU, education, research and innovation are seen for the key potential to contribute to (national) economic growth in a multicultural knowledge society, and for global competitiveness, hence linking them to broader policy agendas, including more recently in the EU to those related to social and democratic challenges.

All these achievements in the EU have not been without their challenges, and continue to be so. The many shortcomings need to be addressed on a daily basis. Yet through an ongoing and open dialogue at EU level, between Member States, higher education institutions, faculty and students, major changes can be made, as has been seen in the shaping of EU education policy and programmes in the last 30 years.

There is strength in diversity and preserving the rich and diverse culture of higher education systems continues to be a local and global concern for higher education. In its interactions with other parts of the world, European higher education continues to address these challenges. Looking back at the results achieved through closer international cooperation, there are many fascinating examples and success stories of positive changes in international higher education.

Notes

1. Among them quality assurance and transparency instruments, the adoption of the three-tier system, and national and European qualifications frameworks.
2. 28 EU Member States, Turkey, the former Yugoslav Republic of Macedonia, Norway, Iceland and Liechtenstein. In addition, the Erasmus+ programme is open to the rest of the world through partnerships.
3. Students who undertake the entire degree programme, from enrollment to graduation, in another country.
4. The third "tier" concerns doctoral education specifically and was officially added in 2003.
5. Through Erasmus+, The European Structural Investment Fund, and the European Fund for Strategic Investment.
6. A second round is scheduled in the autumn of 2019.

References

Bergan, S., & Deca, L. (2018). Twenty years of Bologna and a decade of EHEA: What is next? In A. Curaj, L. Deca, & R. Pricopie (Eds.), *European higher education area: The impact of past and future policies.* doi.org/10.1007/978-3-319-77407-7_19

Bologna Process. (2001). *Towards a European higher education area.* Communiqué of the meeting of European Ministers in charge of Higher Education in Prague on May 19th 2001. http://www.ehea.info/media.ehea.info/file/2001_Prague/44/2/2001_Prague_Communique_English_553442.pdf

Bologna Process. (2003, September 19). Realizing the European higher education area. In *Communiqué of the Conference of ministers responsible for higher education.* Berlin. http://www.ehea.info/Upload/document/ministerial_declarations/2003_Berlin_Communique_English_577284.pdf

Bologna Process. (2005, May 19–20). The European higher education area – Achieving the goals. In *Communiqué of the Conference of European ministers responsible for higher education.* Bergen. http://www.ehea.info/Upload/document/ministerial_declarations/2005_Bergen_Communique_english_580520.pdf

Bologna Process. (2007, May 18). *London communiqué.* European Higher Education Area. London. http://www.ehea.info/Upload/document/ministerial_declarations/2007_London_Communique_English_588697.pdf

Bologna Process Committee. (1999). *Joint declaration of the European Ministers of Education convened in Bologna on 19 June 1999* (The Bologna Declaration). http://www.ehea.info/Upload/document/ministerial_declarations/1999_Bologna_Declaration_English_553028.pdf

Council of the European Union. (2009). Council conclusions of 12 May 2009 on a strategic framework for European cooperation in education and training (ET 2020). *Official Journal of the European Union, C 119*, 2–10. https://eur-lex.europa.eu/legal-content/EN/ALL/?uri=CELEX%3A52009XG0528%2801%29

ERA-LEARN. (2018). *Partnerships in a nutshell: Types of partnerships*. Retrieved September 29, 2019, from https://www.era-learn.eu/partnerships-in-a-nutshell/type-of-networks

European Commission. (2006a). *Communication from the commission to the council and the European parliament. Delivering on the modernisation agenda for universities: Education, research and innovation.* COM, 2006, 208. https://eur-lex.europa.eu/legal-content/EN/TXT/?uri=celex:52006DC0208

European Commission. (2006b). *Communication from the commission to the council, the European parliament, the economic and social committee and the committee of the regions: Towards a European research area.* COM, 2000, 6. https://eur-lex.europa.eu/legal-content/EN/ALL/?uri=CELEX:52000DC0006

European Commission. (2010). *Communication from the commission EUROPE 2020 A strategy for smart, sustainable and inclusive growth.* https://doi.org/10.1016/j.resconrec.2010.03.010

European Commission. (2013). *Communication from the commission to the European parliament, the council, the European economic and social committee and the committee of the regions: European higher education in the world.* COM, 2013, 0499. https://eur-lex.europa.eu/legal-content/EN/ALL/?uri=COM:2013:0499:FIN

European Commission. (2017). *Communication from the commission to the European parliament, the council, the European economic and social committee and the committee of the regions: On a renewed EU agenda for higher education.* COM/2017/0247. https://eur-lex.europa.eu/legal-content/EN/ALL/?uri=CELEX:52017DC0247

European Commission. (2018a). *Erasmus+ annual report 2017*. Publications Office of the European Union. doi:10.2766/465575

European Commission. (2018b). *Erasmus+ annual report 2017: Annex*. Publications Office of the European Union. doi:10.2766/148879

European Commission/EACEA/Eurydice. (2018a). *The European higher education area in 2018: Bologna process implementation report*. Publications Office of the European nion.

European Commission/EACEA/Eurydice. (2018b). *National student fee and support systems in European higher education – 2018/19*. Eurydice – Facts and Figures. Publications Office of the European Union.

European Council. (2000, March 23–24). *Presidency conclusions*. Lisbon. https://www.consilium.europa.eu/uedocs/cms_data/docs/pressdata/en/ec/00100-r1.en0.htm

European Institute of Innovation and Technology. (2019). *EIT at a glance*. Retrieved September 27, 2019, from https://eit.europa.eu/who-we-are/eit-glance

European Parliament. (2019). *Higher education: Fact Sheets on the European Union.* Retrieved September 29, 2019, from http://www.europarl.europa.eu/factsheets/en/sheet/140/higher-education

European Union. (2019a). *About higher education policy.* Retrieved September 27, 2019, from https://ec.europa.eu/education/policies/higher-education/about-higher-education-policy_en

European Union. (2019b). *Erasmus master degree loans.* Retrieved September 28, 2019, from https://ec.europa.eu/programmes/erasmus-plus/opportunities/individuals/students/erasmus-plus-master-degree-loans_en

European Union. (2019c). *European universities initiative.* Retrieved September 27, 2019, from https://ec.europa.eu/education/education-in-the-eu/european-education-area/european-universities-initiative_en

European Union. (2019d). *Horizon Europe – The next research and innovation framework programme.* Retrieved September 27, 2019, from https://ec.europa.eu/info/horizon-europe-next-research-and-innovation-framework-programme_en

European Union. (2019e). *International cooperation and policy dialogue.* Retrieved September 29, 2019, from https://ec.europa.eu/education/policies/international-cooperation/international-cooperation-and-policy-dialogue_en

Eurostat. (2019). *Learning mobility statistics.* Retrieved September 29, 2019, from https://ec.europa.eu/eurostat/statistics-explained/index.php/Learning_mobility_statistics#Credit_mobile_students

ICEF. (2019, August 19). Erasmus supported nearly 800,000 international placements in 2017 [Blog]. Retrieved September 27, 2019, from https://monitor.icef.com/2019/03/erasmus-supported-nearly-800000-international-placements-2017

Klemenčič, M. (2019). 20 years of the Bologna process in a global setting: The external dimension of the Bologna process revisited. *European Journal of Higher Education, 9*(1), 2–6. doi:10.1080/21568235.2019.1570670

Sorbonne Declaration. (1998, May 25). *Joint declaration on harmonisation of the architecture of the European higher education system by the four ministers in charge for France, Germany, Italy and the United Kingdom.* Paris, The Sorbonne. http://www.ehea.info/media.ehea.info/file/1998_Sorbonne/61/2/1998_Sorbonne_Declaration_English_552612.pdf

PART 3

The Context of Higher Education Cooperation and Internationalisation in Countries of the Four Continents

CHAPTER 4

Brazil-EU Cooperation in Higher Education

Creso M. Sá and Magdalena Martinez

Abstract

This chapter provides an overview of Brazil-EU cooperation in higher education, situating the discussion in the context of relevant actors, government agencies, and long-term patterns of engagement in internationalisation. Recent policy developments are discussed, as well as the challenges raised by the current political context for the near future of international academic cooperation.

The chapter situates the Brazil-EU cooperation in higher education in the context of Brazil's efforts to promote internationalisation. Federal and state governments have developed programmes to promote international academic cooperation. Universities, in spite of administrative and policy infrastructures that do not prioritise internationalisation, respond to government initiatives and create programmes that respond to particular institutional interests. Academic careers, while rooted in a context of relatively limited internationalisation, are marked by institutional incentives to establish international engagement.

Keywords

Brazil – Europe – academic cooperation between Brazil and Europe – Brazil policies for higher education internationalisation – global science – internationalisation

1   Introduction

European academic traditions have been influential in the development of the Brazilian higher education system since the establishment of the first post-secondary institutions during Portuguese colonisation. Brazil remained relatively isolated from the Anglo-Saxon scientific world well into the 20th century, seeing in continental Europe its main intellectual influences. During the so-called "Brazilian Enlightenment" between the late 19th century and the early 20th century, intense interactions with France and Germany brought scientific ideas that were circulating at the time in Europe (Schwartzman, 1991). A generation of Brazilian scientists trained in Europe, particularly in France, went on to lead the research institutes and higher education institutions that emerged in the first few decades of the 20th century. Ideas about how to organise research and higher education were brought to the country, not only by them but also by European émigrés.

In the post-World War II period, the spectacular ascendancy of American science gradually shifted the gaze of Brazilian scientists and higher education policy makers away from Europe. By one estimate, 90% of Brazilian researchers going abroad for their doctoral studies earned their degrees in the United States (de Moura Castro, 1983). The major higher education reform of 1968 brought elements of the American system to Brazilian universities, including the departmental model, the credit system, and the structure of graduate degree programmes (Balbachevsky & da Quinteiro, 2003). Still, Europe remained a major influence for the research community for a number of cultural, social, and ideological reasons (de Moura Castro, 1983; Schwartzman, 1991). To date, the European Union is a major destination for Brazilian researchers studying abroad or spending time away from their home institutions, and a significant level of research collaboration takes place between Brazilian and European universities and researchers.

The purpose of this chapter is to situate Brazil-EU cooperation in higher education in the context of Brazil's efforts to promote internationalisation. Federal and state governments have developed programmes to promote international academic cooperation. Universities, in spite of administrative and policy infrastructures that do not prioritise internationalisation, respond to government initiatives and create programmes that respond to particular institutional interests. Academic careers, while rooted in a context of relatively limited internationalisation, are marked by institutional incentives to international engagement.

The chapter is organised into four sections. It begins with an overview of the context of higher education in Brazil and the main agencies involved in internationalisation. In the following section, we discuss the governmental efforts to promote internationalisation. In Section 3, we explore the role of universities in developing international programmes, with a focus on Europe. In Section 4, we review current educational changes in the Brazilian context that might affect internationalisation.

2   Context and Actors

While Brazilian higher education owes its late development to an intense exchange of people, ideas, and expertise with Europe and the United States (Schwartzman, 1991), in this century the country has arguably been a marginal player in some of the recent policy trends driving internationalisation. These trends are rooted in a contemporary understanding of academic "excellence", which entails an orientation towards so-called "global" norms: the pursuit of prestige through research achievement as determined by international disciplinary communities and recognition systems; the promotion of inter-institutional status competition increasingly cast in global terms; the internationalisation of faculty and students, along with increasing use of English as an academic language; and an emphasis on collaborating with foreign institutions. Such an orientation has motivated policy efforts in many countries to internationalise their higher education systems and induce stronger cross-national partnerships in a variety of formats (Vaira & Rostan, 2011). In Brazil, they have not become a major policy focus at the national level. The assumption that higher education is a national asset to be compared and evaluated against those of other countries, which rationalises a number of "excellence" initiatives in European and Asian countries, does not carry political purchase in national policy debates.

Absent a stronger political mobilisation around higher education as a national asset to be compared to those of other countries considered as references or "competitors", policy initiatives to promote international cooperation have been more circumspect (Sá & Grieco, 2015). With few exceptions, they take place within the technocratic environment of federal agencies operating in higher education and science policy.

The main actors promoting internationalisation in the federal government are the Ministry of Education, the Ministry of Science and Technology, and the Ministry of Foreign Relations (Pereira Laus & Costa Morosini, 2005). The Coordination for the Improvement of Higher Education Personnel (CAPES) Foundation was created in 1951 within the Ministry of Education (MEC) to contribute to the expansion and development of graduate education in the country. Among several objectives, promoting and funding international scientific cooperation is one of the main mandates of CAPES. The Brazilian National Council for Scientific and Technological Development (CNPq), created in 1951 under the Ministry of Science and Technology, has as its main objectives to promote science and technology research, including international collaboration.

Moreover, the Brazilian Agency for Cooperation, part of the Ministry of Foreign Relations, promotes technical cooperation.

The State of São Paulo, which has the largest and most dynamic economy in the country, is unique in having a historically well-supported state research foundation (FAPESP). This agency has played a major role in sponsoring international cooperation programmes as part of its research support programmes. The long-term stability of FAPESP's operating budget and funding schemes have been critical to the development of the main public universities in São Paulo as flagship research universities in Brazil (Schwartzman, 2007).

These government agencies, along with the Ministry of Education, interface with a large higher education system. Brazilian higher education is very diverse, including public universities supported and controlled by federal, state, and municipal governments, and a massive private sector composed of both non-profit and for-profit institutions (Balbachevsky & da Quinteiro, 2003; Neves, 2015). Generally speaking, most research takes place at public universities and a few elite private non-profit institutions, although there is great variability in the public sector in terms of research intensity. Enrolment expanded substantially since the 1990s with an increasingly competitive and differentiated private sector absorbing most of the demand, albeit through different policy tools reflecting the political preferences and agendas of different governments (Schwartzman & Balbachevsky, 2011).

While Brazil's constitution enshrines university autonomy, in practice many aspects of academic decision-making are regulated by central agencies (Pereira Laus & Costa Morosini, 2005; Schwartzman & Balbachevsky, 2011). The Ministry of Education issues curriculum standards and oversees degree recognition. The CAPES Foundation evaluates and accredits graduate programmes, and funds graduate students. Control exerted from the central government over key aspects of curricular development and research performance influences institutional priorities and individual orientations towards international engagement.

3   Government Programmes

The Brazilian government has long supported internationalisation through programmes aimed at fostering mobility and international research collaboration. EU countries are among the most important destinations and partners in these policy initiatives. The development of these programmes through the main federal agencies has been marked by ebbs and flows caused by the state of the economy and changes in government.

Investments in academic mobility have been a consistent strategy of the federal government for decades (Morosini, 2011). When CAPES was first established in the 1950s, there were few graduate programmes in Brazil, and the foundation sponsored students to go abroad, earn PhDs and return to work in Brazilian universities. This modality of mobility for graduate studies remains important to this day, along with 'sandwich' scholarships for graduate students to have a stay abroad during the doctoral studies. Another important instrument for mobility are the so-called 'post-doctoral' fellowships aimed at faculty members, which fund the equivalent of a sabbatical year at a foreign university. As national graduate schools developed, CAPES gradually shifted support towards 'sandwich' scholarships to the point that they became the predominant funding tool for mobility. For instance, in 2017, from more than 9,500 awards for graduate students, researchers and professors, about 4,190 were granted for sandwich doctoral studies abroad (Ministério da Educação, 2018). As a major research funding source, CNPq also plays a role in supporting mobility through fellowships and project funding.

In uncharacteristic fashion, the federal government during president Dilma Rouseff's government (2011–2016) launched a large and visible policy initiative to stimulate academic mobility in 2011, the Science Without Borders (SWB) programme. President Rousseff herself announced the programme with the goal of sending 100,000 students and scholars abroad, and also supporting visiting professors from abroad in Brazilian universities. Nonetheless, this programme was mired in controversy since the beginning. Funding for the scholarships was initially announced as resulting from a mix of new government funds and private sponsorship, which never materialised as envisaged. As a result, funding was redistributed from federal science agencies (CAPES and CNPq) leading to severe cutbacks in research funding and other programmes. Moreover, policy design left unclear how the government expected to reach their goals (Sá, 2016). The emphasis on sending a massive number of undergraduate students abroad for a year – they represented 76% of the scholarship recipients – met several obstacles, including language proficiency among applicants, the lack of recognition of academic credits, and a disconnect between the curriculum at the home and host universities (Knobel, 2012; Mcmanus & Nobre, 2017; Nery, 2018). As the economy slowed down and fiscal constraints became more pressing, the programme was phased out in 2017, and CAPES reverted to the older model of supporting graduate study abroad at a smaller scale – about 5,000 scholarships per year (Ministério da Educação, 2017).

The experience of SWB illustrates traditional mobility patterns among Brazilian students. While the most popular country of destination was the US (c. 27.821 student), the region receiving the most SWB students was Europe. The most popular European destinations were the UK (10,740 students), France (7,279), Germany (6,595), Spain (5,025), Italy (3,930), and Portugal (3,843) (Ciências Sem Fronteiras, 2016).

Over the last two decades, Brazilian funding agencies have supported international research collaboration through a number of specific funding schemes. For most of the 2000s, under president Lula da Silva's government which emphasised "South-South" diplomacy, efforts were made to position Brazil's higher education and research systems as partners to South American and African countries. For instance, CNPq launched programmes such as PRO-SUL and PROAFRICA to support joint research projects and scientific events involving South American and African countries, respectively (Sá, Kretz, & Sigurdson, 2015). These programmes, arising out of foreign policy consideration, co-existed with other significant international partnerships driven by scientific objectives such as those involving spatial research and geo-monitoring (de Brito Cruz & Chaimovich, 2010).

Brazilian funding agencies have worked with a number of European countries on agreements to coordinate joint research funding opportunities. For example, a bi-lateral Science & Technology Agreement established in 2007 between the EU and Brazil has led to more than 350 projects (European Commission, 2018). In addition, CAPES has bilateral programmes with a number of countries in Europe, including Germany, Austria, Belgium, Spain, France, Italy, Netherlands, Norway, Portugal, the UK, and Sweden. In 2017, 30 funding schemes were in place with international partner universities (Ministério da Educação, 2018). Similarly, FAPESP has cooperation agreements with several European public institutions in France, the UK, Germany, and Spain. Severe cuts to the national science budget in recent years, discussed below, have affected these programmes (Escobar, 2019).

Departing from the more conventional focus on supporting individual researchers or research teams in the programmes discussed above, CAPES launched in 2017 the Institutional Programme of Internationalisation (CAPES-PrInt) with a R$300 million (c. US$75,505,000) budget. This initiative was presented as a new approach to internationalisation, following sectoral consultations (Ministério da Educação, 2018). Generally, CAPES' objectives were to encourage universities to develop their own internationalisation strategies, to create and strengthen international research networks, and expand the internationalisation graduate programmes. Support is provided over four years for projects that contribute to those objectives. This programme had the effect of inducing several universities to devise internationalisation plans as they sought to apply for funding. In 2018, CAPES supported 36 higher education institutions (Fundação CAPES, 2018).

These institutional programmes supported by PrInt provide a glimpse into the international orientation of Brazilian universities. The University of Brasilia provides an illustrative account of priorities and obstacles to be addressed (Universidade de Brasília, 2018a, 2018b). The main areas of focus for internationalisation were related to increasing academic mobility, research collaboration, and strategic networks with existing partners in a number of countries, including a majority of European nations such as France, Germany, the Netherlands, Italy, Spain, the UK, Norway, and Portugal. Other universities similarly pointed to established collaboration with European nations. For example, the Pontifical Catholic University of Rio Grande do Sul, has most of its partner countries for PrInt funded projects in Europe, including Germany, Austria, Belgium, Spain, Finland, France, Italy, Ireland, and more (PUCRS, n.d.). Similarly, the Universidade Federal do Ceará states that it has predominant collaborations with France, Germany, and the UK, in addition to the US and Canada (Universidade Federal do Ceará, 2017). The Universidade Federal do Rio Grande do Sul describes a long history of international relations with Western Europe and North America, having most of its collaboration with countries from these regions (Universidade Federal do Rio Grande do Sul, 2017).

The University of Brasília recognised a number of barriers to be overcome, which are arguably common among Brazilian universities (Universidade de Brasília, 2018b). They encompass academic and policy frameworks that are not responsive to the demands of internationalisation, lack of infrastructure to support international collaboration, and an insufficient administrative apparatus to aid research and innovation.

4 Bottom-up Initiatives

Apart from the policy frameworks for internationalisation in Brazilian universities, much of the impetus to engage in international cooperation comes from the bottom-up. Historically and presently, students and professors have pursued research training and collaborators in European countries, forging ties that are harnessed when funding opportunities arise. As discussed above, it is common for Brazilian researchers to secure funding from federal agencies to go abroad for a partial PhD, postdoc, or a visiting position. PhDs abroad were the norm until the mid-1990s, when the number of doctoral programmes in Brazil expanded and met national demand for graduate training (Balbachevsky, 2005). More recently, the emphasis has been on partial doctoral studies or post-doctoral training overseas. A study by Furtado et al. (2015) on the career trajectory of around 6,000 scientists found that 20% of PhDs were completed abroad, while 60% of post-docs were completed abroad.

These international experiences are most often acquired in Europe and North America. Furtado et al.'s (2015) survey found that about 12% of PhDs were completed in Europe and around 7% in North America. For 21% of the researchers, a post-doc was their only international career experience. Those postdoctoral stints help researchers establish networks of collaboration with international research groups. Indeed, internationally co-authored publications by Brazilian researchers have consistently included peers at European and North American institutions (Leta & Chaimovich, 2002). Like their Latin American counterparts, Brazilian researchers mostly co-publish with colleagues in the US and Western European countries such as Spain, France, Germany, and the UK (UNESCO, 2015).

The impact of this pattern in academic careers can go beyond the immediate outcomes related to visiting appointments and post-doctoral training. They provide a basis for long-term cooperation, as faculty members use the networks they establish to develop research partnerships when opportunities arise, and to enable further mobility by future graduate students.

One EU-funded research centre, the Institute for Brazil-Europe Studies at the University of São Paulo, provides a formal venue for these kinds of relationships. Created in 2010, the Institute supports and promotes communication and exchange among Brazilian and European researchers (USP, 2015). By 2015, it had involved 27 European and Brazilian universities in partnership arrangements. Through the IBE, students, faculty, and staff have participated in the Erasmus Mundus programmes.

But how common are university-based initiatives to foster cooperation with the EU? We analysed the academic plans of a sample of 15 public universities to understand how they articulated their internationalisation objectives, and the extent to which cooperation with the EU is prioritised. Public universities under the control of the federal government ("federal universities") produce Institutional Development Plans for accreditation and evaluation purposes (Dal Magro & Rausch, 2012). We selected the following public universities for the study: Universidade de Brasília; Universidade Federal de Mato Grosso do Sul; Universidade Federal da Bahia; Universidade Federal do Recôncavo da Bahia; Universidade Federal do Ceará; Universidade Federal do Maranhão; Universidade Federal do Vale do São Francisco; Universidade Federal Rural do Semi-Árido; Universidade Federal do Amazonas; Universidade Federal do Pará; Universidade Federal de Minas Gerais; Universidade Federal de Viçosa; Universidade Federal do Estado do Rio de Janeiro; Universidade Tecnológica Federal do Paraná; Universidade Federal de Santa Catarina.

Through these documents, higher education institutions develop a 5-year academic plan delineating their mission, priorities, and objectives (Ministério da Educação, 2004, n.d.). Internationalisation is not one of the aspects that universities are required to report on – these include institutional profile, institutional management, academic organisation, infrastructure, financing, and evaluation of institutional development. Therefore, they allow us to observe how institutions choose to frame and report on internationalisation initiatives. We examined current and the immediate past institutional plans in order to assess the continuity in strategies, and identify possible shifts in priorities and objectives.

Our review of these documents shows growing attention to internationalisation in the early 2010s. All most recent plans, published between 2015 and 2019, mention internationalisation as an important institutional objective. While there were mentions of internationalisation in earlier plans, they were not as common, and in four of the 15 universities it was not addressed at all. That increase seems to be related to the perceived importance attributed to it by government agencies; earlier, mentions of Science Without Borders were common while the programme was at its apex.

More generally, universities profile efforts to establish international agreements with universities abroad, with European countries being among their priorities. They also indicate an interest in opportunities to attract international scholars and researchers, and several universities had Erasmus Mundus and Santander Universities as their main sponsors for academic mobility. Not all have been successful in tapping these sources; the Federal University of Bahia documented a decrease in incoming international students from Europe due to perceived funding limitations.

Moreover, Europe appeared to be one of the main regions of interest for international cooperation. Four university institutional development plans did not give any information regarding the countries of cooperation or interest for internationalisation. From the 11 that did, all mentioned Europe in some way, usually representing their main region of collaboration or one of their priorities of collaboration. Four universities with diverse research profiles gave a detailed account of cooperation agreements (University of Brasilia; Federal University of Mato Grosso do Sul; Federal University of Vale do São Francisco; Federal Technological University of Parana). In these cases, the majority of cooperation agreements were with European universities. Europe is also considered one of the main sources of funding for internationalisation for some of the universities. For example, the Federal University of Viçosa identified the EU alongside CAPES and the International Foundation for Science as relevance funders.

5 2020s: Whither International Cooperation?

For the historical, cultural, and professional reasons sketched out above, the EU will continue to be a central destination for Brazilian scholars and scientists wishing to further their academic careers through study, work, and collaboration. However, the 2020s will start with a dramatic shift in the context, mood, and perspective of Brazilian higher education for international engagement. The optimism of the early 2010s, when Brazil was still in the limelight as one of the emerging economies of the so-called BRICS, was followed by a sustained fiscal crisis and political turmoil. Annual GDP growth has averaged 0.5% per year between 2011–2018 and the decade is projected to end with a meagre 0.9% annual average (Ministério da Economia, 2019). This has resulted in a real decrease in GDP per capita, while government expenditures continued on an upward trajectory. This weak economic performance has only been matched by the 1980s, known as "the lost decade", when average annual GDP growth was 1.6%. The latter half of the 2010s has been particularly challenging for Brazilian academia, with clear impacts on the ability of universities and researchers to engage in international cooperation. This will likely result in a dampening of internationalisation initiatives linking Brazilian institutions and their counterparts in the EU, as well as academic mobility to Europe.

The worsening of the deficit has led to successive cuts to the higher education and science budgets since the mid-decade. In 2015, president Dilma Rouseff's government cut 10% of higher education funding, including R$9.4 billion (US$2.31 billion) from the Ministry of Education budget and a R$1.6 billion (US$390 million) from the Ministry of Science, Technology, and Innovation (Branco, 2015). Budget cuts to education continued in the following years. From 2015 to 2018, CAPES expenditures decreased by almost half (from US$1.9 billion to US$1 billion) (Martelli Júnior et al., 2019). In 2016, the federal budget for science, technology, and innovation was the lowest in 10 years at $1.5 billion, which led to substantial cuts in scholarships and grants (Escobar, 2016), while in 2017 the budget of the Ministry of Science and Technology was the lowest in 14 years (Martelli Júnior et al., 2019).

In 2019, the Bolsonaro government continued the pattern of cuts aimed at redressing the deficit, coupled with politically motivated financial sanctions to public universities perceived to be engaging in partisan politics. For example, in April, a 30% cut to the Federal University of Bahia, Fluminense Federal University, and University of Brasilia were announced, accusing the universities of hosting political events (BBC, 2019). The CAPES scholarship programme had to put 11,000 scholarships on hold due to the freezing of its funding allocation, and a similar measure affected the Ministry of Education blocking allocations to federal institutions of higher education to the tune of R$2 billion (US$490 million) (BBC, 2019). The budget of the Science and Communications Ministry was also cut to nearly half (Angelo, 2019), leading to a reduction of funding to CNPq of R$330 million reais (US$89 million). This has caused the cancellation of 80,000 scholarships and fellowships to researchers and students (Andrade, 2019). CAPES projected having half of the 2019 budget in 2020 (G1, 2019). While the exact magnitude of these cuts will continue to be negotiated, the retrenchment of public expenditures in higher education and science characterising this period is clear and will not be reversed soon.

Altogether, the economic situation and fiscal crisis severely compromise the operation of graduate programmes and research activity in Brazilian universities, as well as their ability to autonomously engage in international cooperation. Their prospects for the start of the 2020s are not encouraging, as attention will be focused on trying to preserve the regular operation of teaching and research activities, with limited scope for innovative initiatives. With federal funding to universities in constant decline, we can expect a general reduction in internationalisation funding and, thus, a decrease in research programmes linking Brazilian researchers to their colleagues overseas. As already observed in the more recent internationalisation plans of Brazilian universities, these institutions have often reached out to European sources of funding as a significant contribution to internationalisation. They will likely be more dependent upon external sponsorship to initiate new internationalisation activities. To the extent that the European Union continues to invest in academic cooperation and exchange programs with third countries such as Brazil, they will find an eager audience among cash-starved Brazilian universities.

Not only is the current political context characterised by budget woes for higher education, but it is also marked by an explicit antagonism to academia and science which arguably detracts from the country's ability to exercise soft power through these institutions. This has been evident in the appointment of two unqualified and ideologue ministers of education in its first year who have engendered a series of faux-pas (Filho, 2019). Through anti-intellectual positions and rhetorical attacks on universities, the Minister of Education has created an environment of constant polemic and conflict with the higher education sector (Ferreira, 2019). Furthermore, this government has engaged in a brand of right-wing populism that shuns the autonomy of scientific institutions and the values of multilateral engagement (McCoy, 2019). In less than a year, its reckless disregard for environmental protection has undermined Brazil's international standing, with clear implications for the country's ability to exercise soft power in the international community (Lupion, 2019).

In conclusion, the first year of this government suggests that international academic cooperation will hardly register as an area deserving of special support in the next four years, both domestically and as part of its foreign policy agenda. The longstanding means through which federal agencies have enabled academic mobility and research collaboration have been affected by financial demands, and will likely remain threatened in the near future. Alongside the retrenchment in general support for higher education, universities will be constrained in maintaining and developing their own internationalisation initiatives. Barring a dramatic reversal of fortune in Brazil's economic and fiscal conditions, the 2020s will start with a reduction in the autonomous engagement of Brazilian universities and researchers with their counterparts in the EU, and greater dependence on international sources of support for such activity.

Acknowledgement

The authors would like to thank the Social Sciences and Humanities Research Council of Canada for their support.

References

Andrade, R. de O. (2019). Brazil's budget cuts threaten more than 80,000 science scholarships. *Nature, 572*, 575–576. https://doi.org/10.1038/d41586-019-02484-w

Angelo, C. (2019). Brazil's government freezes nearly half of its science spending. *Nature, 568*, 155–156. https://doi.org/10.1038/d41586-019-01079-9

Balbachevsky, E. (2005). A pós-graduação no Brasil: Novos desafios para uma política bem-sucedida. *Os Desafios Da Educação No Brasil. Rio de Janeiro: Nova Fronteira, 1*, 285–314.

Balbachevsky, E., & da Quinteiro, M. C. (2003). The changing academic workplace in Brazil. In P. G. Altbach (Ed.), *The decline of the guru: The academic profession in the third world* (pp. 75–106). Palgrave Macmillan. https://doi.org/10.1057/9781403982568_4

BBC. (2019, May 15). Saiba o que já é verdade e o que ainda é ameaça sobre os cortes na educação. *BBC News Brasil.* https://www.bbc.com/portuguese/brasil-48283522

Branco, M. (2015, July 17). *Pesquisadores pedem a Dilma revogação de cortes na educação e ciência.* EBC. http://www.ebc.com.br/noticias/politica/2015/07/pesquisadores-pedem-dilma-revogacao-de-cortes-na-educacao-e-ciencia

CAPES. (2019). *CAPES libera mais de 3 mil novas bolsas de pós-graduação.* http://www.capes.gov.br/36-noticias/9821-capes-libera-mais-de-3-mil-novas-bolsas-de-pos-graduacao

Ciências Sem Fronteiras. (2016). *País de Destino do Bolsista* (Painel de Controle Do Programa Ciência Sem Fronteiras). http://www.cienciasemfronteiras.gov.br/web/csf/painel-de-controle

Dal Magro, C. B., & Rausch, R. B. (2012). Plano de desenvolvimento institucional de universidades federais brasileiras. *Administração: Ensino e Pesquisa, 13*(3), 427–453.

de Brito Cruz, C. H., & Chaimovich, H. (2010). Brazil. In S. Schneegans (Ed.), *UNESCO science report 2010* (pp. 103–121). UNESCO.

de Moura Castro, C. (1983). The impact of European and American influences on Brazilian higher education. *European Journal of Education, 18*(4), 367–381. https://doi.org/10.2307/1503099

Escobar, H. (2016, October 18). Budget cap would stifle Brazilian science, critics say. *Science | AAAS*. https://www.sciencemag.org/news/2016/10/budget-cap-would-stifle-brazilian-science-critics-say

Escobar, H. (2019). Brazilian scientists lament 'freeze' on research budget. *Science, 364*(6436), 111. https://doi.org/10.1126/science.364.6436.111

European Commission. (2018). *New mechanisms to support EU–Brazil cooperation in research and innovation*. https://ec.europa.eu/info/news/new-mechanisms-support-eu-brazil-cooperation-research-and-innovation-2018-may-22_en

Ferreira, P. (2019, November 22). Reitores das universidades federais querem processar ministro da Educação. *Jornal O Globo*. https://oglobo.globo.com/sociedade/educacao/reitores-das-universidades-federais-querem-processar-ministro-da-educacao-24094315

Filho, J. (2019, April 14). Por dentro da paranoia olavista do novo ministro da Educação, Abraham Weintraub. *The Intercept*. https://theintercept.com/2019/04/14/mec-olavo-weintraub-educacao-comunismo/

Fundação CAPES. (2018). *Divulgado resultado final do Programa de Internacionalização*. http://www.capes.gov.br/36-noticias/9090-divulgado-resultado-final-do-programa-de-internacionalizacao

Furtado Jr., C. A., Gonçalves, M. A., & de Almeida, J. M. (2015). A spatiotemporal analysis of Brazilian science from the perspective of researchers' career trajectories. *PLOS ONE, 10*(10), e0141528. https://doi.org/10.1371/journal.pone.0141528

G1. (2019). *Corte em bolsas da Capes vale também para programas de pós-graduação com alta nota de avaliação | Educação | G1*. https://g1.globo.com/educacao/noticia/2019/09/10/capes-vai-congelar-bolsas-de-pesquisa-ate-em-cursos-com-alto-nivel-de-avaliacao.ghtml

Knobel, M. (2012). Brazil's Student Mobility Initiative. *International Higher Education, 66*. https://doi.org/10.6017/ihe.2012.66.8836

Leta, J., & Chaimovich, H. (2002). Recognition and international collaboration: The Brazilian case. *Scientometrics, 53*(3), 325–335.

Lupion, B. (2019). *Brasil é cínico ao cobrar engajamento ambiental de países desenvolvidos*. DW. https://www.dw.com/pt-br/brasil-%C3%A9-c%C3%ADnico-ao-cobrar-engajamento-ambiental-de-pa%C3%ADses-desenvolvidos/a-50194465

Martelli Júnior, H., Martelli, D. R., Silva, A. C. S. e, Oliveira, M. C. L., & Oliveira, E. A. (2019). Brazil's endangered postgraduate system. *Science, 363*(6424), 240. https://doi.org/10.1126/science.aav9015

McCoy, T. (2019, August 7). Brazil's Amazon monitor, fired after dispute with Bolsonaro, speaks out on deforestation. *Washington Post*. https://www.washingtonpost.com/world/the_americas/the-amazon-monitor-who-was-fired-by-bolsonaro-speaks-out-on-deforestation/2019/08/06/f436af92-b844-11e9-bad6-609f75bfd97f_story.html

Mcmanus, C., & Nobre, C. A. (2017). Brazilian scientific mobility program – Science without borders – Preliminary results and perspectives. *Anais Da Academia Brasileira de Ciências, 89*(1), 773–786. https://doi.org/10.1590/0001-3765201720160829

Ministério da Economia. (2019). *Nota Informativa: Comparando o Crescimento do PIB nas Décadas de 1980 e atual*. https://observatorio3setor.org.br/wp-content/uploads/2019/03/2019.02.28_NI-compara%C3%A7%C3%A3o-do-PIB-d%C3%A9cadas-1980-x-2010.pdf

Ministério da Educação. (2004). *Plano de Desenvolvimento Institucional – PDI: Diretrizes para Elaboração*. https://sites.unipampa.edu.br/pdi/files/2013/04/Diretrizes-para-elabora%C3%A7%C3%A3o-do-PDI-2004.pdf

Ministério da Educação. (2017). *MEC afirma que o Ciência sem Fronteiras terá 5 mil bolsistas na pós-graduação*. http://portal.mec.gov.br/ultimas-noticias/212-educacao-superior-1690610854/46981-mec-afirma-que-o-ciencia-sem-fronteiras-tera-5-mil-bolsistas-na-pos-graduacao

Ministério da Educação. (2018). *Relatório de Gestão do Exercício de 2017*. https://www.capes.gov.br/images/banners/18092018_Relat%C3%B3rio_de_Gest%C3%A3o_CAPES_2017.pdf

Ministério da Educação. (n.d.). *Formulários do Plano de Desenvolvimento Institucional – PDI*. Retrieved September 13, 2019, from http://www2.mec.gov.br/sapiens/Form_PDI.htm

Morosini, M. C. (2011). Internacionalização na produção de conhecimento em IES Brasileiras: Cooperação internacional tradicional e cooperação internacional horizontal. *Educação em Revista, 27*(1), 93–112. https://doi.org/10.1590/S0102-46982011000100005

Nery, M. B. M. (2018). Science without borders' contributions to internationalization of Brazilian higher education. *Journal of Studies in International Education, 22*(5), 371–392. https://doi.org/10.1177/1028315317748526

Neves, C. E. (2015). Demand and supply for higher education in Brazil. In S. Schwartzman, R. Pinheiro, & P. Pillay (Eds.), *Higher education in the BRICS countries* (pp. 73–96). Springer.

Pereira Laus, S., & Costa Morosini, M. (2005). Internationalization of higher education in Brazil. In H. de Wit, I. C. Jaramillo, J. Gacel-Avila, & J. Knight (Eds.), *Higher education in Latin America: The international dimension* (pp. 111–147). World Bank.

PUCRS. (n.d.). *PUCRS PrInT*. Projeto Institucional de Internacionalização – PUCRS PrInt. Retrieved September 13, 2019, from http://www.pucrs.br/print-pt/

Sá, C. M., & Grieco, J. (2015). International collaboration in Brazilian higher education. *Frontiers of Education in China*, *10*(1), 7–22. https://doi.org/10.1007/BF03397050

Sá, C. M., Kretz, A., & Sigurdson, K. (2015). Research and the 'third mission' in light of global events. In S. Schwartzman, R. Pinheiro, & P. Pillay (Eds.), *Higher education in the BRICS countries: Investigating the pact between higher education and society* (pp. 379–398). Springer. https://doi.org/10.1007/978-94-017-9570-8_19

Schwartzman, S. (1991). *A space for science: The development of the scientific community in Brazil*. Pennsylvania State University Press.

Schwartzman, S. (2007). Brazil's leading university – Original ideas and contemporary goals. In P. G. Altbach & J. Balán (Eds.), *World class worldwide: Transforming research universities in Asia and Latin America* (pp. 143–172). The John Hopkins University Press.

Schwartzman, S., & Balbachevsky, E. (2011). *Brazil: Diverse experiences in institutional governance in the public and private sectors*. http://archive.org/details/BrazilDiverseExperiencesInInstitutionalGovernanceInThePublicAnd

UNESCO. (2015). *UNESCO science report: Towards 2030*. Author. http://uis.unesco.org/sites/default/files/documents/unesco-science-report-towards-2030-part1.pdf

Universidade de Brasilia. (2018a). *Plan of Internationalization Universidade de Brasilia (UnB) 2018–2022: Executive Summary*. http://www.int.unb.br/images/Normativas/Internationalization_Plan_-_EXECUTIVE_SUMMARY.pdf

Universidade de Brasilia. (2018b). *Projeto PrInt Aprovado Capes (com read orçamentária)*. https://drive.google.com/file/d/1MVrXY2Et7R4y-IWmFu_W-N4pl_AYSJ9k/view

Universidade Federal do Ceará. (2017). *Plano de Internacionalização da Universidade Federal do Ceará*. http://www.ufc.br/images/_files/a_universidade/plano-internacionalizacao-ufc/plano-internacionalizacao-ufc.pdf

Universidade Federal do Rio Grande do Sul. (2017). *Plano de Internacionalização da Universidade Federal do Rio Grande do Sul*. http://www.ufrgs.br/propg/print-ufrgs/arquivos/plano-institucional

USP. (2015). *Instituto de Estudos Brasil-Europa conecta pesquisadores brasileiros e europeus*. Universidade de São Paulo. https://www5.usp.br/95044/instituto-de-estudos-brasil-europa-conecta-pesquisadores-brasileiros-e-europeus/

Vaira, M., & Rostan, M. (Eds.). (2011). *Questioning excellence in higher education: Policies, experiences and challenges in national and comparative perspective*. Sense Publishers.

CHAPTER 5

China's Policies and Practices with Respect to Higher Education Cooperation with the EU

Yuzhuo Cai and Gaoming Zheng

Abstract

When it comes to the second decade of the 21st century, the cooperation between the European Union (EU) and China in higher education has been evolving from 1.0 era, when the focus was on policy dialogues and practical collaboration in the higher education sector only, to 2.0 era, when EU-China higher education cooperation becomes an integral and important part of the EU-China strategic partnership. Nevertheless, the many stakeholders in EU-China higher education cooperation are not yet aware of such change. Primarily from China's perspective, the chapter aims to provide an overview of policies and practices of EU-China higher education cooperation in 1.0 era, and also discuss the transition to EU-China higher education cooperation in the context of building an EU-China strategic partnership in 2.0 era. The analysis shows that the EU and China have achieved fruitful outcomes in higher education cooperation in 1.0 Era, especially in the increase of joint education provision, the deepening and expansion of research collaboration, and also the growth of individual mobility between both sides. The positive outcomes have also enhanced the compatibility of the EU's and China's expectations in cooperation with each other in higher education and led them into a more comprehensive partnership development in 2.0 era, fitting into the EU-China strategic partnership framework. The chapter also highlights that the recently launched China's New Silk Road Policy has brought in a new perspective in the current landscape of international higher education cooperation and may affect the EU-China higher education cooperation in the future. The study applies an on-desk qualitative research method by analysing secondary data, such as academic literature, governmental policy documents, and strategic documents.

Keywords

EU – Europe – China – higher education – cooperation – internationalisation

1   Introduction

Higher education cooperation between the People's Republic of China and many European countries has a long history, dating back to student exchanges in the 1950s. More profound cooperation between China and the European Union (EU) has taken place since the 1990s and especially the beginning of the millennium, owing to the rapid development of reciprocal relationships between China and the EU (Cai, 2019a). In 2003, China issued its first-ever policy paper on the EU and on the EU side the European Commission (EC) issued a communication on *A Maturing Partnership – Shared Interests and Challenges in EU-China Relations* (Zhou, 2017). Following this, the most significant change in the nature of China-EU cooperation is that both sides consider each other to be an important innovation partner, not merely trade partners (Cai, 2019a). The burgeoning interests of both China and the EU in science, technology and innovation (STI) co-operation have been expedited by the signing of the *EU-China Innovation Cooperation Dialogue* in 2012, which complements and ensures synergy with the *Agreement on Science and Technology Cooperation between the EU and China* in 1998.

Higher education cooperation is an integral part of the larger picture of EU-China strategic partnership building. The future of such cooperation is more than achieving prosperous student/teaching mobility, joint degree provision and research collaboration. As proposed by Cai (2019b), EU-China higher education cooperation is expected to move up a notch, reflected in a paradigm change from the form 1.0 to the form 2.0. Compared to the current EU-China higher education cooperation 1.0, consisting of policy dialogues and practical collaboration in the higher education sector only, it is expected that in EU-China higher education cooperation 2.0, the next phase, the higher education collaboration between both sides is seen as an integral part of building an EU-China strategic partnership. This change requires Chinese policies and practices concerning EU-China higher education cooperation to be analysed from the strategic partnership perspective of cooperation.

However, there is a gap in both research and practice with few interactions between higher education cooperation and cooperation in other sectors (Cai, 2019a; Cai, Ferrer, & Lastra, 2019). Although having an ambitious intention to fill the gap, the goal of this chapter is modest. It tries to achieve two objectives: (1) to provide an overview of policies and practices of EU-China higher education cooperation, primarily from the Chinese perspective and (2) to briefly discuss the development of this higher education cooperation in the context of building an EU-China strategic partnership. The two objectives are respectively related to the two forms of EU-China higher education cooperation, namely 1.0 and 2.0. The chapter will be concluded with some suggestions on how to strengthen higher education cooperation in the context of broader EU-China relations.

2   EU-China Higher Education Cooperation 1.0

2.1   *China's Internationalisation of Higher Education*

The internationalisation of higher education is an inevitable outcome of China's integration into the global economy as well as an essential measure to improve its higher education system. Major activities of internationalisation have been undertaken in the areas of student mobility, internationalisation of activities of teaching and research, and joint education provision (Yang, 2014), with remarkable achievement though mainly in a quantitative sense (Cai, 2014).

In spite of the dramatic expansion of China's higher education system, the surging demand from its younger generation for high quality higher education has not yet been met (Cai & Yan, 2015). To resolve the tension, a use of foreign educational resources is a possible solution (Shumilova & Cai, 2016). The number of students pursuing study abroad has increased dramatically in the last four decades. According to the latest published statistics, from 1978 to 2018 the population of Chinese students overseas reached 5.85 million, among whom 3.65 million have completed their study and returned to China (Ministry of Education in China, 2019c).

China also attaches importance to attracting international students to study in China. In 2018 there were 4.92 million international students undertaking their studies in 1,004 universities in China (Ministry of Education in China, 2019a). These international students came from 196 different countries, and among them the top five sources were Korea, Thailand, Pakistan, India and America (Ministry of Education in China, 2019a). The booming numbers of international students in Chinese universities can be explained in two ways. Firstly, legislation has to a large extent transferred the power of recruiting international students to institutions (Shieh & Wang, 2007). Secondly, the growing interest among many countries in cooperating with China and entering the Chinese market has driven many of their students to study in Chinese universities.

While the main activity of internationalisation of higher education until the late 1990s was student mobility, since then the focus has changed to internationalise the profiles of teaching and research. This internationalisation has three dimensions: increasing English taught courses; a higher percentage of overseas trained teachers; and institutionalised structures specifically for research cooperation (Cai, 2014).

In terms of cooperation on degree education, the most important achievement is the development in Sino-foreign cooperation in establishing educational institutions. The term Sino-foreign Cooperation in Running Schools (SFCRS) is explicitly defined as: "the activities of the cooperation between foreign educational institutions and Chinese educational institutions in establishing educational institutions within the territory of China to provide education service mainly to Chinese citizens" (Article 2, Regulations on Chinese-Foreign Cooperation in Running Schools, Ministry of Education 2003). In practice, foreign institutions must partner with Chinese institutions in establishing joint educational provision in China. By 2019, all together 109 international joint institutes and 1,087 international joint academic programmes in China had been established and approved by the Chinese government (Ministry of Education in China, 2019b).

2.2 *China's Ongoing Policies of Internationalisation of Higher Education*

The activities of China's internationalisation of higher education are facilitated by steering policies and funding mechanisms mainly concerned with mobility, education and research collaboration. For instance, in terms of student mobility, the China Scholarship Council (CSC) was established in 1994, and since then it has been supporting Chinese students to study abroad with state funding. However, nowadays self-funded students have become the majority of Chinese overseas students. Since 2003, the CSC has set an "Excellent Self-funded Students' Prize" to award outstanding self-funded Chinese overseas students. Besides supporting Chinese students studying abroad, the CSC also provides scholarships for international students to undertake degree studies in China.

In another aspect of importing international education resources, *The 2003 Regulations on SFCRS* and follow-up regulations play a key role. The Regulations manifest the self-interest of the Chinese government to support cooperation between Chinese and international universities to provide education jointly inside China at institutional level (Qu & Feng, 2018). By allowing foreign universities to enter into the Chinese higher education system, the Chinese government recognised that joint ventures in higher education (joint institutions and joint programmes) were a potential way to introduce advanced educational resources from abroad and to provide opportunities for receiving internationally grounded education to its students who were not able to attend top tier universities locally or abroad (Onsman, 2013).

With respect to international research cooperation, the twelfth and thirteenth Five-Year Plans of the National Natural Science Foundation of China

(NSFC) in 2011 and 2015 explicitly supported Chinese academics in international collaboration in scientific research (NSFC, 2011, 2015). The NSFC has acted as the core funding organisation in China to support scientific research (especially basic research), innovation, and the cultivation of talent since its establishment in 1986 (NSFC, 2019). For instance, the NSFC launched the NSFC *Regulation on International (Regional) Collaboration in Research* to support Chinese scholars in conducting international joint research projects on the frontier of scientific development (NSFC, 2009). In 2014 the NSFC published another policy in order to attract international, especially young, academics to undertake research activities in mainland China (NSFC, 2014). By 2018, through the two policies, the NFSC had supported 432 joint research projects between China and international partners costing 834 million Ren Min Bi (RMB), and 140 international young researchers costing 45 million RMB (NSFC, 2018). Another funding and coordinating organisation in the area of social sciences, the National Social Science Fund of China (NSSFC) was also established in 1986 and a series of policies to support international collaboration in social science research have been launched.

The Guidelines of the *National Mid- and Long-Term Educational Reform and Development Planning* (2010–2020) (hereafter referred as Education 2020) is the most fundamental policy. Launched by the Chinese government in 2010, Education 2020 determined that an international strategy would be an important long-term policy for higher education development in China (Zhu & Zhang, 2017). It has supported the development of a comprehensive policy framework for the internationalisation of higher education in China through highlighting and encouraging the outward and inward international mobility of students and staff, joint institutions and joint programmes, and other international exchanges and cooperative activities (Zhu & Zhang, 2017). China's commitment to the internationalisation of higher education has been further affirmed by the *Modernisation of Chinese Education 2035* promulgated by the Central Committee of Chinese Communist Party and the State Council (Xinhua-Net, 2019). The new strategy (in Article 9) particularly states that China should enhance international collaboration in education comprehensively, promote the mutual recognition of academic degrees between China and other countries, encourage international communication and the sharing of experiences on the quality assessment of education (Xinhua-Net, 2019).

All these policies constitute a comprehensive internationalisation policy framework for Chinese higher education, which has allowed and motivated China to cooperate with other countries and regions in higher education development. Against such a background, practices in China-EU higher education cooperation take place.

2.3 Practices of China-EU Higher Education Cooperation

EU-China higher education cooperation has resulted in fruitful outcomes in practice. These are mainly reflected in the increase of joint higher education institutions and joint academic degree programmes, the expansion and deepening of research collaboration, and the growth of the exchange mobility of students and academics.

In terms of joint institutions and programmes in 2019 there were 28 EU-China joint higher education institutions and 171 EU-China joint academic programmes (including bachelor's, master's and doctoral degree programmes) based inside China (Ministry of Education in China, 2019ab). Inside the EU, the development of joint institutions and programmes between EU partner institutions and Chinese institutions has also been under exploration. For instance, in 2012, the first Erasmus Mundus Masters' Joint Degree (EMJD) Programme that has a Chinese university as partner institution in the programme consortium, a Masters Course in Research and Innovation in Higher Education (MARIHE), was implemented with financial support from the EC. It is a pioneering approach to explore the possibilities of Erasmus Mundus joint programmes with Chinese partners (Cai, 2013). Chinese universities have also been seeking opportunities to open offshore campuses or joint institutions in Europe in recent years, although their geographic focus has been largely placed in the UK (d'Hooghe, Montulet, de Wolff, & Pieke, 2018).

The deepening and expanding EU-China research collaboration is another achievement (Cai, 2019a). The Ministry of Sciences and Technology in China (MOST) has been actively promoting international research collaboration between the EU and China. For instance, in 2019, MOST launched a call for research proposals under the EU-China Co-funding Mechanisms for Research and Innovation (CFM) to support nine broad priority areas including food, agriculture, and biotechnology, for which MOST would invest about one billion RMB (about 13 million euros) (Delegation of the European-Union to China, 2019). Another example has been the development of an effective networking platform to connect researchers, higher education institutions and research institutes from China and the EU, providing useful information in terms of research funding, careers, collaboration opportunities and organising relevant events (EURAXESS, 2019b). Joint laboratories and joint research institutes have been established with EU-China cooperation, for instance in 2010, the EU-China Clean Energy Centre was launched, jointly financed by the Chinese government and the EU (EURAXESS, 2019a).

Although the increasing numbers of exchange students and academics between EU countries and China are applauded, there is a lack of sufficient statistics on the mobility. Where available, statistics from a joint study by the

EC and the Ministry of Education in China in 2011 indicates that in 2010, the total number of Chinese students in the EU was between 118,700 and 120,000, a figure which increased about 6 times from 2000 (GHK-Consulting & Renming-University, 2011). In terms of students' mobility from EU to China, in 2009 the number of EU students in China was over 22,600, which had nearly doubled from 2004 (GHK-Consulting & Renming-University, 2011). The same source indicates that from 2008 to 2009, at least 6,697 academics from China worked in EU countries, and in 2008 about 156 EU academics travelled to China on exchange schemes. It is noticeable that there exists an imbalance of exchange numbers between the two sides. It should also be mentioned that China has been among the top five non-EU partner countries sending students to participate in the Erasmus+ programme (European-Commission, 2019). The mobility of students and academics between EU and China have brought many benefits to European universities: for instance, a supply of much-needed doctoral candidates, tuition fees from fee-paying students, and access to cutting-edge research in Chinese universities (d'Hooghe et al., 2018).

2.4 Opportunities and Challenges in EU-China Higher Education Cooperation

The growing compatibility of the EU's and China's expectations in terms of collaboration in higher education has become a reliable foundation for more cooperation between both sides in the future (Cai, 2013, 2019a; Zheng & Cai, 2018). The review of the EU's and China's internationalisation strategies and practices in recent decades suggests that EU-China higher education cooperation has been developing in line with the needs/interests of the two sides (summarised in Table 5.1).

In spite of the fit between both the EU's and China's expectations of international cooperation between both sides at the policy level, the challenges lie in how the interests which match both sides can be realised (Cai, 2019a). Among many challenges, here we highlight three that urgently need our attention: the first is a lack of mutual trust between EU and China. Despite the recognition of the fruitful outcomes in EU-China higher education cooperation and its promising future benefits, recent research on this still expresses a concern from European researchers on collaboration with China in higher education (d'Hooghe et al., 2018; Kirby & Van der Wende, 2018). In the practice of joint degree provision between EU and China, a lack of mutual trust and understanding has often become a barrier (Cai, 2013; Zheng, Cai, & Ma, 2017). This may take a long time and more cooperative initiatives to overcome in the future.

Second, there is a lack of transparent, accessible information sharing between both sides. The language barrier may be one issue which hinders accessibility to information, e.g. information for research funding from China

TABLE 5.1 Compatibility of the EU's and China's expectations for the internationalisation of higher education

EU	China
Recruiting more Chinese students to study in European universities	Encouraging more Chinese students to study abroad, particularly in advanced systems, such as Europe
Exporting educational programmes and services to China	Meeting growing demands for higher education by importing high quality education resources from advanced higher education systems
Enhancing education and research cooperation with Chinese universities	Increasing international reputation and competitiveness through cooperation with (prestigious) foreign universities
Sending more European students to study in Chinese higher education	Attracting more international students to study in China

SOURCE: CAI (2019A, P. 171)

for European researchers and vice versa (d'Hooghe et al., 2018). Fortunately both the EU and China have been aware of this and now make information more available on the relevant websites by using English as a lingua franca.

The third challenge comes from the difficulties in reconciling the structural differences and incompatibility of higher education systems of EU countries and China. This may discourage further cooperation between European and Chinese universities. For instance, differences in legislative oversight, institutional regulations, communication channels and schemes would cause difficulties in the provision of joint academic degrees between European and Chinese universities and in recognising the learning outcomes of students from both sides (Cai, 2013). There are also challenges in reconciling the differences among EU member states' higher education systems when cooperating with Chinese partners (Zheng et al., 2017).

3 EU-China Higher Education Cooperation 2.0

3.1 *China's Internationalisation of Higher Education from the Perspective of Building EU-China Strategic Partnerships*

The increasingly strengthened higher education cooperation between China and Europe is associated with the rapid development of reciprocal relationships between China and the EU. The EU and China are looking for a comprehensive strategic partnership between both sides (European Commission, 2013) to improve cooperation in education, culture, youth, and research. This is reflected in three pillars: the strategic dialogue initiated in 2005; the economic and trade dialogue commenced in 2008; and the EU-China High-level-People-to-People Dialogue (HDDP) launched in 2012. The most significant change in the nature of China-EU cooperation is that both sides consider each other to be important innovation partners (China, 2017) and not merely trade partners as previously perceived. Indeed, China is becoming a global player in STI.

The strategic partnership entails a higher education dimension (Pinna, 2009), supporting both research and education collaboration between the EU and China. The cooperation has been greatly facilitated by the *EU-China Higher Education Platform for Cooperation and Exchange* (HEPCE), jointly set up in 2012 by the EC and the State Council of People's Republic of China within the framework of High Level People-to-people Dialogue (HPPD). The Platform has a clear aim of promoting sectoral policy dialogues, identifying common interest and strengthening mutual exchanges of best practices between EU and China (European Commission and State Council of China, 2012).

With respect to research, in May 2005, China and the EU signed a joint declaration in the EU-China Science and Technology Forum, in which it stated that it was high time for them to take cooperation forward based on mutual benefits to and reciprocal access and participation between both sides (Ministry of Science and Technology in China, 2005). Guided by the joint declaration, both sides have undertaken to support effective interaction between European and Chinese academia, facilitating research mobility, and improving and coordinating academic expertise more effectively. The EC has reinforced higher levels of collaboration between Europe and China, for example, via various programmes, such as the Innovative Training Network (ITN) Project under the Marie Skłodowska Curie Actions (MSCA), the COFUND Project and the Erasmus Mundus Scholarship Programme (Zhu, Cai, & François, 2017). Meanwhile, China opened its national research funding schemes, e.g. the 973 Programme and the 63 Programme, to European applications and encouraged joint research among European and Chinese researchers (Cai, 2019a).

Meanwhile, the EU and China have been exploring co-funding mechanisms to support joint research of mutual interest. In 2009, the Science and Technology Partnership Scheme between the Chinese MOST and the EC was established to support the launching of joint strategic projects by planning coordinated calls on topics of mutual interest between EU and China (EURAXESS, 2019a). In 2015, an EU-China initiative for co-funding for research and innovation was launched and opened its call for proposals to a wide range of disciplines (EURAXESS, 2019a). For instance, the EU-China flagship initiative, co-funded by Horizon 2020 of the EC and the NSFC, is planned to support joint projects on specific subjects of mutual interest, such as new biotechnologies for environment remediation in the 2018 call, and microorganism communities for plastics biodegradation and custom-made biological scaffolds for specific tissue regeneration and repair in the 2019 call (Business Finland, 2018). Co-funding for this initiative is jointly envisaged from Horizon 2020 with 35 million euros and from NSFC with 105 million RMB (approximately 13.4 million euros) (Business Finland, 2018). In 2015, NSFC and the European Research Council also signed an agreement on fostering cooperation between top level young researchers between China and Europe (EURAXESS, 2019a). While not essential, most of the research collaboration is based in universities.

Educational collaboration between the EU and China has been elevated to a new level since it has become an important part of the HPPD. The EC committed to welcome 5,000 Chinese students and academics to the EU and 2,000 EU students and academics to China during 2012–2016 under the EU mobility programmes. As a response, China's government scholarship has opened an EU window to attract and support 200 European annually students to study in Chinese universities (European Commission and State Council of China, 2012). For outbound mobility from China to the EU, the CSC has been actively supporting Chinese university students to study abroad all over the world including EU countries, for both short-term exchanges and degree studies. Several long-standing EU-China collaborative education programmes have been reinforced in the EU-China cooperation frameworks. For instance, the China-Europe International Business School (CEIBS), established in 1994 as a joint venture between EU and China, which by 2015 had successfully provided management training for over 80,000 executives (European Union External Action Service, 2015).

The studies on China-EU relations have stressed that the key to developing EU-China strategic partnerships lies in how to find effective ways to align the EU's and China's interests and expectations in different areas of cooperation, but the research has not so far provided satisfactory evidence on this (e.g., Men & Linck, 2017; Telò, Chun, & Xiaotong, 2018; Zhou, 2017). As a possible solution, Cai (2019a) suggested leveraging EU-China university cooperation, which has a relatively high level of mutual understanding (Liu, 2017; Navracsics, 2017), with a special cultural mission (Yang, 2017) to enhance trust in EU-China cooperation in other sectors, such as industry and government.

In recent years, the changing nature of EU-China cooperation has particular implications for EU-China higher education cooperation. The most significant change is that both sides consider each other to be important innovation partners (European Union Chamber of Commerce in China, 2017), and not merely trade partners as previously perceived. Indeed, China is becoming a global player in science, technology and innovation. Thus universities, which hold the most importance place in generating knowledge, developing technology and cultivating future scientists, will have a more significant role in EU-China relations. This particularly holds true when recent geopolitical events in the world, such as Brexit and the move away from globalisation by the US, have created more uncertainty for higher education development in Europe. The EU is recognising the importance of strengthening relations and collaboration with Asia, particularly China (Kirby & Van der Wende, 2018). Such recognition is of importance to China not only in terms of higher education development and of a large educational market for fee-paying students, but also as a partner working jointly towards a more cooperative and rule-based global order and a collaborator in global leadership (Kirby & Van der Wende, 2018).

3.2   Towards the Future of EU-China Higher Education Cooperation

In the future EU-China higher education cooperation is expected to be further integrated into the larger framework of EU-China strategic partnership building. For instance, Cai et al. (2019) call for attention to be given to the synergy building between higher education and other sectors in EU-China cooperation. They argue that the roles of transnational university cooperation are more than producing and transferring knowledge across national borders, along with cultivating "global talent" (Shumilova & Cai, 2016). There are two additional roles of such cooperation: fostering institutional change (concerning norms and values) and developing reliable networks between various actors in transnational contexts (Cai, 2018). Performing these two functions are likely to be new but important features in the future. For instance, given that EU-China higher education cooperation is challenged by a recent perception of China as both a collaborator and competitor on the EU side (European Commission, 2019), higher education cooperation between both sides may play a significant role in developing sustainable China-EU relations.

From the perspective of EU-China higher education cooperation phase two, one must take into account the broad policies/strategies concerning EU-China cooperation. Besides the three pillars of this cooperation and their related policy dialogues, China's New Silk Road Policy, also called "One Belt One Road" (OBOR) Policy, is influencing higher education cooperation at present and will do so in the near future.

The "Silk Road" originally refers to land-based trading which connected East and Central Asian markets to those of the Middle East and Mediterranean (Kirby & Van der Wende, 2018). The New Silk Road Policy was launched by

China in 2013 as a key instrument for reconsidering China's international relations, international economic policy and the enhancement of its soft power, so as to expand its global influence (Kirby & Van der Wende, 2018). The policy also indicates China's keenness to show its commitment to gain a more hegemonic role in the international community through the globalisation of its economy and the internationalisation of its culture and values (Perez Garcia, 2016). Despite the geographic focus of the policy being largely on Central Asia (Kirby & Van der Wende, 2018), of the 65 countries along the Belt and Road, 25 are European countries (Tijssen, 2018), which suggests Europe is also considered as an important partner in China's OBOR policy. While Brexit and the retreat from global cooperation by the U.S. have overshadowed the prospects of globalisation in the West, cooperation with China may bring Europe a more sustainable and inclusive version of globalisation, thus making it more attractive for the EU (Kirby & Van der Wende, 2018).

When it comes to higher education, the OBOR has introduced a new network for EU-China cooperation. Higher education cooperation has been included as an important dimension of OBOR Policy since 2015 (Kirby & Van der Wende, 2018). Guided by this policy, the University Alliance of the New Silk Road (UASR) was established in 2015, followed by the establishment of several sub-alliance groups in the area of management, law, mechanical and chemical engineering, aerospace, etc. (UASR, 2019). Currently, there have been 148 universities involved in UASR. Eighty-two come from Asia (56%), 56 from Europe (38%), six from Oceania (4%), two from America (2%) and two from Africa (2%). Thus, European universities are the second largest component in the network. UASR has fostered synergies in the globalisation of higher education, which is considered by European stakeholders to be a positive influence for the development of the European Higher Education Area (EHEA) and the European Research Area (ERA) (Kirby & Van der Wende, 2018). The UASR aims to build up a China-led collaborative platform in higher education (Kirby & Van der Wende, 2018) and advance international exchanges and partnerships among universities along the New Silk Road (UASR, 2019), which would be different from the previous landscape where the UK and the U.S. led higher education development.

Thus, the UASR has brought new perspectives to consider in relation to EU-China higher education cooperation. For instance, the role of the China-European joint ventures in higher education may not only be a mechanism to introduce educational resources into Chinese system, but also a mechanism to export China's advanced educational experience to other countries along the Belt and Road (Sharma, 2018). Thus, combined with the scholarship in support of international mobility of students from OBOR countries to China, the imbalance of inward and outward mobility between Europe and China may well change.

4 Conclusions

Higher education cooperation between EU and China consists of both opportunities and challenges. The opportunities are more reflected in the policy/interest match between both sides, whereas the challenges are concerned with realising the fit in practice. The difficulties in realising a policy match are mainly due to a lack of mutual understanding, and of incentives to follow up policy drives; and resources provided for their implementation. In order to resolve these problems, it is essential to consider EU-China higher education cooperation from the perspective of a more inclusive and broader partnership, rather than concentrating on concrete practices and policy dialogues as previously. In this regard, we propose the following suggestions.

First, we suggest taking a critical view of the problem of a lack of mutual understanding in EU-China higher education cooperation. Certainly, the mutual understandings between both sides should be enhanced to produce reciprocal cooperation in higher education. However, this is a too general and abstract claim. If we really want to improve the situation, we must be aware of two facts. One is that for those who have been deeply engaged in concrete activities of the collaboration, they are already quite aware of all the possible benefits and tensions involved in this. What is needed is the development of a more effective information sharing mechanism to help impart their experiences and insights with other actors, such as policy makers, university managers, academics and students from both the EU and China. The second fact is that mutual understanding in the domain of higher education cooperation is generally more advanced than that in other areas, such as politics and business (d'Hooghe et al., 2018). Thus, EU-China higher education can be utilised to support the building of trust between both sides in other sectors.

Second, both policy makers and practitioners in EU-China higher education cooperation should be more active in communication and collaboration with actors in other domains of EU-China cooperation. There is a great opportunity to use the university cooperation to support industry cooperation, because higher education cooperation has reached an unprecedented level, demonstrated by not only the large scale of student/staff exchange but also increasingly deeper research collaboration and joint educational programmes. For instance, the university cooperation can support industrial cooperation by creating reliable networks (Cai et al., 2019). However, such potential has not been realised by the industrial actors as well as the policy makers who set broader frameworks for EU-China cooperation. Once the relevant stakeholders are convinced about the significant role of university cooperation in the overall picture of EU-China cooperation, universities are more likely to receive additional resources to support their international activities. Meanwhile, actors engaged the higher education cooperation would be more motivated when they recognised the larger impact of their commitment.

Third, the two suggestions mentioned above require the expansion of research on EU-China higher education cooperation. Studies this cooperation should consider the issue from a broader perspective. For instance, one important line of research could be about responses to the need for synergy between different areas of EU-China cooperation. Moreover, the research could be used for supplementing the information flow between practitioners and policymakers. Compared to the overall positive messages implied by existing studies on this cooperation, there are few efforts to investigate negative experiences and even failures in EU-China higher education cooperation. To advance the cooperation in practice, it is crucial to first discover the most difficult cases and then find solutions. This is especially helpful for policy makers in fully understanding the realities and enables them to design better policy frameworks.

Fourth, both sides could also learn from each other in relation to the experiences in higher education reforms. For instance, the lessons of over 400 university mergers taking place in China during the 1990s and 2000s may be helpful for European higher education where mergers are emerging (Cai & Yang, 2016). The relatively long-time practices of transforming universities for the better servicing of regional development and innovation in Europe would be very useful for the Chinese when they have just embarked on similar reforms (Cai, Yang, Lyytinen, & Hölttä, 2015).

Finally, it has to be remembered that as the EU consists of member states with different social structures, histories and economic conditions, there is no simple approach for China to cooperate with the EU. The same kind of reminder holds true for the EU and EU member states. Although China is a single country, it also is diverse. There are regions with different economic development levels, industrial advantages and cultures. There are over 2000 Chinese universities of different types located in various regions (Cai & Yan, 2017). Thus, policy makers and universities in EU member states need to adjust their strategies when collaborating with different universities in China.

Acknowledgement

We want to thank Pinna Cristina for her initial ideas shared with us about the topic of the chapter.

References

Business Finland. (2018). *EU-China flagship initiative on biotechnologies for environment and human health.* https://www.businessfinland.fi/globalassets/finnish-customers/horizon-2020/esitysaineistot/faq-eu-china-flagship-ce-biotec-04-2018.pdf

Cai, Y. (2013). Erasmus Mundus joint programme and EU's strategy on higher education collaboration with China: Lessons from the MARIHE programme. *Journal of European Higher Education Area, 2,* 95–112.

Cai, Y. (2014). Institutionalization of internationalization of higher education in China. *Frontiers of Education in China, 9*(2), 175–181. doi:10.3868/s110-003-014-0015-x

Cai, Y. (2018). Towards a socially responsible entrepreneurial university: Conceptual and analytical framework building. *SPIRAL, 2018*(1), 1–4.

Cai, Y. (2019a). China-Europe higher education cooperation: Opportunities and challenges. *Frontiers of Education in China, 14*(2), 167–179. https://doi.org/10.1007/s11516-019-0009-5

Cai, Y. (2019b, September 27). *Opportunities and challenges in EU-China higher education cooperation: From 1.0 to 2.0.* Paper presented at the Network Meeting on EU-China High Education Cooperation and University Academic Leadership, Helsinki.

Cai, Y., Ferrer, B. R., & Lastra, J. L. M. (2019). Building university-industry co-innovation networks in transnational innovation ecosystems: Towards a transdisciplinary approach of integrating social sciences and artificial intelligence. *Sustainability, 11*(17), 1–23. doi:10.3390/su11174633

Cai, Y., & Yan, F. (2015). Supply and demand in Chinese higher education. In S. Schwartzman, P. Pillay, & R. Pinheiro (Eds.), *Higher education in the BRICS countries: Investigating the pact between higher education and society* (pp. 149–169). Springer.

Cai, Y., & Yan, F. (2017). Higher education and university. In W. J. Morgan, Q. Gu, & F. Li (Eds.), *Handbook of Chinese education* (pp. 169–193). Edward Elgar.

Cai, Y., Yang, P., Lyytinen, A., & Hölttä, S. (2015). Seeking solutions though the mirror of Finnish experience: Policy recommendations for regional university transformation in China. *Journal of Higher Education Policy and Management, 37*(4), 447–458. doi:10.1080/1360080X.2015.1056597

Cai, Y., & Yang, X. (2016). Mergers in Chinese higher education: Lessons for studies in a global context. *European Journal of Higher Education, 6*(1), 71–85. doi:10.1080/21568235.2015.1099458

European Union Chamber of Commerce in China. (2017). *European Business in China – Business confidence survey.*

d'Hooghe, I., Montulet, A., de Wolff, M., & Pieke, F. N. (2018). *Assessing Europe-China collaboration in higher education and research.* https://www.merics.org/sites/default/files/2019-02/LeidenAsiaCentre%20Report%20-%20Assessing%20Europe-China%20Collaboration%20in%20Higher%20Education%20and%20Research_2018.pdf

EURAXESS. (2019a). Collaboration opportunities. *EURAXESS Researchers in Motion.* https://euraxess.ec.europa.eu/

EURAXESS. (2019b). *EURAXESS China.* https://euraxess.ec.europa.eu/worldwide/china

European Commission. (2013). *EU-China 2020 strategic agenda for cooperation.*

European Commission. (2019). *Erasmus+ higher education impact study.*

European Commission. (2019). *EU-China – A strategic outlook.*

European Commission and State Council of China. (2012, April 18). *Follow-up actions of the first round of the EU-China High Level People-to-people Dialogue (HPPD).* https://ec.europa.eu/assets/eac/education/international-cooperation/documents/china/follow_en.pdf

European-Union-External-Action-Service. (2015). *Factsheet/memo: The EU-China comprehensive strategic partnership.*

GHK-Consulting & Renming-University. (2011). *EU-China student and academic staff mobility: Present situation and future developments.* ec.europa.eu/assets/eac/education/international-cooperation/.../china/mobility_en.pdf

Kirby, W., & Van der Wende, M. (2018). The new silk road: Implications for higher education in China and the West? *Cambridge Journal of Regions, Economy and Society, 12*(1), 127–144. doi:10.1093/cjres/rsy034

Liu, Y. (2017, November 14). Speech at fourth meeting of China-EU high-level people-to-people dialogue, Shanghai.

Men, J., & Linck, A. (2017). *China and EU: Reform and governance.* Taylor & Francis.

Ministry of Education. (2003). Regulations of the people's Republic of China on Chinese-foreign cooperation in running schools.

Ministry of Education in China. (2019a, April 12). International students in China 2018. *News.* http://www.moe.gov.cn/jyb_xwfb/gzdt_gzdt/s5987/201904/t20190412_377692.html

Ministry of Education in China. (2019b). *List of programs and institutions of Chinese-Foreign cooperation in running schools.* http://www.crs.jsj.edu.cn/index/sort/1006

Ministry of Education in China. (2019c, March 27). Statistics of China overseas students 2018. *News.* http://www.moe.gov.cn/jyb_xwfb/gzdt_gzdt/s5987/201903/t20190327_375704.html

Ministry of Science and Technology in China. (2005, May 16). *EU-China Joint declaration on developing a knowledge-based strategic partnership between EU and China: Leading EU-China cooperation in science and technology into new era.* http://www.most.gov.cn/xinwzx/xwzx/xwfb/200505/t20050516_21606.htm

Navracsics, T. (2017, November 14). Speech at fourth meeting of China-EU high-level people-to-people dialogue, Shanghai.

NSFC. (2009). *NSFC regulation on international (regional) collaboration in research with international regions and organizations.* Bureau of International Cooperation. http://bic.nsfc.gov.cn/Show.aspx?AI=1019

NSFC. (2011). *12th five year plan of national Natural Science Foundation of China (NSFC)*. http://www.nsfc.gov.cn/nsfc/cen/bzgh_125/ml.html

NSFC. (2014). *NNFS international early-career researcher funding regulation*. http://bic.nsfc.gov.cn/Show.aspx?AI=1023

NSFC. (2015). *13th five year plan of national Natural Science Foundation of China (NSFC)*. http://www.nsfc.gov.cn/publish/portal0/xxgk/043/info72249.htm

NSFC. (2018). *Achievement*. http://bic.nsfc.gov.cn/Show.aspx?CI=24

NSFC. (2019). *Brief introduction*. http://www.nsfc.gov.cn/publish/portal0/jgsz/01/

Onsman, A. (2013). International students at Chinese joint venture universities: Factors influencing decisions to enrol. *Australian Universities' Review, 55*(2), 15.

Perez Garcia, M. (2016). The global dimensions of "one belt, one road" strategy in China-Latin America international relations: Toward a sustainable economic growth model. In M. Perez Garcia & S. Cui (Eds.), *China and Latin America in transition: Policy dynamics, economic commitments, and social impacts* (pp. 131–156). Palgrave Macmillan.

Pinna, C. (2009). EU–China relations in higher education. *Asia Europe Journal, 7*(3), 505. doi:10.1007/s10308-009-0238-y

Qu, X., & Feng, Y. (2018). The developmental path of internationalization of higher education in China. [我国高等教育国际化发展路径研究]. *Study & Exploration, 5*(274), 32–37.

Sharma, Y. (2018, 23/03/2018). One belt one road towards a China-led HE area? *University World News*. https://www.universityworldnews.com/post.php?story=20180323045239515

Shieh, C. J., & Wang, I.-M. (2007). Development of export of China's higher education. *Connexions Module: m14289*. http://cnx.org/content/m14289/latest/

Shumilova, Y., & Cai, Y. (2016). Three approaches to competing for global talent: Role of higher education. In B. Krishna & F. Charlotte (Eds.), *Global perspectives and local challenges surrounding international student mobility* (pp. 114–135). IGI Global.

Telò, M., Chun, D., & Xiaotong, Z. (2018). *Deepening the EU-China partnership: Bridging institutional and ideational differences in an unstable world*. Taylor & Francis.

Tijssen, R. (2018). *China's research links with belt & road countries: Mapping the 'academic traffic' space*. Paper presented at The New Silk Road: Implications for higher education and research cooperation between China and Europe, Oxford.

UASR. (2019, 27/12/2018). *University alliance of the silk road*. http://uasr.xjtu.edu.cn/S_R.htm

Xinhua-Net. (2019, February 23). *Central committee of communist party, state council of China launched "modernization of education in China 2035"*. http://www.moe.gov.cn/jyb_xwfb/s6052/moe_838/201902/t20190223_370857.html

Yang, R. (2014). China's strategy for the internationalization of higher education: An overview. *Frontiers of Education in China, 9*(2), 151–162. http://dx.doi.org/10.3868/s110-003-014-0014-x

Yang, R. (2017). The cultural mission of China's elite universities: Examples from Peking and Tsinghua. *Studies in Higher Education, 42*(10), 1825–1838. doi:10.1080/03075079.2017.1376873

Zheng, G., & Cai, Y. (2018). Collaboration between Europe and China in doctoral education: Historical development and future challenges. In A. V. Oleksiyenko, Q. Zha, I. Chirikov, & J. Li (Eds.), *International status anxiety and higher education: Soviet legacy in China and Russia* (Vol. 35, pp. 335–361). Springer & Comparative Education Research Centre (CERC).

Zheng, G., Cai, Y., & Ma, S. (2017). Towards an analytical framework for understanding the development of a quality assurance system in an international joint programme. *European Journal of Higher Education, 7*(3), 243–260. doi:10.1080/21568235.2017.1290877

Zhou, H. (2017). *China-EU relations: Reassesing the China-EU comprehensive strategic partnership*. Springer & Social Sciences Academic Press.

Zhu, C., Cai, Y., & François, K. (2017). Perceptions of European and Chinese stakeholders on doctoral education in China and Europe. *European Journal of Higher Education, 7*(3), 227–242. doi:10.1080/21568235.2017.1290866

Zhu, W., & Zhang, H. (2017). The review of internationalization policy in China's higher education [我国高等教育国际化政策变迁述评]. *Journal of Higher Education Management, 11*(2), 116–124.

CHAPTER 6

Russia-EU Internationalisation of Higher Education: Cooperation vs Competition?

Svetlana Shenderova

Abstract

Russia, due to its unique location simultaneously in Europe and Asia, has more than three centuries of higher education cooperation with the European states. The role of higher education cooperation has been defined by the changes in general political context, international relations. Approaches to interaction have varied from attempts to transplant European academic culture into national culture to the severe limitations of any contacts with Western higher education institutions.

The chapter explores the rationale and evolution of the role of higher education cooperation between Russia and Europe under the pressure of foreign policy and its changing priorities. In particular, the author considers Russia-EU internationalisation as part of the common trend of rising competition between different countries and regions of the European Higher Education Area (EHEA).

To understand the challenges for Russia-EU higher education cooperation in terms of the common framework provided by EHEA, the author studies different institutional environments where the universities of Russia and the EU member states implement internationalisation activities. The chapter overviews the policy tools to support the internationalisation of higher education in Russia, highlights the opportunities for Russia-EU cooperation and investigates the challenges produced by national traditions, EHEA and national law enforcement, and university governance practices, which have constrained Russia-EU higher education cooperation.

Keywords

higher education institutions – institutional environment – Russia-EU cooperation – internationalisation of higher education – Bologna Process

1 Introduction

The geographical location of Russia and the EU has provided unique opportunities for cooperation in higher education and research. Common borders, complicated history and the spirit of competition with Europe constitute the fundamental differences in the internationalisation of higher education (IoHE) in Russia compared to Brazil, China and South Africa. Brazil's cooperation with European higher education emulates the USA's approach (Granja & Carneiro, Chapter 8, this volume), while South Africa bases its cooperation in higher education on the strategic partnership with the EU, and active participation in the EU North-South cooperation framework (Langa & Wolhuter, Chapter 7, this volume). The Federal Governments of Brazil and South Africa enforce IoHE, cooperating with the EU mainly through the programmes of student and staff mobility. Meanwhile China has developed a wider range of IoHE activities and embeds higher education cooperation with the EU into the general policy of building strategic partnerships (Cai & Zheng, Chapter 5, this volume). But Russia tries to use higher education cooperation as a tool of competition, implementing IoHE policy to catch up and overtake the EU – its closest neighbour and historical rival.

Russia's accession to the Bologna Process expanded the European Area of Higher Education (EHEA) and strengthened internationalisation in cooperation with the EU. The series of programmes funded by the Government of the Russian Federation (RF Government) supported Russia-EU IoHE activities to achieve ambitious objectives worldwide. The constantly reformed and renamed RF Ministry of Education (the Ministry) has been the core, but not the only administrative body responsible for the development and implementation of IoHE policy in Russia.

This chapter explores the rationale and evolution of the development of higher education cooperation between Russia and Europe, influenced by changing priorities of foreign policy. In particular, we overview the policy tools of support for IoHE in Russia, and discuss the challenges constraining Russia-EU higher education cooperation, and where these challenges come from.

2 Russia and Europe: Three Centuries of Cooperation and Competition

Russia, being a natural bridge between Europe and Asia, has had more than three centuries of higher education cooperation with European states. The changing general political context has impacted on how the country has understood the role of higher education cooperation, which has varied from the attempts to transplant European academic culture into Russian culture to the total control of any interaction between Russians and Europeans.

The development of Russian higher education institutions (HEIS) has been inspired by the idea of building them in cooperation with Europe to enhance further competition. This ambivalent policy has manifested itself since Russia became a European competitor in XVIII century (Kristinsson, 2010, pp. 268–271). On the one hand, European academics from Germany and France laid the basis for the first Russian university and Academy of Science in St. Petersburg shortly after being established by Peter I in 1724 (Madariaga, 1998; Frolov, 2010). But the fact that the Russian higher education system arose from a Decree of an absolute monarch imposed severe restrictions on university autonomy and academic freedoms. Since their foundation Russian HEIS have perceived any opportunity to organise their internal life not as their own right, but as something which a supreme authority may give or take away without explanation. The serfdom empire took 80 years to grant three universities the right to award their own degrees and to elect rectors and academics. And a few decades later these academic freedoms disappeared with a stroke of the tsar's pen.

In the XIX century Russian universities behaved much like regular army troops. They reported to one Minister; one Charter enacted one list of degrees, courses, departments, and the number of obligatory contact hours for a professor (not less than 8 hours per week). International degree holders were discriminated against: foreign doctoral degrees should be recognised only as master's degrees. (Dneprov, 2017; Novikov & Perfilova, 2014). Students must at all times wear a uniform and salute superiors and academics were likewise military. They were forbidden from getting married during study period (Vititneva & Lushchaeva, 2018). It is not surprising that many Russian HEIS actively supported Russian revolutions. In the later decades of the XXth century the growth of the higher education sector skyrocketed, embedding it into a planned economy, and under the total control of the state.

The concepts of world revolution, internationalism and the competition of socialist and capitalist systems had echoed down through Soviet times. The USSR's geopolitical priorities in higher education cooperation concentrated more on student enrollment than on academic collaboration; secret services severely controlled both (Kuraev, 2014). The People's Friendship University was founded in 1960 specially to offer courses to students from developing and nonaligned countries (Kastakioris, 2019) as a soft power tool. While the 'third world' countries provided the largest numbers of international student enrollment, socialist countries including Eastern European ones developed academic cooperation with the USSR. Higher education cooperation with

Western European countries was not considered a priority (de Wit & Merkx, 2012, pp. 50–51). However, several Soviet HEIs had some experience of cooperation even during the Cold War (Fischl, 2018). In the 1980s the USSR became the third country in the world after USA and France in terms of numbers of international students enrolled. Frumina and West (2012, pp. 12–13) estimate the number as 180,000 including 18,500 who studied in the military colleges and 30,000 in the system of Communist education. Gurko et al. (2019, p. 36) indicate that there were 126,500 international students in the USSR in 1990, 70% of whom studied in the territory of the largest among the 15 Soviet Republics, namely Russia.

In the 1990s the USSR crumbled and abandoned its support of socialist-oriented regimes worldwide; people's friendship increasingly had been replaced by armed conflicts. Independent Russia embraced the age of political turbulence. Those who were able to go abroad to study still had to have the permission of the secret services. However, they did not dictate directly how the cooperation of Russian and European HEIs should be organised.

Russia, the EU and its member states signed the Agreement of partnership and cooperation in 1994. It focused on updating the higher education system and methods of training in Russia, and cooperation between European and Russian HEIs, mobility for academics, young researchers, administrators and youth. Russia became an active participant of the EU funded TEMPUS Programme. Many Russian and European HEIs have evolved from sporadic cooperation of researchers to the development of student and academic staff mobility ("Results of joint research activity", 2014). Moreover, the vast majority of current partnerships in IoHE activities has been based on the cooperation agreements concluded in the 1990s (Burquel, Shenderova, & Tvorogova, 2014a).

As a result, EU-Russia partnerships in the 1990s considered cooperation as the cornerstone of policy and implementation of such IoHE activities as internationalisation of the curriculum, and student and staff exchanges. However, the opportunities for Russian HEIs to expand their autonomy, academic freedoms and international dimensions in the degree programmes were still limited. Despite permission for rector's elections, the appearance of private HEIs, and a general weakness of control on the quality of education, the RF Government continued having a say in the provision of degree programmes. The Ministry strictly regulated the list, structure and content of any degree; and it specified the number of students enrolled on each degree programme. Reallocation of state funded places between different fields of study within each HEI required special negotiations with the Ministry. The number of academic positions corresponded with the number of full-time student equivalents (FTE); for particular named universities the proportion of one academic to four FTE students was set, but the rectors of the other universities had to agree the proportion by negotiation with Ministry officials. (Shenderova, 2002, 2011). Russian HEIs were not allowed to recognise the period of study their students spent in the EU in the curricula. That is why the description of the first post-Soviet decade in higher education sector as 'laissez-faire' (Platonova & Semyonov, 2018) is untrue.

The XXI century brought new opportunities for Russia-EU higher education cooperation. The EU became Russia's largest neighbour after the accession of Finland in 1995; Latvia, Lithuania, Estonia, Slovakia, and Poland in 2004; Bulgaria and Romania in 2007. In 2003 Russia joined EHEA, which, as a result, included an area from Lisbon to Vladivostok and united its participant countries – to some extent. Russia started using these opportunities to cooperate and compete with the EU. The next section suggests a theoretical framework for the changing roles of higher education cooperation and competition in IoHE.

3 Internationalisation of Higher Education: Cooperation for Competition as a Common Trend

The IoHE is understood here as 'the intentional process of integrating an international, intercultural or global dimension into the purpose, functions and delivery of post-secondary education, in order to enhance the quality of education and research for all students and staff, and to make a meaningful contribution to society', following the definition of de Wit, Hunter and Coelen (2015, p. 281).

Some authors consider IoHE as a national response on globalisation and its challenges (Chan, 2004; Altbach & Knight, 2007; Beerkens et al., 2010; Elken, Hovdhaugen, & Stensaker, 2016). Korhonen and Alenius (2018) mention that the cooperation of HEIs and cross-border study programmes create the networks which transcend national boundaries. Burquel and Ballesteros note in this book (Chapter 3, this volume) that the Erasmus programme has concentrated on support for higher education cooperation in terms of European global competition.

Other researchers focus on the reciprocity of internationalisation and competition. Trondal, Gornitzka & Gulbrandsen (2003) allot to competition the role of a push towards internationalisation. It is seen in the emerging patterns of IoHE which succeeded such traditional cooperation activities as student and academic mobility. Competition has made IoHE strategies more formal and top-down at supranational, national and institutional levels. De Wit, Hunter, and Coelen (2015, p. 277) emphasise that IoHE in Europe has been used more and more in the competition of higher education systems to pursue short-term economic goals (the UK and the Netherlands) and soft power (Germany and Scandinavian countries). Murray (2018) notes the non-neutrality, politicisation and inequality of IoHE, while Guri-Rosenblit (2015) specifies its uneven benefits and particular risk for different types of HEIS.

Opportunities for higher education cooperation in IoHE have therefore become more limited by national and regional interests and growing competition on the global stage. Moreover, there is a common trend in the recent decade. Russia's internationalisation policy is not an exclusive example of the changed role of competition caused by the advancing of national and regional interests in the face of globalisation. In particular, since 2003 Russia in liaison with the EU member states has promoted the international competitiveness of European (i.e. regional) higher education worldwide in accordance with the Bologna Declaration (EHEA, 1999). Beside this common objective Russia and the EU called their HEIS 'to further internationalise their activities and to engage in global collaboration for sustainable development' (EHEA, 2009, 2012). However, implementation of IoHE in Russia and in the EU led to markedly different and uneven results.

For example, Russia-EU degree mobility remains asymmetrical. 62.8% of Russian students (35,568) who studied abroad moved to the EU to study. Germany hosted 9,620 of them, Czech Republic 5,979, the UK 3,920, and France attracted 3,691 Russian students. Meanwhile far fewer students from the EU arrived in Russia to study, mostly from neighbouring former USSR republics: 452 Latvian, 270 Estonian, and 249 Lithuanian students. Among the others were 191 French, 163 Italians, 146 Greeks, 74 Bulgarian, 69 Finnish and 49 Polish students (UNESCO UIS, 2017). The academic mobility of foreign students in Russia (2016, p. 11) specifies 2,480 students who may approximately be identified as EU citizens, i.e. coming to Russia from Northern, Western, Southern and Eastern Europe (CIS countries excluded). It is 1% of the total number of international students.

To understand where the challenges for higher education cooperation come from within the EHEA common framework, we might consider different institutional environments as a set of Russian dolls *'matryoshka'* where HEIS implement IoHE activities (Shenderova, 2018b). If we apply Magna Charta Universitatum (1998), an HEI is 'an autonomous institution at the heart of societies differently organised because of geography and historical heritage', which 'produces, examines, appraises and hands down culture by research and teaching'. From this perspective, an HEI is a core institution in several institutional environments. Any HEI by itself has its own internal institutional environment. The latter includes a set of formal and informal rules related to internal strategies, policies, regulations, traditions etc. IoHE activities are developed within the internal institutional environment of an HEI. Thus, any partner HEI becomes another '*matryoshka*' for IoHE activity implemented in cooperation.

There are at least two external institutional elements affecting any HEI and their partnerships. Each country shapes its national institutional environment which comprises policies, laws and regulations including those related to IoHE activities (education, migration, labour etc.). Russian and European HEIS cooperate within their national institutional environments, as smaller '*matryoshkas*' within those which are larger. EHEA, the largest of them, provides a common institutional environment through a framework of supranational alignments for all countries including the EU member states and Russia, and their HEIS.

The awareness of the dissimilarities between internal and external institutional environments where HEIS and countries cooperate is critical for the success of the IoHE activities that are developed. The lack of understanding of the distinctions between higher education systems and partner's traditions hampers cooperation both for the countries and for their HEIS. That means that partners have to spend additional resources just to recognise the barriers that they are unaware of at the start of cooperation, then to spend additional time and money to travel, meet, negotiate, and develop new procedures, to monitor their implementation and revise them, when new unexpected cultural differences appear. Imperfect information and uncertainty about the partner's internal and external institutional environments increase the transaction costs of internationalisation between the HEIS of different countries.

The transaction costs of IoHE could be defined as comprising all the unforeseen effort, time, and expenditure of stakeholders involved in IoHE strategies and policies, and their implementation at supra-, national, and HEI levels. Transaction costs could be produced both externally and internally by any partner HEI; or they could appear within their partnerships.

Within HEIS transaction costs result from multiplication of decision-making centres and their influence on the allocation of funding. The more complicated a particular IoHE activity, the more resources may be needed to implement it, and the more likely it is that transaction costs appear. At the policy level transaction costs are caused by vaguely allocated responsibilities or counterproductive multiplication of key performance indicators (KPIS) for the agencies operated in IoHE. They try to prove their efficiency as the control bodies by provision of new KPIS and on reporting of their implementation (Shenderova, 2018a).

On the one hand, there is no partnership without transaction costs, as there is no physical world without friction (Pesch & Ishmaev, 2019). However, each HEI and country at the start of cooperation is able to discuss the partner's and its own peculiarities in order to recognise which IoHE activities are possible within the given frameworks of external institutional environments. In particular, the limits of HEIs' autonomy and academic freedoms determined by national history and policy are important to develop an understanding of the paths of cooperation from a transaction costs perspective.

The sections below investigate national IoHE policy and its challenges for Russia-EU higher education cooperation.

4 Internationalisation Policy in Russia: From Bologna to Crimea

Initially President Putin authorised Russia's accession to the Bologna Process as part of a general policy to cooperate with the EU in terms of irreversible mutual recognition of higher education qualifications for an extended labour market (RF Ministry of International Affairs, 2003). Then Russia and the EU agreed the Road Map on Common Space of Research and Education including Cultural Aspects (2005) that stressed 'the strengthening of competitiveness of economies in the EU and Russia' as the common objective of their higher education cooperation. Russia-EU cooperation has been long recognised as the important factor for the common growth and competitiveness of both economies and their higher education sectors on the global stage (President of Russia, 2005). In 2011 the EU considered Russia as a strategic partner (EU and Russia, A Strategic Partnership, 2011).

The TEMPUS-TACIS programme provided financial support for the EU-Russia higher education cooperation funding joint research centres, curriculum development, reforms and studies of university management. Russian applicants became the most active recipients of TEMPUS among non-EU nationalities (Gänzle, Meister, & King, 2009). However, the Mid-term evaluation of Tempus in Russia (2008, p. 20) showed that Russian students have been little involved in the Bologna Process: staff mobility dominated over student mobility in 60% of the projects.

In 2006 Russia started the series of programmes supporting internationalisation activities in the HEIs selected as leaders of the sector, and funded by the RF Government (Platonova & Semyonov, 2018). Exchange rate fluctuations between the Euro and the Russian Rouble and its influence on EU-Russia higher education cooperation are described in the next section of this chapter. The National Project 'Education' funded 17 Russian HEIs to develop innovations including new IoHE activities. At least four of the selected HEIS had already had solid experience of long close cooperation with EU partners in academic exchanges and in building collaborative programmes. The second call in 2007 supported 40 Russian HEIS, funding for which varied from ₽210 mln to ₽930 mln. All HEIS increased the number of staff exchanges and training courses offered. Some HEIS developed collaborative degree programmes to combine national support with funding from the EU and/or its member states.

The other set of measures in 2008–2010 financed 29 National Research Universities (₽49.8 bln) and nine Federal Universities (₽13 bln since 2006–2010) established in each Federal District of Russia. All participants had to demonstrate ten-year Development Programmes with growing numbers of IoHE activities including some implemented in cooperation with the EU HEIS. 55 HEIS received funding for their Programmes of Strategic Development to a maximum of ₽200 mln in 2011; a significant number of them later entered the pool of 'pillar universities' specially chosen to respond to the needs of their regions. In 2006–2011 the ability of an HEI to demonstrate the increase of international competitiveness was considered an important reason for funding, along with lobbyist and geopolitical potential (Shenderova, 2011).

The year 2012 marked the primacy of competition in IoHE national policy. The President of Russia (2012) signed a Decree aimed at enhancing the competitiveness of 'leading Universities' among the leading world research-education centres. The Decree aimed to enable at least five Russian HEIS to be placed in the top 100 of those in the 'world university ranking' (WUR) by 2020. RF Government Resolution (2012) and the related documents requested that IoHE activities be developed in cooperation with the leading world universities including the EU universities. The latter were defined as belonging to the top 300 of WURs with a preference for QS (Shenderova, 2018a).

The Russian Academic Excellence Project 5–100 (2020) named after the indicator identified in the Presidential Decree, has, since 2013, become an important tool of IoHE policy. In 2013–2016 the Ministry of Education funded 21 Russian HEIS with an average support of ₽592.4 mln. Russian HEIS who participated in the 5–100 project received a total of ₽9.9 bln in 2019; the number of HEIS is expected to be up to 30 with a budget of ₽5 bln. The supported HEIS are expected to develop such IoHE activities as collaborative study programmes, and outcoming and incoming mobility (credit, degree and staff) to include the leading European HEIS.

The 'Global Education' Programme (₽3.75 bln), started in 2014, offered reimbursement for 718 Russian citizens to study abroad in training programmes, master's and PhD degrees before returning to further employment in Russia. 'Global Education' (2020) mentions 416 EU HEIS along with the others where the 751 participants studied. 423 participants are indicated as having been provided with employment.

The Priority Project 'Development of the export potential of Russian higher education system' (RF Government, 2017) seeks to increase the number of international students in Russia by 425,000 in a consortium of 40 Russian HEIs (Gurko et al., 2019, p. 39). Collaborative degree programmes are considered as a tool of incoming mobility along with short-term mobility and seasonal schools.

The current reincarnation of the National 'Education' Project includes ten Federal Projects (RF Government, 2018). Among them there is 'Export of Education' (₽107.5 bln) which aims to move the country to the 'tenth position in the world among national universities in the top-500 of global university rankings' calculated as an arithmetic average of positions held in such rankings as QS, THE and ARWU by 2024. Another Federal Project 'Young professionals' (₽156.2 bln) provided new KPI for Russian HEIs supported by 5–100: their 'presence in the top-1000 of global institutional rankings for not less than two years'.

RF Ministry of Science and Higher Education administers IoHE supported projects in liaison with at least 13 bodies. Among them there are the Federal State Autonomous Research Centre 'Sociocenter' (for National Project 'Education' and 5–100), and 'Skolkovo Management LTD' based in the private Moscow Scholl of Management 'Skolkovo' (for 5–100, 'Global Education', 'Development of the export potential of the Russian higher education system'). Besides, the latter project involves the responsibilities of nine Federal Ministries, the Federal agency 'Rossotrudnichestvo', and the State Russian Export Center. In addition, the Federal State Budget Organisation 'Interobrazovaniye' is involved in 'Global Education'.

The year 2014 signified a dramatic change in Russia-EU relations. The EU interpreted the accession of the Crimean Peninsula to Russia as its annexation, and imposed economic sanctions. These developments undermined the foundation of Russia-EU cooperation (Mogherini: Russia is no longer the EU's strategic partner, 2014). Since 2014 the capacity-building funding does not allow Russian HEIs to be leaders of the projects. However, Russian HEIs actively participated in one tenth of selected projects and received €4.1 mln in grants.

The other IoHE activities implemented in cooperation with the EU were recognised as important for people-to-people contacts and for those least affected by political tensions. In 2014–2017 the EU continued to fund higher education cooperation with Russia for such IoHE activities as exchanges (€36.0 mln) for students (three to 12 months) and staff (up to two months), 130 scholarships for joint master's and 23 doctorate degrees (€9.4 mln), and Jean Monnet funding (€3.9 mln). It is noteworthy that in comparison with the situation analysed above, in 2017 staff exchanges (1,198) from Russia to the EU slightly dominated over students' (1,066) and barely above the number of exchanges from the EU to Russia (1,035). However, Erasmus+ student exchanges have remained asymmetrical: only 642 students used this option for mobility (Russell, 2017).

Other challenges for Russia-EU higher education cooperation lie in the institutional environments where IoHE is implemented at the policy level.

5 The Challenges for Internationalisation in Higher Education Cooperation

Reporting on the RF Government programmes which support internationalisation presents a major challenge in itself. Each of the 13 organisations listed above is responsible for developing a set of data, which do not overlap and contradict other data. In addition, the Ministry charged with responsibility for education reforms has been several times reformed itself, renamed, and the work allotted to several different Ministries in 2018. During these transfigurations the responsibilities have been repeatedly redeployed among the multiplying departments, namely 23 in the current Ministry of Science and Higher Education.

A grave challenge to Russia-EU cooperation comes from IoHE policy makers who have misunderstood the historical context of the country. For example, Volkov and Melnyk (2019) propose the selection of a 'group of universities to the special academic zone [*zona* in Russian] with the special rules of autonomy, financial support and heightened requirements to internationalisation'. However, in the Russian thesaurus of the possible meaning of the word '*zona*' is a forced-labour camp where imprisoned scientists did research on atomic weapons which provided the USSR with strongly competitive potential during the Cold War. An Orwellian offer to restrict the number of HEIs available for internationalisation while simultaneously excluding them from the common law, would impede Russian and EU HEIs in their ability to cooperate with the provisions of the European Higher Education Area. In addition, the need for 'special zone with the special rules' stresses the lack of intention to make common law, regulation, statistics and funding in the entire higher education sector more relevant to the named objectives of IoHE policy.

We shall not discuss here why Russian IoHE policy makers rely on international rankings with widely different and frequently changed methodologies to understand the competitiveness enhancement of national HEIs. However, the discrepancies between the statistics provided for the Ministry, and data requested by the RF Government programmes and WURs, significantly distort the picture of IoHE policy implementation including such basic parameters as the numbers of FTE domestic and international students (Shenderova, 2018a).

Confusion between one-cycled and two-cycled degree programmes, with both leading to the third-cycle, is another source which blurs the findings of IoHE policy. Despite the announcement of the Bologna reforms, Russia still allows the holders of first-cycle qualifications (specialist degrees, 5–6 years of study) to obtain third-cycle degrees (*kandidat nauk* or PhD), bypassing the second-cycle master's degree (RF Government, 2013, amend. 2018). In 2019 the number of 1st year FTE students who studied on specialist degrees amounted to 19.1% of the total FTE in the state HEIs. The proportion of students who studied on specialist programmes in the total national FTE is even larger: 25.1%. Moreover, the RF Ministry of Science and Higher Education (2020) considers all specialist's, bachelor's and master's students as undergraduate, while WURs include master's in graduate enrollment.

In trying to respond to all requests for data, Russian HEIs have to build up new project offices and hire managers whose job is to report to different offices in the organisations in the capital, but not necessarily on the implementation of IoHE activities in the relevant HEIs. The other option is to prepare data occasionally without further systematisation. As a result, the Ministry and WURs have different perceptions of IoHE (Shenderova, 2018a). For example, it is obvious that different teams do not communicate with each other in preparing data for WURs and for the domestic authorities in Lomonosov Moscow State University (MSU, 2020). It estimates the share of international students as 10% FTE for the RF Government, for which it is specially funded; however, the same indicator for THE (2020a) is 29%, and 19% for QS (2020a). A similar situation is found in Kazan Federal University supported by the 5–100 project: it mentions 15.5% of international students in FTE in the self-assessment report for the Ministry (KFU, 2019), 13% in THE (2020b), and 21% in QS (2020b).

Volatility of national currency has seriously reduced the effect of Government support for Russia-EU higher education cooperation. The exchange rate EURO/RUR (€/₽) was €1/₽34 in 2006, became €1/₽45 in 2009 to 2014, and achieved €1/₽91 in 2016. At the beginning of 2020 the exchange rate is €1/₽70 (RF Central Bank, 2020). Considerable fluctuations of the exchange rate make difficulties in planning any internationalisation activity linked to travel, study and work abroad, thus hampering the achievement of the listed KPIs.

Fedotova et al. (2019) analyse two projects on closely related topics: Priority Project 'Development of the export potential of Russian higher education system' (2017–2025), and Federal Project 'Export of Education' (2019–2024). The authors emphasise the significant duplication of these RF Government projects implemented almost simultaneously, the weak coordination of the administrative bodies involved and a lack of concrete solutions to simplify recognition of the foreign qualifications and period of study abroad. In addition, two similar export-oriented projects appeared a year apart without previous public consultations with Russian HEIs. Such an attitude demonstrates the power of traditions laid down during the tsarist regime: current policy makers still perceive Russian HEIs as subordinates.

University autonomy remains an abstraction in Russia. The rectors of leading Russian HEIs are appointed without internal elections by the President of Russia, Prime-Minister, or Minister of Science and Higher Education. Some rectors have held their positions since 1992 (e.g. Lomonosov Moscow State University and National Research University Higher School of Economics). RF Ministry of Science and Higher Education still dictates to Russian HEIs on how to interact with foreign colleagues. Russian academics (Fradkov, 2019) initiated a campaign to abolish the Ministry's order which created additional administrative barriers for internationalisation. In accordance with this order, each HEI must have a list of employees allowed to contact foreigners. A rector has a personal responsibility to approve people on this list, and to report each meeting of his subordinates with foreigners to the Ministry. Taking into account the additional time, people and papers needed to meet all the articles of the order, it contributes to the exponential growth of IoHE transaction costs both at the level of HEIs and the Ministry. However, the campaign has had little effect: there is still no document published to confirm the promises given by the Ministry.

Academic freedoms are still restricted even for the leading Russian HEIs. Although 46 of them are granted the right to implement their own educational standards, they have to agree the curricula and content of their degrees with the Federal State Standards. The latter require Russian HEIs to implement their bachelor's, master's and doctoral study programmes only within the fields of studies which are listed by the Ministry's orders (2013 amend. 2019; 2017 amend. 2018). The compliance of any degree with its Federal Educational Standard is confirmed by the obligatory procedures of licensing and state accreditation in order to have the degrees recognised and to provide male students deferment from military service. The boundaries between fields of study for the degree programmes become a barrier for cross-disciplinary programmes developed with the EU partners (Ustyuzhantseva et al., Chapter 10, this volume). In those cases, transaction costs are generated by the arduous procedure of the state accreditation each five years. In addition, the Federal State Standards and their implementation has led to the isolation of Russian and European curricula and quality assurance systems. They do not allow partner HEIs to provide a united double degree programme and diminish its added value (Shenderova, 2020).

Heavy contact hours as the main part of the teaching workload do not provide enough time for research and internationalisation activities. The EDU neighbours' study (2020) revealed the average number of contact hours as 16–18 per week during the study year, per one academic position. But in modern Russia, unlike USSR, the Ministry does not specify contact hours per academic position. Instead, funding can be cut simultaneously with salary rises, with the result that the workload of academics becomes overloaded.

As a result, Russian HEIs are not able to confirm their students' choice of courses within a certain degree programme. That drastically reduces the opportunities to implement a double degree as an individual study track. Students study on a Bachelor's degree programme whose enrollment might have, for instance, 120 persons. Any student, who studied a certain degree, has the same or very similar set of courses. Some universities provided their student with a track within a degree which may be chosen after two years of study. However, students are not allowed to follow an individual curriculum by choosing any course outside a specified track, either on a Bachelor's or a Master's degree. Students within each degree programme study in groups of 30–35 persons on Bachelor's degrees and not less than ten on Master's degrees. For example, St Petersburg State University requests academics to provide the new courses; however, a course (or their track) will be available if its enrollment is not less than 10 students (SPbSU, 2019). Because Russian HEIs combine state-funded and self-funded students, a 'group approach' maximises the contact workload per academic, simultaneously minimising the average salary and maximising the profit. The HEIs are given the right to spend the revenue from tuition fees as they choose; their budgets are not open to public scrutiny.

For some HEIs it is easier to hire additional managers to report to the different control bodies, and/or to agree to their administrative demands, than to hire more academic staff with a reasonable workload who are allowed to combine IoHE development, teaching and research.

6   Conclusion

Modern Russia has developed a national policy aimed at enhancing the competitiveness of Russian HEIs worldwide, using Russia-EU higher education cooperation for this purpose. Historically and geographically Russia stands in a unique position for cooperation with the EU, being its largest eastern neighbour and sharing time zones with five EU countries. It is not surprising that the EU countries are among the preferred destinations for Russian students, while not many EU students are eager to study in Russia.

Russia-EU higher education cooperation comes into conflict with growing competition, commercialisation, managerialism, and global uncertainty. These are the challenges which arise from supranational and global external institutional environments where Russian and EU HEIs cooperate. Statutory micromanagement of Russian HEIs, their degree programmes and international contacts from federal authorities are among the other challenges.

At the same time the degree system in Russia has not yet built in consistent and coherent levels of higher education in accordance with the European Qualification Framework. Authoritarian top-bottom decision-making has had deep roots in Russian state policy and university governance. The RF Government programmes support IoHE but multiply the number of control bodies and confuse their responsibilities. The Federal Education Standards' lists of the fields of study, the incompleteness of the reform of the degree system and the arbitrariness of supervisors remain challenges for the development of internationalisation activities.

Multiple administration and time-consuming cross-reporting are combined with the permanent increase of other obligatory reports. They produce transaction costs of IoHE at the level of national IoHE policy. Their volume and unpredictability severely undermine the IoHE activities implemented in cooperation with European partners. While the number of staff recruited specially to provide data for reporting at the HEI and policy levels snowballs, transaction costs related to IoHE activities are passed on to students and staff, some of whom unexpectedly have to spend time and money on translation of the transcripts of their records and Diploma Supplement in English, visa or travel (Shenderova, 2020).

However, Ustyuzhantseva, Zvonareva, Hortsman & Popova (Chapter 10, this volume) shows that Russian and European academics are able to rise above the deteriorating international situation and disadvantaged institutional environments in order to continue cooperating. Their endeavours offer the most powerful opportunity to continue building Russia-EU higher education cooperation from Lisbon to Vladivostok.

Acknowledgements

I would like to express my deep gratitude to Dr. Sirke Mäkinen, University of Helsinki, for fruitful discussions of university autonomy and academic freedom and her support of my research; the colleagues from Higher Education Group and Politics, Faculty of Management and Business, Tampere University, for creating an inspiring institutional environment for my study; Dr. Dmitry

Lanko, St. Petersburg State University, Dr. Alexey Malygin, Ivanovo State University, and all Russian colleagues for their generous sharing of their experience of the implementation of national higher education policy in Russian universities.

References

5–100 Russian Academic Excellence Project. (2020). Retrieved January 4, 2020, from http://5top100.com/documents/

Academic mobility of foreign students in Russia. (2016). *Facts on Education, 7.* https://ioe.hse.ru/data/2016/08/04/1119531130/ФО7.pdf

Agreement on partnership and cooperation. (1994). https://eur-lex.europa.eu/legal-content/EN/TXT/HTML/?uri=CELEX:21997A1128(01)&from=EN

Altbach, P. G., & Knight, J. (2007). The internationalization of higher education: Motivations and realities. *Journal of Studies in International Education, 11*(3–4), 290–305. https://doi.org/10.1177/1028315307303542

Beerkens, E., Brandenburg, U., Evers, N., van Gaalen, A., Leichsenring, H., & Zimmermann, V. (2010). *Indicator projects on internationalisation – IMPI research report.* CHE. Retrieved January 16, 2020, from https://www.che.de/download/indicator_projects_on_internationalisation___impi_100511-pdf/

Burquel, N., Shenderova, S., & Tvorogova, S. (2014a). *Joint education programmes between higher education institutions of the European Union and Russian Federation. Innovation and transformation in transnational education.* European Union. https://publications.europa.eu/en/publication-detail/-/publication/6bb2175a-75f9-11e8-ac6a-01aa75ed71a1/language-en/format-PDF/source-78326987

Burquel, N., Shenderova, S., & Tvorogova, S. (2014b). *Catalogue 'sampled joint programmes between European and Russian higher education institutions. Innovations and transformation in transnational education'.* European Union. https://publications.europa.eu/en/publication-detail/-/publication/b01303b3-fba4-415b-8d36-b8e10663f9dd/language-en

Chan, W. W. Y. (2004). International cooperation in higher education: Theory and practice. *Journal of Studies in International Education, 8*(1), 32–55. https://doi.org/10.1177/1028315303254429

de Wit, H., Hunter, F., & Coelen, R. (2015). Internationalisation of higher education in Europe: Future directions. In H. de Wit, F. Hunter, L. Howard, & E. Egron-Polak (Eds.), *Internationalisation of higher education: Study* (pp. 273–280). European Union. Retrieved January 10, 2020, from https://op.europa.eu/en/publication-detail/-/publication/1b743fec-8b6c-45c2-aa9e-2fdf0967757b/language-en de Wit, H., & Merkx, G. (2012). The history of internationalization of higher education. In D. K. Deardorff, H. de Wit, J. D. Heyl, & T. Adams (Eds.), *The Sage handbook of international higher education* (pp. 43–60). Sage Publications.

Dneprov, E. (Ed.). (2017). *Russian legislation on education XIX–beginning of XX century. Collection of documents* (Vol. I). Higher School of Economics Publishing House.

EDUneighbours. (2020). *Towards good neighbourliness with higher education cooperation. Finnish-Russian research and action project.* Retrieved January 4, 2020, from https://research.uta.fi/eduneighbours/papersandpublications/

EHEA. (1999). *Bologna declaration.* The European Higher Education Area. http://www.ehea.info/Upload/document/ministerial_declarations/1999_Bologna_Declaration_English_553028.pdf

EHEA. (2009). *The Bologna process 2020 – The EHEA in the new decade.* Communiqué of the Conference of European Ministers Responsible for Higher Education, Leuven and Louvain-la-Neuve. http://www.ehea.info/media.ehea.info/file/2009_Leuven_Louvain-la-Neuve/06/1/Leuven_Louvain-la-Neuve_Communique_April_2009_595061.pdf

EHEA. (2012). *Making the most of our potential: Consolidating the EHEA.* Bucharest Communiqué. http://ehea.info/media.ehea.info/file/2012_Bucharest/67/3/Bucharest_Communique_2012_610673.pdf

Elken, M., Hovdhaugen, E., & Stensaker, B. (2016). Global rankings in the Nordic region: Challenging the identity of research-intensive universities? *Higher Education, 72*(6), 781–795. https://doi.org/10.1007/s10734-015-9975-6

EU and Russia. A Strategic partnership. (2011). http://eeas.europa.eu/archives/docs/russia/docs/2011_eu-russia_leaflet_en.pdf

Fedotova, O., Platonova, E., Tregubenko, E., & Avanesyan, G. (2019). Development of the export potential of Russian education in the modern strategic discourse. *SHS Web Conf., 70*, 02005. https://doi.org/10.1051/shsconf/20197002005

Fischl, L. (2018). *Very best friends. 1968 to 2018: 50 years of partnerships between the St. Petersburg State University and Freie Universität Berlin were celebrated in St. Petersburg.* Retrieved January 16, 2020, from https://www.fu-berlin.de/en/international/news-events/meldungen/20181203_50jahre_st-petersburg/index.html

Fradkov, A. (2019). A foreigner? Take your watch off! An open letter to the Minister of Science and Higher Education M.M. Kotyukov. *Troitsky Variant*, August 3. https://trv-science.ru/2019/08/13/inostranec-snimaj-chasy/

Frolov, E. (2016). Academic links between Russia and Germany in the 18th–19th centuries. *Vestnik of St. Petersburg State University, Series 2, History, 3*, 57–67.

Frumina, E., & West, R. (2012). *Internationalisation of Russian higher education: The English language dimension.* British Council. https://www.britishcouncil.ru/sites/default/files/internationalisation_of_russian_higher_education.pdf

Gänzle, S., Meister, S., & King, C. (2009). The Bologna process and its impact on higher education at Russia's margins: The case of Kaliningrad. *Higher Education, 57*(4), 533–547. https://doi.org/10.1007/s10734-008-9187-4

Global Education Programme. (2020). Retrieved February 13, from http://educationglobal.ru/ns/overview/employed/#{"employed-list":{"page":1,"directionId":"","fio":"","employerId":"","cityId":""}}

Guri-Rosenblit, S. (2015). Internationalization of higher navigating between contrasting trends. In A. Curaj, L. Matei, R. Pricopie, J. Salmi, & P. Scott (Eds.), *The European higher education area between critical reflections and future policies* (pp. 13–26). https://doi.org/10.1007/978-3-319-20877-0

Gurko, D., Trostyanskaya, I., Sema, E., Barsukov, A., & Polikhina, N. (2019). *Education of international students in Russian higher education institutions/The Ministry of science and higher education of the Russian Federation.* State Autonomous Sociological Research Center.

Katsakioris, C. (2019). The Lumumba University in Moscow: Higher education for a Soviet-Third World alliance, 1960–91. *Journal of Global History, 14*(2), 281–300. https://doi.org/10.1017/S174002281900007X

KFU. (2019). *Self-assessment report for 2018.* https://stat.kpfu.ru/content/uploads/2019/05/Otchet-o-samoobsledovanii-KFU-za-2018-god-1.pdf

Korhonen, V., & Alenius, P. (2018). Introduction: International and transnational dimensions in higher education. In V. Korhonen & P. Alenius (Eds.), *Internationalisation and transnationalisation in higher education* (pp. 15–37). Peter Lang AG. https://doi.org/10.3726/b11212

Kristinsson, A. (2010). *Expansions: Competition and conquest in Europe since the Bronze age.* Reykjavíkur Akademían.

Kuraev, A. (2014). *Internationalization of higher education in Russia: Collapse or perpetuation of the soviet system? A historical and conceptual study* (PhD dissertation). Boston College, Lynch School of Education. http://hdl.handle.net/2345/3799

Madariaga, I. (1998). *Politics and culture in eighteenth-century Russia.* Routledge. https://doi.org/10.4324/9781315840116

Magna Charta Universitatum. (1998). http://www.magna-charta.org/resources/files/the-magna-charta/english

Mid-Term Evaluation of Tempus in Russia. (2008). *Assessing the contribution of Tempus to the Bologna process in Russia.* Brussels. Retrieved January 22, 2020, from http://www.russianenic.ru/publications/DOC/3%20Mid%20term%20Evaluation%20TEMPUS%20.pdf

Mogherini: Russia is no longer the EU's strategic partner. (2014). EURACTIVE. https://www.euractiv.com/section/global-europe/news/mogherini-russia-is-no-longer-the-eu-s-strategic-partner/

MSU. (2020). *General information.* https://www.msu.ru/science/2010/sci-study.html

Murray, D. (2018). Living in a world different from the one in which we think. *Journal of Higher Education Policy and Management, 40*(6), 520–532. https://doi.org/10.1080/1360080X.2018.1529132

Novikov, M., & Perfilova, T. (2014). The university Charter of 1884: Illusion of the academic freedom (Part I). *Yaroslavl Pedagogical Bulletin, 4*(1), 27–40.

Pesch, U., & Ishmaev, G. (2019). Fictions and frictions: Promises, transaction costs and the innovation of network technologies. *Social Studies of Science, 49*(2), 264–277. https://doi.org/10.1177/0306312719838339

Platonova, D., & Semyonov, D. (2018). Russia: The institutional landscape of Russian higher education. In J. Huisman et al. (Eds.), *25 years of transformations of higher education systems in post-Soviet countries* (pp. 337–362). Palgrave Macmillan. https://doi.org/10.1007/978-3-319-52980-6_13

President of Russia. (2005, May 10). *Press statement and responses to questions following the Russia-European Union Summit.* http://en.kremlin.ru/events/president/transcripts/22967

President of Russia. (2012). Decree No 599 from 07.05.2012 'on measures of implementation of the state policy on education and science'. Art. 1, 1v. https://rg.ru/2012/05/09/nauka-dok.html

QS. (2020a). Retrieved February 14, from https://www.topuniversities.com/universities/lomonosov-moscow-state-university

QS. (2020b). Retrieved February 14, from https://www.topuniversities.com/universities/kazan-volga-region-federal-university

Results of joint research activity of scientists from Saint-Petersburg State Polytechnical University and Leibniz University of Hannover. (2014). Polytechnical University Publishing House.

RF Central Bank. (2020). Retrieved January 22, 2020, from https://www.cbr.ru/eng/currency_base/dynamics/

RF Government. (2012). *Resolution No 2006-p. On approval of the plan of measures providing leading Universities' competitiveness enhancement among the leading world research-education centres.* http://archive.government.ru/gov/results/21298/

RF Government. (2013, amend. 2018). *Resolution No 842. On the procedure to award scientific degrees p. 3, par. 3.* http://government.ru/docs/all/117525/

RF Government. (2017). *Passport of the priority project 'development of export potential of Russian education system'.* http://government.ru/projects/selection/653/28013/

RF Government. (2018). *Passport of national project 'education'.* http://government.ru/projects/selection/741/35566/

RF Ministry of Education and Science. (2013, amend. 2019). *Order No 1061. On approval of the list of specialties and fields of study for degree programmes in higher education.* https://base.garant.ru/70480868/

RF Ministry of Education and Science. (2017, amend. 2018). *Order No 1027. On approval of nomenclature for scientific specialties and the fields of study, for which scientific degrees are allowed to award. Annex No 1. Scientific specialties, their groups and the fields of studies for awards kandidat nauk and doctor nauk scientific degrees.* http://www.consultant.ru/document/cons_doc_LAW_283150/

RF Ministry of International Affairs. (2003, November 10). *From the speech of the President of Russia at the meeting with the members of the Government.* https://www.mid.ru/web/guest/maps/fr/-/asset_publisher/g8RuzDvY7qyV/content/id/497610

RF Ministry of Science and Higher Education. (2020). *Forma VPO-1.* https://minobrnauki.gov.ru/ru/activity/stat/highed/

Road Map on Common Space of Research and Education including Cultural Aspects. (2005). https://russiaeu.ru/userfiles/file/road_map_on_the_common_space_of_research_and_education_2005_english.pdf

Russell, M. (2017). *EU-Russia cooperation on higher education. At a glance, 21 September.* EPRS, European Parliamentary Research Service. http://www.europarl.europa.eu/thinktank/en/document.html?reference=EPRS_ATA(2017)608701

Shenderova, S. (2002). Problems of teaching economic disciplines in technical institutes. *Voprosy Economiki, 8,* 102–114.

Shenderova, S. (2011). *Multi-level higher education institutional arrangement in the Russian Federation: Formation and development.* St. Petersburg State University Economics and Finance Publishing.

Shenderova, S. (2018a). Internationalisation of higher education in Russia: National policy and results at institutional level. In V. Korhonen & P. Alenius (Eds.), *Internationalisation and transnationalisation in higher education* (pp. 69–100). Peter Lang AG. https://doi.org/10.3726/b11212

Shenderova, S. (2018b). Permanent uncertainty as normality? Finnish-Russian double degrees in the post-Crimea world. *Journal of Higher Education Policy and Management, 40*(6), 611–628. https://doi.org/10.1080/1360080X.2018.1529134

Shenderova, S. (2020). Finnish-Russian double degree programmes: When partner's responsibilities become a challenge for internationalisation. In B. Broucker, V. Borden, T. Kallenberg, & C. Milsom (Eds.), *Responsibility of higher education systems: What? Why? How?* (pp. 185–203). Brill | Sense. https://doi.org/10.1163/9789004436558_011

SPbSU. (2020). *St. Petersburg State University, Order No. 3773/1 from 12.04.2019.* Retrieved January 22, 2020, from https://spbu.ru/sites/default/files/20190412_3773_1.pdf

THE. (2020b). https://www.timeshighereducation.com/world-university-rankings/kazan-federal-university

THE. (2020a). https://www.timeshighereducation.com/world-university-rankings/lomonosov-moscow-state-university

Trondal, J., Gornitzka, Å., & Gulbrandsen, M. (2003). Conceptual lenses. In Å. Gornitzka, M. Gulbrandsen, & J. Trondal (Eds.), *Internationalisation of research and higher education. Report 2/2003*. NIFU. https://nifu.brage.unit.no/nifu-xmlui/handle/11250/274410

UNESCO UIS. (2017). *Global flow of tertiary-level students*. Retrieved January 22, 2020, from http://uis.unesco.org/en/uis-student-flow

Vititneva, E., & Lushchaeva, G. (2018). Everyday life of Siberian students in the pre-revolutionary period and its law regulation by the example of higher educational institutions in Tomsk. *Issues of Social-Economic Development of Siberia, 32*(2), 109–115. https://brstu.ru/static/unit/journal_2/docs/number-32/109-115.pdf

Volkov, A., & Mel'nyk, D. (2019, April 9). Why international students for Russia. *Vedomosti*. https://www.vedomosti.ru/opinion/articles/2019/04/09/798618-zachem-rossii-studenti

CHAPTER 7

The Policy Context of EU-South Africa Higher Education Cooperation: An Overview of Policies and Practices

Patrício V. Langa and Charl Wolhuter

Abtract

This chapter examines the South African policy framework and practices of cooperation with the European Union (EU) in the field of higher education. More specifically, it examines the cooperation protocols and programmes with the two jurisdictions post 1994, the year that officially marks the end of apartheid in South Africa. The EU existed prior to 1994, but the meaningful policy frameworks which cover the democratic South Africa occurred after the Amsterdam treaty, which includes a chapter on research and technical development. The most prominent of these framework programmes has been the Erasmus Programme, a university exchange programme which began in 1987. The chapter describes the policy environment and development by the government departments accountable for higher education, research, technology and innovation (DHET) and the Department of Science and Technology (DST).

Since the fall of the racial and segregationist Apartheid regime in 1994, South Africa started a journey of transforming its institutions and society at large towards becoming a democratic, non-racial, non-sexist `rainbow` nation, representing the countries' multiracial and multicultural aspirations (Tutu & Allen, 1995). The pursuit of political, financial and economic stability to enable the country to further develop to the benefit of all who live in it has led to partnerships with the EU, including in the sector of higher education, science, technology and innovation. The South African government has since 1993 attempted to forge multiple sectorial and global partnerships and cooperation with strategic partners. South Africa established and maintained strategic alliances with them prior to 1994, but the meaningful policy frameworks which cover the democratic South Africa occurred after the Amsterdam treaty, which includes a chapter on research and technical development (Amsterdam Treaty, 1997).

Keywords

South Africa – South African higher education cooperation with the European Union – South African Higher Education policies for HE internationalisation – South African higher education system

1   Introduction

This chapter examines the South African policy framework and practices of cooperation with the European Union (EU) in the field of higher education. More specifically, it examines the cooperation protocols and programmes with the two jurisdictions in post 1994, the year that officially marks the end of apartheid in South Africa. The EU exists prior to 1994, but the meaningful policy frameworks which cover the democratic South Africa occurred after the Amsterdam treaty, which includes a chapter on research and technical development. The most prominent of these framework programmes has been the Erasmus Programme, a university exchange programme which began in 1987. The chapter describes the policy environment and development by the government departments accountable for higher education, research, technology and innovation (DHET) and the Department of Science and Technology (DST).

The EU is an acronym for European Union, a political and economic union of 28 member states that are geopolitically located primarily in Europe (European Commission, 2018). Relationships between the EU and South Africa operate on the basis of bilateral, regional and international frameworks and platforms to enhance strategic cooperation, and integration at both economic, geo-political and cultural levels.

Since the fall of the racial and segregationist Apartheid regime in 1994, South Africa started a journey of transforming its institutions and society at large towards becoming a democratic, non-racial, non-sexist 'rainbow' nation, representing the countries' multiracial and multicultural aspirations (Tutu & Allen, 1995). The pursuit of political, financial and economic stability to enable the country to further develop to the benefit of all who live in it has led to partnerships with the EU, including in the sector of higher education, science, technology and innovation. The South African government has since 1993 attempted to forge multiple sectorial and global partnerships and cooperation with strategic partners. South Africa established and maintained strategic alliances with them prior to 1994, but the meaningful policy frameworks which cover the democratic South Africa occurred after the Amsterdam treaty, which includes a chapter on research and technical development (Amsterdam Treaty, 1997).

The EU has developed a new approach to North-South cooperation by adopting three key policy papers on the Sustainable Development Goals, the European Consensus on Development and the EU Strategy for Africa. It is strengthening its foreign action and seeks to foster stability, security and prosperity worldwide. South Africa's partnership with Europe is building on shared values and mutual interests as well as profound cultural links. South Africa, the EU and its member states have developed a multifaceted, comprehensive partnership based on Trade, Development and Cooperation Agreements (TDCA).

The chapter is divided into four main parts. After the introduction, the first part looks at the European Union cooperation frameworks with Africa, and particularly with South Africa. The second part is an overview of the societal and higher education context of South Africa. We spell out what both sides can expect from one another on the domestic, regional, continental and global fronts, and do justice to South Africa and the EU's distinctive positions in the new, globalised context. In the third part, we provide a brief overview of the recent developments in South African higher education and in the fourth part, we draw some conclusions.

2   Higher Education Integration in the EU

In 2017, one of the authors of this chapter (PL) attended as a panellist a colloquium jointly organised by the DHET and the European Union Delegation in South Africa to discuss the development of a framework for partnership and collaboration. Some of the reflections in the chapter emanate from the discussion in the 2017 colloquium. EU higher education operates as an integrated area of coordination and policy (Maaseen & Olsen, 2007). Advancement of knowledge as a competitive production factor in a globalised society and economy is at the core of the integration endeavour.

The concept of a Europe of knowledge captures that dynamic of integration and purpose of the higher education system (Gornitzka, Maassen, Olsen, & Stensaker, 2007). The EU higher education system and its relations with research and innovation play a crucial role in individual development and in providing highly skilled human capital and the engaged citizens that Europe needs to create jobs, economic growth, and prosperity (European Union, 2018). Hence, "higher education institutions are crucial partners in delivering the EU's strategy to drive forward and maintain sustainable growth". The Europe 2020 strategy set a target that by 2020 40% of young Europeans should have a higher education qualification (European Commission/EACEA/Eurydice, 2018).

For the year 2020, the EU has defined eight benchmarks including an EU average of at least 20% of higher education graduates that should have had a period of higher education-related study or training, work placements, study abroad, representing a minimum of 15 ECTS credits or lasting a minimum of three months. An EU average of at least 6% of 18–34 year-olds with an initial vocational education and training (IVET) qualification should have had an IVET-related study or training period (including work placements) abroad lasting a minimum of two weeks, or less if documented by Europass (European Commission/EACEA/Eurydice, 2018).

3 The European Higher Education Area

The European Higher Education Area (EHEA) is a unique international collaborative project on higher education and the product of the political will of forty eight countries (which includes the EU nations and adjacent nations as far as Kazakhstan which have bought into the EHEA) comprising distinct political, cultural and academic societies, which, gradually over more than three decades, established an area implementing a shared set of pledges, structural reforms and collective tools. EU nations settled to and implemented reforms on higher education on the basis of common key values - such as freedom of expression, autonomy for institutions, independent student unions, academic freedom, free movement of students and staff (Maassen, Gornitzka, & Fumasoli, 2017). The European Commission's reform agendas for higher education, through coordination processes, drive countries, institutions and stakeholders of the European area to adapt their higher education systems continuously, making them more compatible and strengthening their quality assurance mechanisms (European Commission, 2006, 2011, 2017). For all the EU countries, the foremost objective is to encourage staff and students' mobility and to facilitate employability.

Although primarily geared towards enhancement of its regions, the EU also has a development policy to engage with the developing world. The New European Consensus on Development 'Our World, Our Dignity, Our Future' represents the EU's vision for the 2030 Agenda for Sustainable Development1 (2030 Agenda), adopted by the United Nations in September 2015. The 2030 Agenda is the international community's response to global challenges and trends in relation to sustainable development. With the Sustainable Development

Goals (SDGS) at its core, the 2030 Agenda is a transformative political framework to eradicate poverty and achieve sustainable development globally (European Commission/EACEA/Eurydice, 2018).

In the education sector, including higher education, the EU's vision entails ensuring access to quality education for all, which is a prerequisite for youth employability and long-lasting development. The EU and its individual countries support a policy framework for inclusive lifelong learning and equitable quality education, particularly during early childhood and the primary years. The EU also promotes education at secondary and higher education level, technical and vocational training, and work-based and adult learning, including in emergency and crisis situations. In their education policy framework, special attention is paid to education and training opportunities for girls and women (European Commission/EACEA/Eurydice, 2018).

The EU ensures that every citizen in their region "has the knowledge, skills, capabilities and rights they need to enjoy a life of dignity, to be fully engaged in society as responsible and productive adults, and to contribute to the social, economic and environmental well-being of their communities" (European Commission, 2017, p. 11). In addition, the EU as well as its individual countries vow to work with both developed and developing countries to promote North-South as well as South-South and a triangular cooperation framework that is consistent with the principles and practices of its International Development Policy. It is within this policy framework that we can situate the South African-EU cooperation framework in higher education.

4   Contextual Background: South African Society and Higher Education

4.1   *South African Society*

South Africa occupies 1.2 million square kilometres at the southernmost part of the African continent. Even in this day and age of globalisation, an information, communications and technological (ICT) revolution and a "flat" world, this location at the periphery of the world scientific, technological, educational, and economic system, with its central nerve centre far away in North-America and Western Europe, places the country in a disadvantageous position. To connect physically to their peers in Western Europe or North America is an expensive undertaking for South African scholars.

The total population of South Africa now stands at 58 million. The South African population is made up of Blacks (people of African descent) making up 80.2% of the total population of the country, Whites (people of European descent) making up 8.4% of the total population, Indians (people from Indian descent making up 2.5% of the total population), and "Coloureds" (as this group was historically named, these are people from mixed racial descent) making up 8.8% of the total population.

The Black population group has been in the country for many centuries, their ancestors having migrated into the current territory of South Africa from Western and Central Africa. White settlement dates from the establishment of a refreshment station by the Dutch East Indian Company, where Cape Town is today, in 1652. In the course of time, interbreeding led to the "Coloured" segment of the population (cf. Van Jaarsveld, 1976, p. 29): however to complicate matters, descendants of slaves brought in from Asia (mainly from where Malaysia and Indonesia are today) as well as the Khoisan (that is descendants from the very oldest inhabitants of the country, comparable to what in North America is known as the "first nation people") have historically also been placed in this very problematic category with the name of "Coloureds". The most recent population sector, the Indians, dates from 1855, when Indians were imported from India, to work as indentured labourers on sugar farms.

The current population growth rate is 1.33% per annum. The growth rate has been declining for a number of years.

South Africa has eleven official languages. These are (in bracket after each language appears the percentage of the population who speak that particular language as first language): isiZulu (23.8%), isiXhosa (17.6%), Afrikaans (13.3%), Sepedi (9.4%), English (8.2%), Setswana (8.2%), Sesotho (7.9%), Xitsonga (4.4%), siSwati (2.7%), Tshivenda (2.3%) and isiNdebele (1.6%).

Socio-economic inequalities are stark. At 62.5, South Africa has the second highest Gini index in the world (Central Intelligence Agency, 2019). What makes the inequality more alarming is that, while decreasing, the contours of the socio-economic stratification largely correspond to the racial divide – with Whites concentrated in the top strata, Blacks in the lower strata, and in-between the Coloureds and Indians.

South Africa is, according to the taxonomy of the World Bank, an upper middle income country. The annual per capita income stands at US$ 5,720. The economic growth rate at present stands at a very dispiriting 0.8% per annum (ibid.). Other economic problems besetting the country include a high rate of unemployment (29.1%, figure November 2019), and the relatively low productivity and competitiveness of the labour force (see IMD, 2019).

The political system before 1994 was characterised by policies of extreme segregation of the four population groups enumerated above. The right to vote was reserved for White South Africans. Resistance to this took the form of rising levels of socio-political turmoil, at times reaching the level of a low key civil war (cf. Johnson, 2004). A new political dispensation began in 1994, based on a Constitution, of a liberal Western European kind and a Bill of Human Rights widely hailed as one of the most progressive in the world. The African National Congress took over government after the 1994 elections, and is still the government (although with a reduced majority, compared to 1994).

4.2 South African Higher Education

Formal education in South Africa commenced after the Dutch East Indian Company established a refreshment station at the Cape in 1652. A typical colonial situation, university education lagged; neither the Dutch colonial authorities, nor at first the British colonial authorities (which took over the Cape Colony in 1806) turned their attention to the establishment of a university. The first university to be established was the University of Good Hope founded in 1873. This university was not involved in teaching but, instead, laid down curricula, conducted examinations, and conferred degrees for teaching done at colleges such as the South African College (Cape Town) and the Victoria College (Stellenbosch). The University Act No. 12 of 1916 made provision for the establishment of a federal examining university to be called the University of South Africa, located in Pretoria. This university would incorporate the University of the Cape of Good Hope. In time its constituent colleges became autonomous universities: Stellenbosch University (Victoria College in 1916), University of Cape Town (South African College in 1916), Witwatersrand University in 1922, University of Pretoria in 1930, University of Natal in 1949, University of the Orange Free State in 1950, Rhodes University in 1951, and Potchefstroom University in 1951. After the constituent colleges had become independent universities, the University of South Africa became a correspondence (distance teaching) university in 1951. All these institutions were meant to cater for the White population.

The roots of university education for Black South Africans can be traced back to the founding of Lovedale College in 1916. This institution became autonomous in 1949, under the name of the University of Fort Hare. An important date in South African history is 1948. In that year the National Party took over government and began to implement a policy of total segregation (Apartheid). Ten territories (Bantustans) were created for Black South Africans, the idea was that Black South Africans should have their own governments, health services, houses, farms, education institutions, etc. in these Bantustans. As part of that project universities were established in these Bantustans, i.e. a host of Black universities came into being in the decades after 1948, such as the

University of Zululand, the University of the Transkei and the University of the North. A university meant for the "Coloured" population group (The University of the Western Cape) and one for the Indian population group (The University of Durban Westville) also came into being.

During the course of the twentieth century a second type of higher education institution, called the technikons, and offering higher education of a vocational kind, came into being. These were also racially segregated. By 1994 there were thirteen technikons: seven for Whites, three for Blacks, one for Indians, one for Coloreds, and the Technikon RSA – a distance education institution.

When the socio-political reconstruction of South Africa commenced in 1994, the African National Congress took over government in 1994, and education, including higher education, was in for a major overhaul too. Part of the new government's policy on higher education was to increase access to and participation in higher education, and to equalise access to higher education (see Wolhuter, 2015). To belabour the first two points (increased access and equalisation), it should be mentioned that in 1994 the gross higher education enrolment ratio of South Africa stood at a paltry low of 14%. At that stage of higher education, enrolment ratios of other typical upper middle income countries such as Mexico, Argentina or Malaysia, were easily three times, in some cases even more, than that of South Africa (see Wolhuter, 2015). Furthermore higher education participation rates were very unequal, with participation rates amongst Whites very high, those among Blacks and Coloureds very low, and those of Indians somewhere betweeen these two extremes (see Wolhuter, 2009). Another problem that was besetting higher education in 1994 was the effect of the international academic boycott. From about 1960 till the beginning of the 1990s, South African universities were subjected to a boycott by the international academic world (see Harricombe & Lancaster, 1995). This boycott cut South African scholars off from their counterparts abroad and from developments in their academic fields, and was conducive to pernicious parochialism in scholarship and inbreeding of faculty. Thus in 1994 South African academe also faced the challenge of re-integration into the global academic world.

When assessing the South African higher education sector at this point in time, a number of challenges are looming. Enrolments and participation rates have grown impressively since 1994. Higher education enrolments have swollen from 495,355 in 1994 (Wolhuter, 2009) to 1,116,017 in 2017 (latest available figures) (UNESCO, 2020). However, while having expanded impressively since 1994, enrolment ratios are still low compared to those of other upper middle income countries, let alone high income countries. Similarly, while commendable progress has been made on the equalisation front, enrolment patterns still do not correspond to the demographic make-up of the country.

As far as internationalisation is concerned, the results of successive surveys of the academic profession are illustrative. Thus far two international surveys of the academic profession have been carried out. The first was the Carnegie Investigation of the late 1980s. As South Africa was at that stage still subjected to the international academic boycott, South Africa did not participate in that exercise. However, with the permission and encouragement of the Carnegie Investigation principals, three South African scholars surveyed the South African academic profession in 2003, using the questionnaire of the Carnegie survey, and compared the results with those found in the otherthirteen countries which took part in the survey. From this survey it emerged that in the decade after the global academic community had again opened its doors to South Africa, the South African academic profession, by the international norm, had developed an exemplary group of international activities (see Wolhuter & Higgs, 2004). The second international investigation into the academic profession was the CAP (Changing Academic Profession) survey, which took place in 2008 and which involved 23 countries, South Africa included. The evidence which emanated from this survey, however, was that the gains made by the South African academic profession during the first decade after 1994, were reversed, and by 2008 the South African academic profession had, as far as their international activities were concerned, once again fallen below the international par (Wolhuter, Higgs, Higgs, & Ntshoe, 2012).

Another challenge South African universities are facing is that of research output and research capacity. While there is research indicating that South African universities have at least pockets of excellence regarding research (for example, in an analysis of all articles published in all Web of Science indexed journals in the field of Education in 2012, Wolhuter, 2017, found that in the total global author pool of 18,523 authors, South Africa occupied the 14th place in the rank-order of countries, a remarkable achievement in view of the small size of the South African academic profession), and that these pockets of scholars make their mark on the international circuit. However, on aggregate the South African academic profession does not excel as far as research is concerned. For example, in the CAP survey, it was found that of the 23 participating countries, South African academics had the lowest research output (Wolhuter, Higgs, Higgs, & Ntshoe, 2014).

Taking the focus to doctoral education, the supply line of the research cadre for the university sector, South African universities are having considerable challenges too. South Africa produces 46 doctorates per million population per year, placing the country, on this measure, in the 64th rank-order place in the world (Mouton et al., 2019, p. 36). For comparison, the corresponding figure for Switzerland and Slovenia (currently the world leaders) are 485 each, for the United Kingdom 409, for the United States of America 166 and for China 31.

The number of doctoral degrees awarded has grown substantially from 972 in 2000 to 2,525 in 2012 (ibid.). On the other hand, it is still a long way off from the 2030 goal of 100 doctoral graduates per million population as appearing in the National Development Plan (see Auf der Heyde, 2015). On the equalisation front much progress has been made, but the inclination is even steeper than in the case of the aggregate university enrolment figures cited above. The percentage of Black students in the PhD graduation class has grown from 25% in 2000 to 47% in 2015 (latest available figures at time of writing) (Mouton et al., 2019, p. 36). While obviously far from reflecting the demographic reality in the country, the growth curve is heartening, and it has also been empirically demonstrated that the attainment of a doctorate makes a significant difference in the research productivity of South African academics (at least at aggregate level) (see Wolhuter, Naidoo, Sutherland, & Peckham, 2004).

It is a function of a university (deriving from its unique place in society, an autonomous institution occupying itself with the advancement of various branches of higher learning) to be the conscience of society, delivering social critique (see Wolhuter, 2012). While the historically White English universities and (in another aspect) the historically Black universities had particularly excelled in this role in the years up to 1994, after 1994 this critical voice fell silent (see Weeks, Herman, Maarman, & Wolhuter, 2006; Gumede & Dikeni, 2009). While university campuses – particularly in 2015 and for some time thereafter – have become scenes of student activism, two cautionary notes might be made before these could be regarded as part of the university's societal critical function. The first is that protests are about student grievances, rather than national, let alone international issues: issues such as student financing and students' sense of belonging that they are experiencing on campuses (see Habib, 2019; Wolhuter & Van der Walt, forthcoming). An issue such as the global ecological crisis is totally absent. The second problem is the destructive and violent behaviour that mars such protest action, making it hardly the place where societal critique in an secure atmosphere of free speech can flourish. In the spate of activism on campuses in 2015, damage to the extent of South African Rand 150 million (roughly US$ 10 million) was incurred. Even very progressive South African social commentators, such as Mondli Makahnya (2020) have expressed their unreserved objection to this kind of activism.

Finally, in recent times the imperative for the decolonisation of education, higher education in particular, in South Africa has reached the volume of an alarm siren, including calls from the student corps (see Wolhuter & Van der Walt, forthcoming; Seroto, Noor, & Wolhuter, 2020).

5 South Africa and Cooperation with the EU in Higher Education

As we mentioned earlier in the introduction, South African-EU relations are based on the three pillars of trade, development aid and cooperation in various areas, such as economic and social cooperation. The importance of the special and strengthened relationship between the South Africa and EU was consolidated with the establishment of a Strategic Partnership signed in 2007. This Strategic Partnership is one of ten worldwide and the only one the EU has with an African country. The purpose of the partnership is to strengthen political dialogue and pursue strategic cooperation and shared objectives with regard to regional, African and global issues on the one side, and stronger policy dialogue and sectoral cooperation in a number of areas on the other.

Scientific enterprise in Africa still lags behind that of the economically advanced countries especially in the northern hemisphere in terms of outputs, and many knowledge contributions from African science continue to be invisible and not properly captured. Notwithstanding, significant progress has been made despite the often inadequate funding. For instance, South Africa, in particular, has increased its share of global scientific production from 0.39 per cent in 1996 to 0.7 per cent in 2015 (Morrell, 2019; Dell, 2019). According to Morrell (2019),

> in terms of international benchmarking, South Africa has increased its research output and world research share and improved its world rank (28 in 2016). The output of articles indexed on the Web of Science increased from 3668 publications in 2000 to 15,550 in 2016. This annual average growth of 2.9% resulted in a doubling of South Africa's relative world output (from 0.4% in 2000 to 0.91% in 2016). (p. 1)

South Africa is also the most sought after study destination in Africa and 14th among all countries of the world, and this contributes significantly to turn it into a higher education Hub on the continent (Cloete, Sheppard, & Bailey, 2015).

6 EU Supported Programmes in (South) African Higher Education

The long-standing cooperation between the EU and the African, Caribbean and Pacific (ACP) countries is based on the ACP-EU Partnership Agreement

'Cotonou Agreement' (European Union, 2014). This agreement was signed on 23 June 2000 for a 20-year period (revised in 2010 and in 2015) at the 1st Africa-European Union Summit, to provide for a formal political channel of cooperation between the two regions. The agreement was preceded by the 1975 Lomé Convention (European Union, 1998). Seventy-nine ACP countries (48 countries from sub-Saharan Africa, 16 from the Caribbean and 15 from the Pacific) are parties to the Cotonou Agreement (European Union, 2014). EU cooperation with five Northern African countries (Algeria, Egypt, Libya, Morocco and Tunisia) is based on the Southern Neighbourhood policy.

Since the Cotonou Agreement expired on 29 February 2020, negotiations on a new 'post-Cotonou' agreement have taken place to extend the validity of the current agreement to 31 December 2020. On 28 November 2019, the European Parliament adopted a resolution on the ongoing negotiations. After signing the Cotonou Agreement, cooperation was strengthened in 2002 with the launch of the African Union (AU) succeeding the Organisation of African Unity (OAU), a continental body consisting of 55 African member states, with the main objectives being the reinforcement of international cooperation (European Parliament, 2019).

Various AU-EU summits took place in 2007, 2010, 2014 and 2017. The European Parliament has delegations for relations with: (a) South Africa; (b) the Pan-African Parliament; (c) the ACP-EU Joint Parliamentary Assembly; and (d) the Maghreb countries and the Arab Maghreb Union (DMAG), including the EU-Morocco, EU-Tunisia and EU-Algeria Joint Parliamentary Committees. There are also forums for thematic cooperation, for instance, the EU-Africa Business Forum and the Africa-EU civil society forum.

In the field of higher education, ACP-EU, particularly at the Valletta Summit on Migration, on 11–12 November 2015, committed to secure the mobility of students, researchers and entrepreneurs, and to substantially increase the number of Erasmus+ scholarships for African students and academic staff. The Valletta Summit launched the Emergency Trust Fund for Africa (Council of the European Union, 2019). In 2018, the European Commission launched a new Africa-Europe Alliance for Sustainable Investment and Jobs with 'investment in education and matching skills and jobs' as one of the key objectives. The Commission also announced its support for exchange projects between higher education institutions through the Erasmus+ programme, and the mobility of students, staff and academics across the African continent through the Inter-Africa mobility scheme (European Comission, 2018).

For higher education, the priorities agreed for EU-Africa cooperation are: (a) promote the mobility of students, scholars, researchers and staff; (b) harmonise higher education in Africa; (c) enhance quality assurance and accreditation in African universities; and (d) develop centres of excellence in Africa, in particular through the Pan-African University. The academic mobility (of students, scholars, researchers and staff) is supported through the following programmes and schemes: (a) the African Union Mwalimu Nyerere Scholarship Scheme; (b) the Intra-Africa Academic Mobility Scheme; and (c) the Erasmus+ programme and the Marie Skłodowska-Curie actions (European Commission/EACEA/Eurydice, 2018).

Tuning Africa is an important project aiming at Harmonisation of African higher education systems to enable academic mobility and comparability of degrees. The goal is to be achieved through quality assurance, the Harmonising, Quality Assurance and Accreditation (HAQAA) programme. EU-Africa cooperation includes the area of Science Technology and Innovation (STI), as defined by the EU-Africa High-Level Policy Dialogue (HLPD) on STI. Additionally, the launch of the Africa-Europe Innovation Partnership in 2019 is to be supported by funding instruments, such as the EU's Horizon 2020 programme and the African Union Research Grants. The seventh framework programme for research (FP7) funded around 600 collaborative research projects involving around 1,400 participants from 45 African countries. The EU also supports the Kwame Nkrumah Scientific Awards for leading African scientists (European Parliament, 2019). This section presented a sample of programmes and initiatives supported by the EU and its member states in the framework of cooperation with (South) African countries.

7   Erasmus Mundus/Plus as a Flagship Mobility Scheme for (South) Africans

Erasmus Mundus Plus (+) is one of the flagship programmes in the EU-(South) Africa range of joint programmes in the field of higher education and training. The programme is part of a strategic partnership between the EU and South Africa. The Erasmus schemes present opportunities to address the internationalisation of higher education and more broadly globalisation, particularly through promoting academic mobility schemes. Erasmus+ has been the leading programme for student mobility in the EU for years, with about three million beneficiaries. However, this programme is particularly recent in South Africa.

By 2019, about 537 South Africans had benefitted from the scheme that sees South African students given an opportunity to study at any of the participating universities across EU countries. The beneficiaries include students ranging from master's to doctoral candidates, with university staff members also given the opportunity to exchange through research and teaching in Europe for a certain period. For the Erasmus Mundus, the EU allocated €22 million between 2010 and 2014 to support South African beneficiaries going to study, research or teach in Europe. These scholarships cover return flights, medical insurance, tuition fees and a monthly stipend for the duration of the stay of study, teaching or researching in Europe. For the 2014 to 2020 period, the EU has allocated a further €36.7 million to the Erasmus+ programme which succeeded the Erasmus Mundus (Auf der Heyde, 2015).

8 An Overview of EU-South Africa Cooperation Framework

The ultimate objective of the EU-South Africa collaborative framework in higher education is to develop a human capability and resource base to deliver a skilled workforce to support the desired inclusive growth in the economy and larger society. This objective has led to focussing attention on the linkages between equity, equal access and skill development in higher education, addressing the historical problems of inequality of access and the new dynamics of a changing society. The strategic partnership between the DHET, CHE and EU envisages the overall improvement of higher education in South Africa. The broader logical chain representing the framework of higher education cooperation aims at aligning the following elements: *Skills development system*, *Employability* and *Inclusive society*.

Benchmarking against EU concepts and policies, the South African system adopted the concept of employability as more than the "capacity to find jobs" (Gazier, 1998a, 1998b), but linked to the goal of improving opportunities for all and first and foremost the disadvantaged as a means of access to employment. At the EU level two policies, namely the education and Vocational Education and Training policies, have this aim. Each policy has its qualification framework, certification procedures and quality assurance, standard and guidelines.

The relationship between employment and higher education was conceived as not having a direct linkage. The higher education and employment nexus in the policy is not an appendix to academic studies. The employability of graduates is a subset of and contingent to a transformative lifelong learning principle. Thus, the South African policy framework requires the continuing shift and transition from employment to education and from education to employability. Whereas in Europe, each country is responsible for its own education and training systems, EU policy provides support and helps national action to address common challenges, such as skills deficits, a workforce for the knowledge economy and *society* in a global competitive context. In Europe, the legislative framework on Education (Art. 165) and VET (Aart. 166) are separate policies; in South Africa, the National Qualification Framework is an integrated system comprising three coordinated qualification sub-frameworks for general, further education, higher education and trade and occupations (Government Gazette, Republic of South Africa, 2009). Other areas of benchmarking between the EU and South Africa include: National Qualifications Framework, European Credit system, Quality Assurance in EU, Quality Assurance in HE, Quality Assurance in VET, Role of Professional Bodies. All these areas are part of an on-going cooperation between the parts and subject to reviews and improvements to meet the ultimate goal of developing human capability.

9 Conclusion

This chapter has addressed the policy framework for cooperation between South Africa and EU. The EU framework is based on the overall North-South cooperation framework and strategy adopted by the European Commission under SDGs for all developing partners, which then translates into country specific programmes and interventions. While there are promising structures in place, scholars of higher education, and those in leadership positions regarding these structures, should investigate how to best use these structures to address the following pressing challenges in higher education in South Africa:
- increasing participation in higher education in South Africa;
- continuing the drive towards the equalisation of higher education opportunities;
- promote the internationalisation of higher education in South Africa, in a way that is of benefit not only to the EU partners of EU-South African partnerships in higher education, but also for South Africa;
- increase the research output at South African universities, and even more important, strengthen the research capacity of South African universities; and, very challenging,
- the imperative for the decolonisation of higher education, which has become very compelling in the public as well as in the scholarly discourse about higher education in South Africa. EU-South African collaboration in higher education should be ingeniously crafted so as to promote the decolonisation of South African higher education, and care should be taken that such collaboration does not serve the opposite agenda, namely to reinforce neo-colonial or dependency relations.

Mention has been made above of the two international surveys of the academic profession. Currently a third international survey is underway, the APIKS (Academic Profession in Knowledge Society) survey. This survey which will cover an even larger number and variety of countries than the CAP survey, South Africa included, and will provide an updated and new perspective on the academic profession in South Africa, a key constituency in the higher education project. As such it is something to look forward to and the results should be used to take informed, rational decisions regarding South Africa-EU collaboration in higher education.

References

Amsterdam Treaty. (1997). Retrieved November 4, 2019, from http://www.europarl.europa.eu/topics/treaty/pdf/amst-en.pdf

Auf der Heyde, T. (2015, February 9). PhDs hold key to SAs Development. *Mail & Guardian*, https://mg.co.za/article/2015-02-09-phds-hold-key-to-sas-development/

Central Intelligence Agency (CIA). (2019). *World factbook.* https://www.cia.gov/library/publications/the-world-factbook/rankorder/2172rank.html

Cloete, N., Sheppard, C., & Bailey, T. (2015). South Africa as a PhD hub in Africa? In N. Cloete, P. Maassen, & T. Bailey (Eds.), *Knowledge production and contradictory functions in African higher education* (pp. 75–108). African Minds.

Council of the European Union. (2019, May 23–24). ACP-EU council of ministers. Retrieved November, 2019, from https://www.consilium.europa.eu/en/meetings/international-ministerial-meetings/2019/05/23-24/

Dell, S. (2019, October 2). South Africa 'punches above its weight' in research, says study. *University World News*.

European Commission. (2006). *Delivering on the modernization agenda for universities: Education.* https://eur-lex.europa.eu/legal-content/EN/TXT/?uri=celex%3A52006DC0208.

European Commission. (2011). *Supporting growth and jobs – An agenda for the modernization of Europe's higher education systems.* COM, 567 final. https://eur-lex.europa.eu/LexUriServ/LexUriServ.do?uri=COM:2011:0567:FIN:EN:PDF

European Commission. (2017, June 30). Joint statement by the Council and the representatives of the governments of the member states meeting within the council, the European Parliament and the Commission. *Official Journal of the European Union II Information Joint Declaration.* 2017/C 210/01. COM https://ec.europa.eu/assets/eac/education/library/policy/modernisation_en.pdf

European Commission. (2018, September 12). *Communication on a new Africa – Europe alliance for sustainable investment and jobs: Taking our partnership for investment and jobs to the next level.* COM, 643 final. https://eur-lex.europa.eu/legal-content/EN/TXT/?uri=CELEX%3A52018DC0643

European Commission/EACEA/Eurydice. (2018). *The European higher education area in 2018: Bologna process implementation report*. Publications Office of the European Union. https://eacea.ec.europa.eu/national-policies/eurydice/content/european-higher-education-area-2018-bologna-process-implementation-report_en

European Parliament. (2019). *On-going negotiations for a new EU-ACP partnership agreement European parliament resolution of 28 November 2019 on the ongoing negotiations for a new partnership agreement between the European Union and the African, Caribbean and Pacific group of states (2019/2832(RSP). Texts adopted*. Provisional edition. Retrieved December, 2019, from http://www.europarl.europa.eu/doceo/document/TA-9-2019-0084_EN.pdf

European Union. (1998). The agreement amending the fourth ACP-EC convention of Lomé signed in Mauritius on 4 November 1995. *Official Journal of the European Communities*. European Union. https://op.europa.eu/en/publication-detail/-/publication/62e2bc33-18c9-4aa5-a1f7-55867a57666d/language-et

European Union. (2014). *The Cotonou Agreement 2014 Signed in Cotonou on 23 June 2000 Revised in Luxembourg on 25 June 2005 Revised in Ouagadougou on 22 June 2010 and multiannual financial frame work 2014–20*. The Cotonou Agreement 2014. European Union. https://op.europa.eu/en/publication-detail/-/publication/c030c886-b15c-4456-930d-c9488db9cd0a

European Union. (2018). *The European Union – what is it, what it does*. Retrieved November, 2019, from https://op.europa.eu/en/publication-detail/-/publication/9ab2da22-14da-11ea-8c1f-01aa75ed71a1

Gazier B. (1998a). Observations and recommendations In B. Gazier (Ed.), *Employability: Concepts and policies* (pp. 298–315). European Employment Observatory.

Gazier, B. (1998b). Employability – Definitions and trends. In B. Gazier (Ed.), *Employability: Concepts and policies* (pp. 37–71). European Employment Observatory.

Gornitzka, Å., Maassen, P., Olsen, J. P., & Stensaker, B. (2007). "Europe of knowledge": Search for a new pact. In P. Maassen & J. P. Olsen (Eds.), *University dynamics and European integration* (pp. 181–214). Springer.

Government Gazette, Republic of South Africa. (2009, February 17). National qualifications framework act, act 67 of 2008. *Government Gazette*, No. 31909. Government Printer. https://www.dhet.gov.za/SiteAssets/About%20us%20new/2National%20Qualifications%20Framework%20Act%20No.%2067%20of%202008.pdf

Gumede, W., & Dikeni, L. (2009). *The poverty of ideas: South African democracy and the retreat of intellectuals*. Jacana.

Habib, A. (2019). *Rebels and rage: Reflecting on #fees must fall*. Jonathan Ball.

Harricombe, L. J., & Lancaster, F. W. (1995). *Out in the cold: Academic boycotts and the isolation of South Africa*. Information Resources Press.

IMD. (2019). *2018 IMD world competitiveness scoreboard*. http://www.imd.org/uupload/imd.website/wcc/scoreboard.pdf

Johnson, R. W. (2004). *South Africa: The first man, the last nation.* Jonathan Ball.

Maassen, P., Gornitzka, A., & Fumasoli, T. (2017). University reform and institutional autonomy: A framework for analysing the living autonomy. *Higher Education Quarterly, 71*(3).

Maassen, P., & Olsen, J. P. (Eds.). (2007). *University dynamics and European integration.* Springer.

Morrell, R. (2019). Local intellectual labour has a global effect. *South African Journal of Science, 115*(11/12), Art. 7407. https://doi.org/10.17159/ sajs.2019/7407

Mouton, J., Basson, I., Blanckenberg, J., Boshoff, N., Prozesky, H., Redelinghuys, H., Treptow, R., Van Lill, M., & Van Niekerk, M. (2019). *The state of the South African research enterprise.* DST-NRF, Centre for Excellence in Scienceomterics and Science, Innovation and Technology Policy, Stellenbosch. http://wwwo.sun.ac.za/crest/wp-content/uploads/2019/08/state-of-the-South-African-research-enterprise.pdf

Seroto, J., Noor, D., & Wolhuter, C. C. (Eds.). (2020). *Decolonising education in the global south: Historical and comparative international perspectives.* Pearson South Africa.

Tandwa, L. (2016, January 16). South Africa: #FeesMustFall costs country R150Million – Nzimande. *News24.* http://allafrica.com/stories/201601201489.html

Trade Development Cooperation Agreement (TDCA) SA and EU. (1999, December 4). *Official Journal L, 311,* 0003–0415. https://eur-lex.europa.eu/legal content/EN/TXT/?uri=celex:21999A1204(02)

Tutu, D., & Allen, J. (1995). *The rainbow people of God: South Africa's victory over apartheid.* Bantam Books.

UNESCO. (2020). *Statistics.* http://data.uis.unesco.org/

Van Jaarsveld, F. A. (1976). *Van Van Riebeeck tot Vorster.* Perskor.

Weeks, S., Herman, H., Maarman, R., & Wolhuter, C. (2006), SACHES and comparative, international and development education in Southern Africa: The challenges and future prospects. *Southern African Review of Education, 12*(2), 5–20.

Wolhuter, C. C. (2009). The transformation of higher education in South Africa since 1994: Achievements and challenges. *Higher Education Forum (Japan), 2009,* 59–72.

Wolhuter, C. C. (2012). 'n Wêreldklasuniversiteit in Suid-Afrika: ideaal, wenslik, haalbaar, werklikheid, hersenskim? *LitNet Akademies, 9*(2), 284–308.

Wolhuter, C. C. (2015). 1994: New academic profession for a new South Africa. *Studies in Higher Education, 40*(8), 1377–1391.

Wolhuter, C. C. (2017). The geography of authorship regarding research in education. *Croatian Journal of Education, 19*(3), 981–1000.

Wolhuter, C. C., & Higgs, L. G. (2004). How internationalized is the South African academic profession? In J. Van der Elst & C. C. Wolhuter (Eds.), *Internationalisation and human resource development in the African Union: Challenges for the tertiary education sector* (Proceedings of the 7th International Conference of IEASA, North-West University, Potchefstroom Campus, 3–6 September 2003). The Platinum Press.

Wolhuter, C. C., Higgs, P., Higgs, L. G., & Ntshoe, I. M. (2012). Sudáfrica: La delicada posición de la profesión académica en un pais emergente. In N. Fernández Lamarra & M. Marquina (Eds.), *El Futuro de la Profesión Académica: Desafíos para los paises emergentes* (pp. 199–208). EDUNTREF.

Wolhuter, C. C., Naidoo, K., Sutherland, L., & Peckham, G. (2004). Description of a course in research management at a university in New Zealand: A model for the South Afrian scene. *Southern African Review of Education, 9/10*, 69–76.

Wolhuter, C. C., & Van der Walt, J. L. (forthcoming). Student activism in South Africa (2015–2016) and the status of Afrikaans as a university language medium: A preliminary analysis and explanation. In V. Stead (Ed.), *Toward abolishing White supremacy in higher education*. Peter Lang.

PART 4

*Case Studies: How Higher Education
Institutions of the EU and Countries from
the Four Continents Collaborate*

∴

PART 2

CHAPTER 8

EU-Brazil Cooperation: The Science without Borders Programme Experience

Cintia Denise Granja and Ana Maria Carneiro

Abstract

This chapter presents an overview of the *Science without Borders* programme, launched by the Brazilian Federal government in 2011, in order to analyse its contribution to the cooperation with European Union countries. To date, this programme represents the most ambitious initiative of the Brazilian government to fight the country's conspicuous academic isolation. Between 2011 and 2016, it sent more than 92 thousand Brazilian students and scholars abroad, of whom 50.7% went to European Union countries. The chapter presents the main features of the programme and the role of the European Union in this specific international cooperation strategy. In addition to a bibliographic and documentary review of the programme, it also presents the results of a case study carried out at a Brazilian public research university which was one of the most active institutions of origin. It concludes that, even though the programme has contributed to increasing the circulation of students and researchers between Brazil and the European Union, its design was limited in terms of establishing long-term cooperation between Brazilian and foreign higher education institutions.

Keywords

Brazil – student mobility – programme evaluation – internationalisation – Science without Borders programme – UNICAMP

1   Introduction

The internationalisation of Higher Education is a broad and varied phenomenon, which can be defined as the 'intentional process of integrating an international, intercultural or global dimension into the purpose, functions and delivery of post-secondary education, in order to enhance the quality of education and research [...] and to make a meaningful contribution to society' (De Wit et al., 2015, p. 29). Its strategies can include different kinds of policies and programmes, which can be carried out by governments or organisations, within or outside their home countries (Altbach & Engberg, 2014; Altbach, Reisberg, & Rumbley, 2009; Coey, 2017; Guruz, 2008; Knight, 2004).

Until the early 2010s, the international participation of Brazilian science and higher education was considered low when compared to other countries of similar size and level of development (Velho & Ramos, 2014). Even with an increase in the number of mobility grants during the last decades of the twentieth century, the internationalisation of Brazilian higher education was "a fragmentary process, developed in isolated niches in universities, especially in graduate studies" (Laus & Morosini, 2005, p. 112).

In 2011, the Brazilian federal government launched the most ambitious internationalisation programme to date, called Science without Borders (SwB). The programme sent more than 92 thousand Brazilian students and scholars abroad, in which 50.7% went to European Union (EU) countries. Within this larger picture, this chapter discusses to what extent the SwB programme contributed to strengthen the internationalisation activities of Brazilian higher education institutions in partnership with institutions of the European Union. In order to do that, it presents the main features of the programme and the role of the European Union in this internationalisation strategy. It also analyses the experience of one Brazilian public research university, the University of Campinas (UNICAMP), one of the most active institutions within the SwB's framework, and with a wide-ranging experience of internationalisation activities (such as international cooperation and student mobility), even before the SwB was created.

Data used in this article comes from the programme's official documents, with information coming from Brazilian funding agencies and through UNICAMP's administration. These data were merged with qualitative information coming from semi-structured interviews carried out at the University' level administration, with twelve coordinators of undergraduate courses, six internationalisation managers, ten academics and researchers who were beneficiaries of SwB postdoctoral fellowships and fourteen academics responsible for hosting foreign researchers using SwB grants.

This chapter is divided into four sections. The first one describes the Science without Borders programme and its main characteristics, contextualised in the broader context of Brazil's internationalisation. The second one presents information about the SwB within the European Union. The third one presents some results of the programme at the University of Campinas. Lastly, the final section presents a summary of the main conclusions.

2 The Science without Borders Programme

The Science without Borders programme, announced by the Brazilian federal government in July 2011 (CsF, 2011), was a programme focusing on student and academic mobility which offered both international scholarships for Brazilian undergraduate and graduate students and researchers, and fellowships in Brazil to attract researchers from abroad (Brasil, 2011).

The programme was released by the Brazilian federal government a few days after the former president of the United States (US) Barack Obama had visited Brazil (CSF, 2012; Knobel, 2012). In that visit, Obama challenged the Brazilian former president, Dilma Rousseff, to emulate the US initiatives in relation to student mobility, mentioning two programmes known as 100k Strong in the Americas and 100k US-China, programmes dealing with the massive number of American students sent to Latin America, the Caribbean and China (Knobel, 2012; Manços, 2017).

The Brazilian programme had an extensive and ambitious list of goals – established a few months after its announcement – which included increasing international student and academic mobility, as well as international cooperation (Brasil, 2011). Subsequently, the programme was announced as part of the strategy to strengthen support for Brazilian Science, Technology and Innovation Policy (MCTI, 2012).

The list of priority areas included in the programme was released in January 2013 (about one year after the programme's implementation). The priorities were related to the fields of Science, Technology, Engineering and Mathematics (STEM) and Health Sciences (Brasil, 2013). The choice was justified by the need to invest in the training of highly qualified personnel in the skills necessary to improve the knowledge economy, with a focus on major national challenges, particularly in engineering and other technological areas (MCTI, 2012).

The programme adopted a top-down approach. It was set up by the federal government without a previous alignment with Brazilian Higher Education Institutions (HEIS) or even with the two main Federal agencies in charge of implementing the programme, CAPES (Portuguese acronym for Coordination for the Improvement of Higher Education Personnel, an agency for the promotion, evaluation and accreditation of post-graduation, linked to the Brazilian Ministry of Education) and CNPq (Portuguese acronym for National Council for Scientific and Technological Development, an agency under the Brazilian Ministry of Science, Technology, Innovation and Communications) (Bido, 2015; Cunha, 2016). Besides being a top-down programme, the SwB adopted traditional definitions of types of scholarship that were never properly evaluated (Ramos, 2018; Velho & Ramos, 2014).

Furthermore, the SwB had a distinct centralised design, which reserved almost no room for the universities and research teams to participate in the choice of the host HEIs their students should attend, a factor which would affect the cooperation between them, as can be seen later. In the case of undergraduate students – the largest mode of study of the programme – the sending institution had no control over to where the student would go to. Its only role was to select the participants. Following this process, the candidates were evaluated by the funding agencies (CAPES and CNPq) which were in charge of allocating the candidates (CCT, 2015). In the case of graduate students, the host institutions were chosen by expert committees set by CAPES and CNPq (CCT, 2015). Local researchers were only able to select their partners abroad in one minor sub-programme which attracted scholars to Brazil. The programme also ignored any existing links and mechanisms for cooperation, which had been done through agreements which sought to ensure equal participation for both sides and bilateral exchanges (Laus & Morosini, 2005).

According to the data provided by the Brazilian government through an online platform called *Science without Borders Control Panel* (CsF, 2016), the programme, up to January 2016, granted 92.880 scholarships, of which 79% were for short-term mobility for undergraduate students. Another 10% went to support short-term mobility for Brazilian PhD candidates, 5% to support post-doctoral internships abroad, another 4% for PhD studies abroad, and 1% for master's studies abroad. Only 1% of all scholarships supported visiting scholars from other countries.

Thus, it is clear that the programme was based on a strategy that was almost completely centred on the undergraduate student (Bido, 2015). It also focused more on sending students (98% of the scholarships) than on hosting them (Chaves, 2015; Guimarães-Iosif et al., 2016; Knobel, 2012). Finally, it had essentially an internationalisation 'abroad' format, focusing mostly on international mobility. After the SwB was implemented, an initiative of internationalisation 'at home' was established, emphasising learning English and other languages (called English without Borders). However, this programme was a response to problems faced by SwB students caused by their deficiencies in mastering foreign languages (Athayde, 2016; Borges, 2015; Lage, 2015; Tonelli, Wingler, & Uebe Mansur, 2016), a weakness that had been predicted by the academic community since the beginning of the programme (Castro et al., 2012; Cruz, 2016).

Despite these shortcomings, the SwB programme has had a major impact on the Brazilian experience of internationalisation and has been the largest programme for student mobility ever developed by the Brazilian federal government, representing the most ambitious national initiative to fight the country's conspicuous academic isolation. As can be seen from the data from CAPES (2019) and CNPq (2019a), there was a vast expansion of scholarships after 2012. The scholarships awarded by the programme represented 58% of all the international scholarships implemented by both agencies between 2011 and 2015. In addition, according to Manços (2017), under the "SwB effect" the agencies (both at Federal and State level) expanded the number of scholarships abroad in all areas, including those not covered by the programme.

The increase in the number of scholarships and the number of possible host institutions was so large that it exceeded the capacity of the two Brazilian national agencies. According to the 2014 CAPES's report described by Cruz (2016), the number of agency specialists was insufficient to provide quality guidance to students abroad. Thus, the programme had to rely heavily on the foreign placement agencies, who were considered institutional partners. These agencies became responsible for several activities, such as the allocation of candidates at foreign universities, transfer of funds to the destination country and provision of support to students in collaboration with Brazilian Consulates and Embassies (Manços, 2017).

The programme was first designed to be funded by a dedicated public budget, to which other public and private sources were to be added (CCT, 2015). It was expected that 25% of the scholarships would be funded from private sources. However, private sources only covered 16% of the total scholarships granted under the programme. When launched, the programme was estimated to cost R$ 3.2 billion (Castro et al., 2012). However, the total spending on the programme, to May 2017, was R$ 13.2 billion, and the official estimate is that it will be up to R$ 20 billion by the end of 2020, when the last PhD holders supported by the programme are due to return home (Marques, 2017). This considerable amount of resources went to pay for both scholarships and tuition costs at universities abroad (without any evidence of negotiation of those tuition costs).

In 2015, over 60% of the programme's resources came from the Brazilian Ministry of Education and over 30% from the Ministry of Science, Technology, Innovation and Communications (CCT, 2015). Moreover, the programme appropriated resources from a traditional national fund originally designed to support Brazilian research and postgraduate training, the FNDCT (Portuguese acronym for National Fund for the Development of Science and Technology, the main fund supporting research, operating since the beginning of 1970s).

In 2014, the SwB drew on a third of this resource, and in 2015, when the programme was discontinued, it made use of 40% of it (CCT, 2016). At the same time, CAPES also redirected almost 50% of its resources to support the programme, thus seriously limiting support for graduate programmes in Brazil (O Globo, 2016). The total amount of funding allocated to the programme represented more than 15 times CNPq's committed budget in 2016 (Marques, 2017).

When, in 2015, resources became scarce and the country faced the first signs of an economic downturn, the Federal government suspended the programme. It was officially cancelled in 2017.

3 The Science without Borders Programme within the European Union

As was mentioned before, the central focus of the SwB was on student mobility, mostly through scholarships supporting short-term undergraduate mobility, in order to offer an international experience to the student, usually of one or two terms (locally called "sandwich" scholarships) (Ramos, 2018). According to the programme's official data (CsF, 2016), the destination of most of the students was to Europe (51%), followed by North America (38%), with 30% of those travelling to the USA. In general terms, this pattern of distribution is similar to other scholarships granted in the period by CAPES and CNPq, with two small differences: inside the SwB programme there were four times fewer grants directed to the African continent and one third more grants for Oceania, due to the participation of Australia, one of the top hosts of international students worldwide.

Inside Europe, the main destination was the United Kingdom (23%), followed by France (15%), Germany (15%) and Spain (11%) (CsF, 2016). Even though Portugal received only 8% of the total fellows, at the onset of the programme, in 2012, one in five SwB fellows went to Portugal (Righetti, 2016). However, grants for Portugal were cancelled in the following years, when it became clear that the fellows were choosing the country due to the Portuguese language. Given that the programme covered only STEM and health sciences fields, it is noteworthy that, for some destinations (such as the United Kingdom, Spain, the Netherlands, Belgium, Finland, Poland and the Czech Republic), the SwB grants accounted for more than 70% of all the grants awarded in the period by both Brazilian agencies.

Even though, in its design, the SwB was supposed to send students to prestigious, world-class HEIs, a survey carried out in 2015 showed that less than 4% of scholarship holders went to institutions of excellence (CCT, 2015). Engberg et al. (2014) observed that the institutions named in the public calls launched by the SwB to host Brazilian students were not ranked among the top 250 universities worldwide. One explanation of this situation is the fact that the most prestigious institutions do not usually delegate the selection of their candidates to third parties, as adopted by the programme (Castro et al., 2012).

Table 8.1 presents the list of SwB partners in European Union countries. Some of them have a long experience of collaboration with Brazilian science, such as the Deutsche Akademische Austauschdienst (DAAD-Germany), the Dutch Organisation for Internationalisation in Education (Nuffic-Netherlands) and the Centre National de la Recherche Scientifique (CNRS-France). Others, on the other hand, had their first experience with Brazil under the SwB programme.

TABLE 8.1   SwB European Union partners[a]

Country	Undergraduate education	Postgraduate education
Austria	OeAD GmbH	10 HEIs and The International Institute for Applied Systems Analysis (IIASA)
Belgium	Académie de recherche et d'enseignement supérieur (ARES) and De Vlaamse Universiteiten en Hogescholen Raad (VLUHR)	No official partner
Czech Republic	The Centre for International Cooperation in Education (DZS)	Czech Academy of Sciences
Denmark	No official partner	8 HEIs
Finland	The Finnish Centre for International Mobility (CIMO)	No official partner
France	Campus France	Agreenium, Campus France, CIFRE-Brasil,[b] CNRS, COFECUB,[c] INRIA,[d] INSERM,[e] IRD[f]
Germany	DAAD	DAAD, Fraunhofer
Hungary	Hungarian Rectors' Conference (HRC)	HRC

(cont.)

TABLE 8.1   SwB European Union partners (*cont.*)

Country	Undergraduate education	Postgraduate education
Ireland	Higher Education Authority (HEA)	HEA
Italy	Bologna University + 10 HEIS	Bologna University
The Netherlands	Nuffic	Nuffic
Poland	Conference of Rectors of Academic Schools in Poland (CRASP)	CRASP
Portugal	The Portuguese Polytechnics Coordinating Council (CCISP) and CRUP	The Council of Rectors of Portuguese Universities (CRUP)
Spain	Fundación Universidad.es	Fundación Universidad.es
Sweden	Swedish Council for Higher Education (UHR)	No official partner
United Kingdom	Universities UK	Universities UK

a Bulgaria, Croatia, Cyprus, Estonia, Greece, Latvia, Lithuania, Luxembourg, Malta, Romania, Slovakia and Slovenia have not received any SwB students.
b The Convênio Industrial de Formação através da Pesquisa was co-financed by France and Brazil and was implemented through CNPq and ANRT, a research and innovation promotion agency of the French Ministry of Higher Education and Research.
c Programme between CAPES and the Comité Français D'Evaluation de La Coopération Universitaire et Scientifique avec le Brésil.
d The French national institute for computer science and applied mathematics.
e A public scientific and technological institute, which operates under the joint authority of the French Ministries of Health and Research, dedicated to biomedical research and human health.
f The French national research institute for development.
SOURCE: DATA FROM THE SCIENCE WITHOUT BORDERS WEBSITE (CSF, 2011, 2012, 2016).

As a result of the SwB's implementation plan, the placement agencies hired by CAPES and CNPq followed the traditional process of acting as intermediate for the student's placement abroad. Consequently, many students went abroad without a well-defined study plan, which is the opposite of the European experience (Righetti, 2012). With this approach, the SwB programme did not take advantage of the pre-existing multilateral agreements from CAPES and CNPq, or those established between Brazilian HEIs and foreign universities, factors which seriously limited the programme's lasting effects in terms of Brazilian universities' internationalisation strategies.

In the next section, a case study is presented, focusing on the main institutional effects of the SwB inside a Brazilian Research University, which takes into account its previous experience of cooperation with European Union countries.

4   Science without Borders at the State University of Campinas (UNICAMP)

UNICAMP is one of the most research-intensive Brazilian public universities. It was also one of the most important senders inside the SwB (7th place among the Brazilian institutions and 3rd place in the state of São Paulo) (CsF, 2016). Since its foundation, in the 1960s, internationalisation was part of the university's main institutional strategy. Moreover, in the 1980s the university had established a dedicated local agency responsible for conducting internationalisation activities, which had been somewhat of an innovation in the Brazilian experience (Alves Filho, 2012; UNICAMP, 2016a).

Hence, if internationalisation was not a new experience, it was intensified during the period prior to and in the course of the SwB programme. UNICAMP's strategic planning both from 2011–2015 (UNICAMP, 2012) and from 2016–2020 (UNICAMP, 2016b) adopted specific targets for university internationalisation. The university also had its own financial budget for developing and implementing internationalisation strategies, such as increasing student mobility and expanding the number of cooperation agreements with international institutions (Alves Filho, 2012; Sugimoto, 2016; UNICAMP, 2019).

Academic and student mobility traditionally happens as a result of international agreements held with other institutions and initiatives of cooperation linking local academic projects with partners abroad. UNICAMP also actively explores opportunities for promoting academic and student mobility made available by public and private funds. Some university programmes, such as engineering, also have active double-degree agreements with foreign partners.

The field study carried out by UNICAMP, described in detail in Granja (2018), showed that the SwB programme did fulfil its goals of increasing the number of students and academics experiencing mobility. According to the data obtained directly from UNICAMP's International Office, more than half of the scholarships granted to its students and academics (56%) had European countries as their destination, 98% of which were for European Union countries (Figure 8.1).

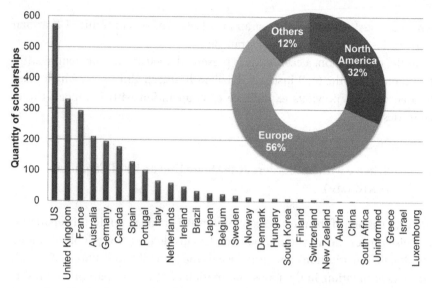

FIGURE 8.1   Destination countries of UNICAMP SwB grants, 2011–2015 (based on data from CsF, 2016)

In total, 85% of the scholarships went to students in the STEM fields. More importantly, the share of European countries as destinations remained high during the whole course of the programme.

Figure 8.2 shows the evolution of new partnership agreements between UNICAMP and international institutions over the past 10 years. As can be noticed, the number of new partnership agreements increased during the SwB period (dashed circle), even if this trend had started before the launching of the programme (Stallivieri, 2015). The trend is similar for both European and non-European countries. With the end of the programme in 2016, a decrease in new agreements can be seen.

When it comes to the effect of UNICAMP's internationalisation initiative, the field work carried out at the university showed that the programme had a positive impact in terms of the systematisation of the procedures for requesting support for mobility and a standardisation of the eligibility criteria for all mobility programmes at the university. These effects follow a pattern noted in similar studies of other Brazilian universities (Bido, 2015; Reschk & Bido, 2017).

However, the field work also identified some relevant negative effects. As noted before, the SwB's design did not consider the universities' experience and their internationalisation strategies. In the case of UNICAMP, its strategy focused mainly on long-term and broad partnerships, most of which included mobility and research collaboration. Despite the increase in the number of

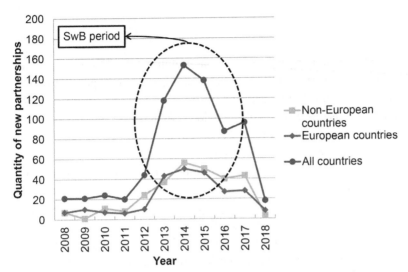

FIGURE 8.2 Evolution of partnerships between UNICAMP and international institutions, 2008–2018 (based on data from UNICAMP, 2019)

partnerships celebrated during the SwB period, most of the new agreements did not support cooperation outside the scope of the SwB. With the end of the programme, consequently, these agreements became null and void. Therefore, even though the programme had the potential to open channels of communication between Brazilian and foreign institutions (Reschk & Bido, 2017; Stallivieri, 2015), it did not foster the establishment of long-term partnerships. Because the university was not involved in the process of deciding the students' destination, it was not possible for UNICAMP to use the SwB as a tool to promote its strategy of internationalisation.

According to three managers involved in implementing UNICAMP's internationalisation strategy, the programme not only took the institution's focus off long-term agreements, but even, in some cases, undermined some partnerships established before launching the programme. As an example, some Portuguese universities preferred to receive UNICAMP's students through the SwB and discontinued the old institutional partnerships, which had exempted international mobility students from academic fees (Granja, 2018).

In addition, three programme coordinators, four internationalisation managers and one supervisor of a visiting scholar at UNICAMP held similar views in that, while the SwB were in place, other programmes and initiatives (which required a high performance profile) experienced a decrease in demand, with some of them even facing difficulties in enlisting candidates for international mobility.

5 Conclusions

During a period of about 5 years, the SwB has mobilised considerable resources to offer 91,601 undergraduate, postgraduate and postdoctoral grants to study outside Brazil and to receive 1,279 scholars from abroad. The countries of the European Union received 50.7% of the fellows. To date, the SwB has been the largest student mobility programme ever developed within such a short period of time by the Brazilian federal government.

In the period before the SwB, the programme of Brazilian higher education internationalisation had been highly conservative in its design. The SwB made extensive use of this old mode of issuing grants to support a student's short-term international experience: this had been the most usual form of scholarship offered by the Brazilian government since the 1980s, even if its efficiency and impact had never been properly evaluated. The programme also focused more on sending students than on receiving foreign students. It promoted student mobility without addressing the Brazilian students' foreign language deficiencies. Furthermore, the lack of planning and funding control compromised its stability. The programme also took place at a time when the number of international cooperation agreements between HEIs had experienced an important growth. At times, despite the successful experiences, the programme undermined some well established local initiatives.

Unlike previous experiences, the programme had a top-down approach and provided little stakeholder involvement in its implementation. Relying on services from placement agencies, it bypassed the institutions' channels. Created at speed (Velho & Ramos, 2014), both the programme's extensive list of goals and priority areas were announced after its creation.

The programme was successful in sending more than 90,000 students abroad. It was the first initiative which focused mainly on supporting undergraduate mobility. However, it did not provide mechanisms for the development of longer-lasting partnerships between Brazilian and foreign HEIs. Thus, the programme did not foster the establishment of strategic partnerships, since the universities of origin had no control over the choice of host universities. One could say, then, that its design ignored the traditional mechanisms of cooperation between HEIs, which had sought to ensure equal participation for both sides and the strengthening of bilateral exchanges. It also lost the opportunity to be aligned with the Brazilian universities' previous strategies for internationalisation, which were mostly aimed at research activities and postgraduate studies.

If we compare the programme's design with its stated objectives, some inconsistencies are clear. Even though the programme's first announcement referred to several goals related to improving the visibility of Brazilian research and fostering cooperation with researchers, research groups and institutions from abroad, its design did not provide sufficient mechanisms to achieve these goals.

If one compares the SwB to the 100K Strong in the Americas, the programme that inspired it, it can be seen that such a huge international mobility strategy can be sustainable. The US programme is funded by a public-private partnership and is based on projects submitted by HEIs that must demonstrate "how they will address on-campus barriers to student mobility, how they will maintain student engagement, and how they will commit to making concrete changes to expand access to study abroad as sending and/or hosting institutions" (100,000 Strong in the Americas, n.d.).

As Manços (2017) points out, the SwB had the potential to increase the international visibility of Brazilian higher education and to connect its institutions with international research cooperation programmes. However, the question is whether this increase in visibility occurred solely from the market point of view, as the Brazilian higher education market became an attractive source of funding for foreign institutions during the SwB.

In 2015, when the SwB was suspended, Brazil had entered an economic and political crisis. The question which remains is whether this programme could have been placed on the Brazilian policy agenda less abruptly, allowing policymakers to design a more sustainable programme. In that case, the monitoring and evaluation of international mobility programmes would have been an important element in the elaboration of a national initiative (Cruz, 2016; Ramos, 2018).

Since a deeper analysis of the collaboration with each EU country was outside the scope of our work for this chapter, a further investigation of the structure and impact of Brazilian collaboration with each country within the SwB programme is suggested as a future research agenda.

Acknowledgements

This chapter is partially based on the results of a Master's thesis "Internacionalização e mobilidade estudantil: o programa Ciência sem Fronteiras na Universidade Estadual de Campinas" [Internationalisation and student mobility: the Science without Borders programme at the University of Campinas], (DPCT/UNICAMP), funded by the São Paulo Research Foundation (FAPESP), process number 2016/10037-7. The authors also thank the reviewer for their insights.

References

100,000 Strong in the Americas. (n.d.). Expand student exchange & training opportunities. Retrieved September 14, 2019, from http://www.100kstrongamericas.org

AEPLAN. (2017). *Anuário Estatístico 2017*. Campinas.

Altbach, P. G., & Engberg, D. (2014). Global student mobility: The changing landscape. *International Higher Education, 77*, 11–13. https://doi.org/10.6017/ihe.2014.77.5676

Altbach, P. G., Reisberg, L., & Rumbley, L. E. (2009). *Trends in global higher education: Tracking an academic revolution*. United Nations Educational, Scientific and Cultural Organization. https://doi.org/10.1016/j.bse.2004.04.006

Alves Filho, M. (2012). Salto nos últimos dois anos consolida internacionalização da UNICAMP. *Jornal Da Unicamp, 550*. http://www.unicamp.br/unicamp/ju/550/salto-nos-ultimos-dois-anos-consolida-internacionalizacao-da-unicamp

Athayde, A. L. M. (2016). *Uma Avaliação Dos Impactos Do Programa Ciência Sem Fronteiras Na Perspectiva De Beneficiários Das Instituições Federais De Ensino Superior De Montes Claros -Mg*. Universidade Federal de Viçosa.

Balbachevsky, E. (2013). Academic research and advanced training: Building up research universities in Brazil. In J. Balán (Ed.), *Latin America's new knowledge economy* (pp. 113–133). Institute of International Education.

Beelen, J., & Jones, E. (2015). Redefining internationalization at home. *The European Higher Education Area*, 59–72.

Bido, M. C. F. (2015). *Ciência com Fronteiras: A mobilidade acadêmica e seus impactos*. Universidade do Vale do Rio dos Sinos – UNISINOS.

Borges, R. A. (2015). *A Interseccionalidade de Gênero, Raça e Classe o Programa Ciência sem Fronteiras: Um Estudo Sobre Estudantes Brasileiros com Destino aos EUA*. Universidade de Brasília.

Brasil. (2011). *Decreto N° 7.642, de 13 de dezembro de 2011. Institui o Programa Ciência sem Fronteiras*. Retrieved February 29, 2016, from http://www.planalto.gov.br/ccivil_03/_Ato2011-2014/2011/Decreto/D7642.htm

Brasil. (2013). Ministério da Educação (MEC). *Portaria Interministerial No.1, de 9 de Janeiro de 2013*. Retrieved January 24, 2017, from http://www.cienciasemfronteiras.gov.br/documents/214072/5058435/MEC_MCTI_temas+prioritarios_Csf.pdf

CAPES. (2019). *GEOCAPES – Sistema de Informações Georreferenciadas*. Retrieved September 14, 2019, from http://geocapes.capes.gov.br/geocapes2/

Castro, C. M., Barros, H., Ito-Adler, J., & Schwartzman, S. (2012). Cem mil bolsistas no exterior. *Interesse Nacional*, 25–36.

CCT. (2015). *Comissão de Ciência, Tecnologia, Inovação, Comunicação e Informática. Relatório de Avaliação de Políticas Públicas. Programa Ciência sem Fronteiras*. Comissão de Ciência, Tecnologia, Inovação, Comunicação e Informática.

CCT. (2016). *Comissão de Ciência, Tecnologia, Inovação, Comunicação e Informática. Relatório de Avaliação de Políticas Públicas. Fundos de Desenvolvimento Científico e Tecnológico*. Brasília.

Chaves, G. M. N. (2015). *As Bolsas de Graduação-Sanduíche do Programa Ciência sem Fronteiras: Uma Análise de suas Implicações Educacionais*. Universidade Católica de Brasília.

CNPq. (2019a). *Investimentos do CNPq em CT&I*. Retrieved September 14, 2019, from http://fomentonacional.cnpq.br/dmfomento/home/fmthome.jsp?

CNPq. (2019b). *Séries Históricas até 2014*. Retrieved September 14, 2019, from http://memoria.cnpq.br/series-historicas

Coey, C. (2017). International researcher mobility and knowledge transfer in the social sciences and humanities. *Globalisation, Societies and Education*. https://doi.org/10.1080/14767724.2017.1401918

Cruz, V. de X. A. (2016). *Programa Ciência sem Fronteiras: Uma avaliação da política pública de internacionali zação do ensino superior sob a perspectiva do Paradigma Multidimensional*. Universidade Federal de Goiás.

CsF. (2011). *Disponibilizadas as primeiras 2 mil bolsas do Programa Ciência sem Fronteiras*. Retrieved September 26, 2017, from http://cienciasemfronteiras.gov.br/web/csf/noticias/-/asset_publisher/Dh91/content/disponibilizadas-as-primeiras-2-mil-bolsas-do-programa-ciencia-sem-fronteiras?redirect=http%3A%2F%2Fcienciase mfronteiras.gov.br%2Fweb%2Fcsf%2Fnoticias%3Fp_p_id%3D101_INSTAN

CSF. (2012). *Presidente do CNPq ressalta a importância do Ciência sem Fronteiras nos EUA*. Retrieved June 4, 2018, from http://cienciasemfronteiras.gov.br/web/csf/noticias/-/asset_publisher/Dh91/content/presidente-do-cnpq-ressalta-a-importancia-do-ciencia-sem-fronteiras-nos-eua;jsessionid=726C91F73746B0A6729 A34E88219F27F?redirect=http%3A%2F%2Fcienciasemfronteiras.gov.br%2F

CsF. (2016). *Painel de Controle do Programa Ciência sem Fronteiras*. Retrieved March 21, 2016, from http://www.cienciasemfronteiras.gov.br/web/csf/painel-de-controle

Cunha, D. A. da. (2016). *Ciência sem Fronteiras: Perspectivas da Internacionalização e a Experiência Australiana*. Universidade Federal do Rio Grande do Sul.

De Wit, H., Hunter, F., Howard, L., & Egron-Polak, E. (2015). *Internationalisation of higher education. European Parliamant's committee on culture and education*. https://doi.org/10.2861/6854

Engberg, D., Glover, G., Rumbley, L., & Altbach, P. (2014). *The rationale for sponsoring students to undertake international study: An assessment of national student mobility scholarship programmes*. http://www.britishcouncil.org/sites/britishcouncil.uk2/files/e002_outward_mobility_study_final_v2_web.pdf

Granja, C. D. (2018). *Internacionalização e mobilidade estudantil: o programa Ciência sem Fronteiras na Universidade Estadual de Campinas*. Universidade Estadual de Campinas.

Guimarães-Iosif, R., Pollom Zardo, S., Veiga dos Santos, A., & Mendonça de Oliveira, L. (2016). Programa Ciência sem Fronteiras: a tradução da política de internacionalização brasileira no Canadá. *Interfaces Brasil/Canadá, 16*(1), 16–39.

Guruz, K. (2008). *Higher education and international student mobility in the global knowledge economy*. SUNY Press.

Knight, J. (2004). Internationalization remodeled: Definition, approaches, and rationales. *Journal of Studies in International Education, 8*(1), 5–31. https://doi.org/10.1177/1028315303260832

Knobel, M. (2012). Brazil seeks academic boost by sending students abroad. *International Higher Education, 66*, 15–17.

Koeller, P., Viotti, R. B., & Rauen, A. (2016). Dispêndios do Governo Federal em C&T e P&D: esforços e perspectivas recentes. *Radar, 48*, 13–18.

Lage, T. S. R. (2015). *Políticas de Internacionalização da Educação Superior na Região Norte do Brasil: uma análise do programa Ciência sem Fronteiras na Universidade Federal do Tocantins*. Universidade Federal do Tocantins.

Laus, S. P., & Morosini, M. C. (2005). *Internationalization of higher education in Brazil. Higher education in Latin America: The international dimension.* https://doi.org/10.1596/978-0-8213-6209-9

Manços, G. D. R. (2017). *Mobilidade acadêmica internacional e colaboração científica: subsídios para avaliação do programa Ciência sem Fronteiras*. Universidade de São Paulo.

Marques, F. (2017). Experiência encerrada – O programa de intercâmbio Ciência sem Fronteiras, que gastou R$ 13,2 bilhões, a maior parte com bolsas de graduação no exterior, deixa de existir. *Revista FAPESP, 256*. http://revistapesquisa.fapesp.br/wp-content/uploads/2017/06/020_financiamento_256-1.pdf

MCTI. (2012). *Estratégia Nacional de Ciência, Tecnologia e Inovação 2012–2015. Balanço das Atividades Estruturantes 2011*. http://www.fortec-br.org/EstrategiaNacionaldeCTIdoMCTI.pdf

Nalon, T. (2013). *Manobra do governo eleva número de programa de bolsas no exterior*. Retrieved September 14, 2019, from https://www1.folha.uol.com.br/ciencia/2013/04/1267095-manobra-do-governo-eleva-numero-de-programa-de-bolsas-no-exterior.shtml

O Globo. (2016). *Acadêmicos apoiam corte de bolsas do Ciência sem Fronteiras; UNE critica*. Retrieved September 14, 2019, from https://oglobo.globo.com/sociedade/educacao/academicos-apoiam-corte-de-bolsas-do-ciencia-sem-fronteiras-une-critica-19783756

Pereira, V. M. (2013). *Relatos de uma política: uma análise sobre o Programa Ciência sem Fronteiras*. Universidade de Brasília. http://repositorio.unb.br/handle/10482/15634

Ramos, A. G. (2016). *Programa Ciência sem Fronteiras: desdobramentos e análise das possíveis contribuições à formação acadêmica dos bolsistas*. Pontifícia Universidade Católica de São Paulo.

Ramos, M. Y. (2018). Internacionalização da pós-graduação no Brasil: lógica e mecanismos. *Educação e Pesquisa, 44*, 1–22. https://doi.org/10.1590/s1517-9702201706161579

Reschk, M. J. D., & Bido, M. C. F. (2017). Potencializando a experiência de internacionalização: reflexões sobre o Programa Ciência sem Fronteiras. *Espaço Pedagógico, 24*(1), 128–138. https://doi.org/10.5335/rep.v24i1

Righetti, S. (2012). *Chefe de "CNPq alemão" critica Ciência Sem Fronteiras*. Retrieved September 14, 2019, from https://www1.folha.uol.com.br/ciencia/1126825-chefe-de-cnpq-alemao-critica-ciencia-sem-fronteiras.shtml

Righetti, S. (2016). *Governo Interrompe bolsas do Ciência sem Fronteiras no Exterior*.

Spears, E. (2014). O valor de um intercâmbio: mobilidade estudantil brasileira, bilateralismo & internacionalização da educação. *Revista Eletrônica de Educação, 8*(1), 151–163. https://doi.org/http://dx.doi.org/10.14244/198271991026 Revista

Stallivieri, L. (2015). *Brazil's science without borders program*. Retrieved January 17, 2017, from https://www.insidehighered.com/blogs/world-view/brazils-science-without-borders-program

Sugimoto, L. (2016). Lançados editais na estratégia de mobilidade internacional. *Jornal Da Unicamp, 649*. http://www.unicamp.br/unicamp/ju/649/lancados-editais-na-estrategia-de-mobilidade-internacional

Tonelli, E., Wingler, S. da S., & Uebe Mansur, A. F. (2016). Regressos do Programa Ciência sem Fronteiras: Impactos da Internacionalização da Educação Superior no Brasil. *Anais Do XII Congresso Latinoamericano de Humanidades, 1*(80), 1089–1108.

UNICAMP. (2012). *Planejamento Estratégico Universidade Estadual de Campinas (PLANES) 2011–2015*. Campinas. http://www.prdu.unicamp.br/areas2/planes/arquivos/PE-TabelaProgsLinhasProjs-2015

UNICAMP. (2016a). *História*. Retrieved July 1, 2017, from http://www.50anos.unicamp.br/a-unicamp/historia

UNICAMP. (2016b). *Planejamento Estratégico Universidade Estadual de Campinas (PLANES) 2016–2020*. Campinas. http://www.prdu.unicamp.br/areas2/planes/planes/arquivos/planes-2016-2020

UNICAMP. (2018). *Sistema Integrado de Dados Institucionais da Unicamp. Matriculados em Cursos Regulares – Graduação – Por Curso e Turno*. Retrieved January 20, 2018, from http://www.siarh.unicamp.br/indicadores/View.jsf;jsessionid=6790A5E74C6C9F8FA5315CF9ACBEEE67

UNICAMP. (2019). *Sistema de convênios da Unicamp*. Retrieved May 7, 2019, from http://www.conveniosderi.gr.unicamp.br/

Velho, L., & Ramos, M. Y. (2014). Internacionalização da ciência no Brasil e mobilidade internacional: políticas, práticas e impacto. In M. G. S. M. C. Marinho, S. Amadeu da Silveira, M. Monteiro, R. de Brito Dias, & C. de Campos (Eds.), *Abordagens em Ciência, Tecnologia e Sociedade* (pp. 1–292). Santo André. https://doi.org/10.13140/2.1.4579.3289

CHAPTER 9

Higher Education Internationalisation and Student Integration: A Case Study of Chinese Students' Social and Academic Integration in Finland

Hanwei Li

Abstract

In recent years, the EU has attracted more and more Chinese students to study in its higher education institutions (HEIs), especially in non-Anglophone EU countries, facilitated by various bilateral agreement programmes and institutional collaborations. This chapter discusses the current internationalisation trends in Finnish education and how they are experienced by Chinese tertiary degree students in Finland. It first explains how Finland developed its higher education internationalisation policies in recent decades, along with a growing awareness of the importance of integration. It then focuses on challenges in Chinese students' academic and social integration into the Finnish academic environment, drawing on qualitative interview data on 30 mainland Chinese students who pursued degree studies in Finland. The data reveals that although the national-level discourse recognises the importance of international students and researchers' integration, in reality there are many deficiencies at the institutional level. Finally, this chapter discusses how the Chinese students' experiences can enlighten the future development of higher education internationalisation policies in Finland and other countries to improve international students' study experiences.

Keywords

higher education internationalisation – Chinese student – Finland – academic integration – social integration

1   **Introduction**

Alongside HEIs' internationalisation and globalisation development, which facilitate international student exchange and mobility, academic communication and relationships, universities increasingly operate on a global scale to expand their income and promote growth (Beech, 2018). As part of this trend, many universities in different parts of the world have been seeking to enhance the diversity of their staff's and students' cultural backgrounds through recruiting international students. Recruitment of international students, who pay higher fees than their domestic and EU counterparts, also helps the universities maintain finances to support teaching, research and development (Zheng, 2014). Universities are also increasingly aware of the importance of ensuring that international students and staff are socially and academically integrated, so that all members of the community benefit from its cultural diversity, as well as from varied learning and social experiences.

Integration is often used as one of the core elements of internationalisation. For instance, De Wit et al. (2015) revised Knight's (2004, 2007) definition of internationalisation as follows:

> the *intentional* process of integrating an international, intercultural or global dimension into the purpose, functions and delivery of post-secondary education, in order to enhance the quality of education and research for all students and staff, and to make a meaningful contribution to society. (De Wit et al., 2015, p. 29)

This definition stresses the importance of the inclusiveness of higher education internationalisation so that education will be meaningful for the individual, the institution and society. Similarly, Hudzik (2011, p. 35) also stresses the importance of integration since 'the integration of all international students and scholars into the campus living and learning environment' is viewed as one of the key goals. Thus, higher education internationalisation is not only about the compositional diversity of students and staff, but also concerns enhancing their study and research experience and improving their integration into the higher education community. The importance of 'integration' points to its multifaceted value for the individual, the institution and the country, and relates to the quality of education and service to the community (within the university and beyond) (Spencer-Oatey & Dauber, 2019b). As more and more countries around the world are making this one of their key objectives for higher education and research development, it is essential to explore how this approach has enhanced the integration of international students.

Finland has had an agenda for its internationalisation process in higher education for several decades. As a Nordic country which has attracted global attention for its outstanding performance in PISA tests for many years, higher education internationalisation has been one of the main aims of its government since the 1980s. In Finland this is closely connected to enhancing the country's global competitiveness in the 1990s and it has taken a strong marketisation shift in the 2000s (Kallunki, Koriseva, & Saarela, 2015). Some scholars also argue that the aim of the internationalisation of higher education is more instrumental since it emphasises the socio-economic benefit for Finnish higher education, businesses and society by becoming more competitive on the global stage (Välimaa & Weimer, 2014). The political-economic motivation of Finnish higher education policy makers is consonant with the discourse for higher educational reforms at the supranational European level and global level, as more and more countries are following a similar rationale: attracting international fee-paying students to supply tertiary education with funding and retain international students as a potentially highly educated labour force (Cantwell, 2019; Shumilova & Cai, 2016).

Chinese students occupy an important position within Finnish education even though the total number of students is relatively low in comparison to Anglophone countries. Although Finland is a non-Anglophone country, its universities still offer one of the highest numbers of higher education (HE) English-taught programmes in Europe (Wächter & Maiworm, 2014). As of 2017, Finland began to charge tuition fees for students from non-EU/EEA countries, yet Chinese students still constitute the largest number of incoming international students in Finnish universities in 2017, and the fourth largest group in the specialist universities of applied sciences (CIMO, 2018). While most of the research on Chinese students' life abroad focuses on those who study in English-speaking countries, such as the USA, the UK and Australia, more and more scholars (Li, 2017; Stensaker et al., 2019; Zheng, Shen, & Cai, 2018) emphasise that a considerable number of non-English speaking countries have invested in educational reforms to attract more international students. Thus greater attention needs to be paid to the experiences of Chinese students in Finland as a non-Anglophone Nordic case in light of its changing internationalisation policy.

The main purpose of this chapter is to provide insight into the following questions: how does Finnish higher education internationalisation affect the social and academic integration of Chinese students and how can the Finnish higher education institutions (HEIs) carry out internationalisation policies at the institutional level to better integrate Chinese students? Despite the increasing awareness of the importance of integration for HE internationalisation, an empirical understanding of how these policies are experienced by students – and the implications for future policy change – remain scant (Spencer-Oatey & Dauber, 2019b). Overall, why integration is vital and what changes are needed remains underexplored. The main focus of this chapter is on the personal aspects of Finnish HE internationalisation prevailing among Chinese students and the implications of the findings for all concerned.

2 Literature Review

2.1 *Internationalisation of Finnish Higher Education*

The internationalisation of higher education has been one of the national higher education policy key strategies in Finland for decades. In the most recent document published by the Ministry of Education and Culture, the "International strategy for higher education and research 2017–2025", the importance of integration for Finnish higher education internationalisation is clearly stressed. The group which prepared the international strategy established a shared vision of ways to promote a smoother integration of the foreign students, researchers and other staff into the Finnish higher education and research community. The strategy states that the goals will be achieved through better arrival and integration services provided for new entrants "they could provide employment, help talented individuals to integrate, and encourage whole families to stay in Finland".

The number of international students nearly tripled from 2000 to 2010, which also led to more international degree programmes being set up in universities and universities of applied sciences to host greater numbers of international degree students (Valimaa & Weimar, 2014). Meanwhile, there was more and more discussion on the financial benefit and implications of such growth, and on whether international students should be charged tuition fees. The initial argument for introducing tuition fees was that it should lead to more quality, efficiency and competitiveness in Finnish higher education. However, it was later perceived as a means of compensating for reduced government funding and to address the need to cut public-sector spending (Kauko, 2014). In spite of resistance and doubts, the Ministry of Education and Culture implemented charging tuition fees for international degree students from non-EU/EEA countries from the autumn term 2017. This shift in the Finnish higher education internationalisation policy agenda resonates with many scholars' explanations for how the motivations behind internationalisation have been changing from academic and socio-cultural to more economic and political (Altbach, 2004; de Wit, 2015).

Another important concrete change was made in 2012, when the Ministry of Education and university vice-rectors and officials drafted a new funding formula in which internationalisation was one of the three main pillars of the new funding model (MinEd, 2011). After this reform, internationalisation has been used as an important contributor to universities' basic funding, which would cover 4.1% of the total (ibid.). Other indicators included teaching-related aspects such as: periods of student exchange; the inclusion of credits taken in a foreign language or abroad; and the number of foreign degree students. There were also research-related aspects such as: numbers of internationally refereed publications; international funding acquired and staff mobility; number of foreign teaching and research staff; and the number of foreigners completing doctoral degrees (Kauko & Medvedeva, 2016).

2.2 Student Integration and Its Importance for Internationalisation

Within the field of education, the earlier work on the integration of students was more focused on academic integration related to students' courses and social integration, which relates to the interactions (or the lack of these) between host and international students within the spaces of the classroom and campus life (Robertson, 2011). Studies on students' integration generally trace back to the work of Vincent Tinto (1997, 1998), which focused particularly on the impact of integration on perseverance in studies and on academic achievement. According to Tinto (1975, 1997), a person's academic integration can be measured on the basis of the grade performance and intellectual development during his/her studies. Tinto (1975) stressed that students not only need to persevere in their studies in order to graduate (i.e. academic integration), but they also need to participate in the student culture, both within and outside the immediate context of the learning environment (i.e. social integration).

Some researchers have explored the meaning of integration building on Tinto's focus on integration and its impact on retention for students from different backgrounds. For instance, Severines and Schnimdt (2009) extended his distinction between academic and social integration to include formal and informal integration. Formal academic integration in general involves the contacts related to studying and the institute itself, while informal academic integration involves contacts between teachers and students outside the formal learning environment. Zepke and Leach (2005), argue that the concept of integration should be modified "to include adaptation, where institutions change to accommodate diverse students" (Zepke & Leach, 2005, p. 47). Adjusting to new ways of studying, living in a different societal environment and building a new network of friends can be a stressful experience for international students.

According to Sawir, Marginson, Deumert, Nyland, and Ramia (2008), many international students report feelings of loneliness and/or isolation including "social loneliness" because of their network of friends, and "cultural loneliness" because of the absence of a familiar and comfortable linguistic and cultural environment. Hence creating stronger bonds between international and local students is particularly important.

This research stresses that the integration of international students can be divided into integration into academic contexts and societal contexts. Academic contexts include the higher education environments in which the international students' academic lives are embedded. Societal contexts refer to the social, cultural and economic environments in which the students live within the host societies (Li, 2018).

The main concern of this chapter is on how Chinese students perceive the education they receive at Finnish higher education institutions, the challenges they encounter and the lessons for higher education reformers to rethink their internationalisation reform strategies and their implementation. While university staff have experienced internationalisation as intensified pressure to compete for international funding or publish in international peer-reviewed journals (Kauko & Medvedeva, 2016), the students may have different perspectives, since their experience of internationalisation mainly relates to studying and research. Although the introduction of tuition fees changed the scenario to some extent, interviews for this research were conducted in 2015 and 2016, before the introduction of tuition fees. Thus, this research will mainly focus on the study and research experiences of students in the academic contexts before the introduction of tuition fees.

3 Methodology

The data were collected through semi-structured interviews with 30 mainland Chinese tertiary-level students in Finland in 2015 and 2016. Permission to collect the data had been approved by the Ethics Committee to the Tampere Region. Two main methods were used to recruit interviewees. International offices of HEIS across Finland were first approached with a request to send an invitation to all mainland Chinese students registered at their universities. Students who volunteered to participate in this research were then contacted by the researcher, either by email, instant message or by phone. Following this, snowball sampling was used as the research participants were encouraged to distribute the invitation letter among their friends for further participant recruitment.

This research looked at the two major types of Finnish tertiary-level study: universities and universities of applied sciences. Approximately half of the interviews were conducted in the Finnish city of Tampere. The rest of the interviews were conducted with students from other major Finnish cities, such as Helsinki, Espoo, Turku, Joensuu and Oulu.

The group of respondents included students from a wide variety of backgrounds, in terms of gender, age, major subject, previous work and study experience, duration of residence in Finland and current location in Finland. Eighteen of the interviewees were female and twelve were male. The participants were studying on bachelor's, master's and doctoral programmes in various fields, including computer science, business management, and engineering. Two of the master's-level students were working full-time while carrying out their master's studies on a part-time basis.

Among the interviewees were students who had moved to Finland to study for one term and students who had been resident in Finland for more than five years. Given the diversity in the durations of sojourn the author was able to explore how different features of integration manifest in different phases. Students who had moved to Finland recently had the fresh experience of 'culture shock', while longer resident students gave lively accounts about how they had managed to overcome integration problems at different stages, reflecting their development trajectories.

The interviews lasted between one and three hours and were conducted in mandarin Chinese by the author. This shared language and cultural background facilitated communication between the interviewer and the interviewees (Welch & Piekkari, 2006). While a list of interview questions was used for all interviews, flexibility and spontaneity were preserved by following up on the specific issues that emerged during the interview. All interviews were audio recorded, transcribed and anonymised for analysis. Citations from the interviews conducted in mandarin Chinese were translated into English by the author.

4   Findings

4.1   *Social Integration*
4.1.1   Lack of English Usage in University Organisational Communication

Although many Finnish universities list internationalisation as a key priority, in reality there is still a long way to go. Many of the interviewees said that at the university management level, many of the internal emails, information and meetings were conducted in Finnish. Since not all the university staff members and teachers were fluent in communicating in English, the environment could be difficult for foreigners unable to speak Finnish fluently.

> The meetings and discussions in the faculty are very often held in Finnish, while sometimes they will give a brief translation in English at the end. Therefore, I feel alienated when I try to participate but could not understand everything. It often happens that they ignore me as foreigner who does not understand Finnish and host the meeting in Finnish. In general, I feel like an outsider. (Female, Medicine)

4.1.2 Lack of Contact between International and Native Finnish Students

Since most of the international students were recruited to study on the English-taught programmes they were isolated from native Finnish students who were taught on programmes in their native language. Some of the interviewees recommended organising more events and activities to facilitate integration between international and local students. One of the interviewees mentioned:

> I think it is not so easy to make friends with Finnish people. […] Unless due to some karma, you met somebody who really gets along with you and share the same hobbies, otherwise, how do you have more in depth talk with them? Most of the time, I just nod and say 'hi' to Finnish people in the corridor, and that's it. (Female, Mathematics)

However, some of the interviewees also mentioned that the barriers to cross-cultural contact between Finnish and Chinese students came from both sides. Some of the Chinese students were likewise not proactive in reaching out to contact the local students, preferring to stay in their own close group of Chinese friends.

> I think many Finnish students are quite friendly towards Chinese students. They are not only friendly, but also quite interested in Asia and Asian culture. But a lot of Chinese students are often not very active or talkative, and prefer to stay in their own small group. If they always act like this, even if the foreigners and Finns want to make friends and communicate with them, it can be quite difficult. (Male, Law)

4.1.3 Finnish Language as a Gateway or Barrier

As the interview quotes above shows, knowledge of Finnish language could be a gateway or barrier to the social integration of Chinese students. The earlier literature often stresses that lack of Finnish language skills is one of the crucial barriers preventing international students from integrating (Pitkänen & Takala, 2012). This research shows that acquisition of Finnish language skills did indeed open doors to wider social networks and also to career potential for Chinese students. One of the few interviewees who actually spoke Finnish fluently said in the interview:

> I think the people that I consider as friends, maybe there are 15 Finnish people, but maybe only one Chinese. I think establishing more contact with Finnish people allows you to understand Finnish culture, society and life style at many levels. For instance, I went to spend Christmas with Finnish families, to see how their family members communicate with each other, and what Finnish family life is like. And, I began to realise that some Finnish people are really just not talkative, even if you speak in Finnish. (Female, Sociology)

Another interviewee who spoke fluent Finnish also said in the interview that Finnish language skills were gateway to social integration:

> I think no matter whichever country you go to, if you want to understand and integrate into the local environment, it is important to learn about the local culture, way of life, values, etc. And, a very important aspect of cultural learning is through language. If a foreigner were to go to China, they would also need to learn Chinese. When you enter into a new environment, you just have to study their language and culture. (Female, Media Studies)

While the university offered Finnish language courses to international students, many of them found it hard to learn Finnish to a standard that allowed them to communicate fluently. One of the interviewees said:

> I have spent time to study Finnish, but you know it is very difficult to learn to an extent that is as fluent as them (native Finns), you know? And, in the university, we conduct research in English, and when we communicate with others, we use English. Therefore, we do not have a lot of opportunities to use this language, to really improve our Finnish language skills. Unless you are already fluent, and your supervisor is willing to communicate with you in Finnish. (Female, Mathematics)

Another interviewee also doubted whether spending time on learning Finnish was worthwhile:

> I think Finnish language can be a big barrier, since if you really invest time to study it, it might not have a big impact. When you are trying to find jobs, they might still look at your skills, since no matter how good your Finnish is, it will not be as good as the natives. If you speak Finnish, you might have wider career choices. But if you don't know any, they might have placed a very high requirement on your skills, so that you cannot find a starting position. Moreover, the Finnish language cannot be used anywhere outside this country. (Male, Computer Science)

In general, the language barrier seemed to be a gateway to access Finnish higher education as well as society, but it was also often perceived as a barrier for many Chinese students. It pointed to the issue that while international students were often asked to integrate into the local host environment, did the local academic community do enough to internationalise itself to welcome those internationals? Some countries in Europe, such as the Netherlands, have adopted a more liberal approach to internationalisation, so that many of its masters' programme are taught in English, and English is commonly used as a working language in academia. It is worthwhile questioning whether Finnish higher education internationalisation should adopt the same approach as the Netherlands to drastically change itself to become more inclusive for foreigners, or insist on the policy that international students and staff need to learn and speak fluent Finnish to survive in the local environment.

4.2 *Academic Integration*

4.2.1   Insufficient Teaching Quality in English

Some of the interviewees complained a lot about the teaching quality in the Finnish education system. In addition to a lack of courses taught in English, some of the interviewees also questioned the overall structure of their study programmes. For instance, one student said in his interview:

> I think the teaching here is not systematic. One of the teachers never teaches herself, so that all her classes are basically guest lecturers. How can a teacher have guest lecturers for almost all her courses? Other teachers will ask you to read the literature for almost all courses. After I had two courses, I still did not know what I had studied. Even though the teacher gave us the study material, it is still difficult to review yourself based on the materials that the teachers gave you. The courses are not based on a book, but some kind of teaching material the teachers produced themselves. After the whole course, I still didn't know what I had studied. I think this is a big problem. (Male, Medicine)

Another interviewee said in the interview that she was not satisfied with the guidance and support she received when she was doing her master's thesis, especially in comparison to the master's education that she could have received from the university where she took her bachelor's degree in China.

> After I came here, I am quite disappointed with the study programme. I didn't expect that this master's programme would be so bad and so relaxed. I know that in China, when the students are doing their master's theses, there will be a teacher guiding and correcting your master's thesis all the way during the master's studies. You need to defend your master's thesis for graduation. There are also external reviews for your master's thesis. You also have a requirement to publish at least one article in one of the key journals. However, here, there is only one professor in charge of all of our students' master's theses. We have a master's thesis class where each of us introduces a progress report on his or her thesis. After I introduced my topic, the supervisor just said my topic was too wide. But this is an obvious problem for me as well. I feel I didn't receive the guidance I wanted from this professor. He also has a lot of tasks, such as travelling and taking care of students from other classes, that he has little time allocated to individual students. (Female, Teacher Education)

One interviewee explained in the interview that since many teachers were teaching in English, which was also not their native language it can be challenging for some students since they also need to adapt to their teachers' Finnish accent. One of the interviewees said:

> Sometimes the teachers who were teaching our course do not speak English well enough, since it is also the second language for them. [...] When I was studying in China, I was more used to the English or American accent of English, while the teachers' Finnish accents were quite a challenge for me in the beginning. (Female, Media Education)

4.2.2 Lack of Equal Academic Opportunities for Foreigners

Several of the interviewees mentioned a lack of equal opportunities for the foreigners in Finnish academia. Academic job opportunities and funding opportunities may give priority to Finnish people or projects with a strong Finnish orientation. One of the interviewees made the following comment about his concern about the glass ceiling in Finland:

> Most of the professors in Finnish universities are native Finns. Or even if a particular foreigner can be a university professor, can they become a dean or university rector? This is basically systematically determined, that for some positions they would only consider Finnish people. Moreover, if you see the most common jobs that Chinese people do in here, to some extent, we are just academic migrant workers. Rarely does anyone make it to a higher level, right? I think this is basically a glass ceiling for your career. This kind of situation can be quite a big setback for people with more career ambitions. (Male, Computer Science)

Two of the interviewees also mentioned the difficulty of finding equal job opportunities in Finnish academia:

> I have tried to talk to the members of the faculty and other administrative staff several times that I would like to teach some English-taught courses in the faculty. But I never got any opportunity to teach. However, the other Finnish doctoral students easily got the opportunity to teach, also for the English-taught courses in the faculty. (Male, Signal Processing)

> If your skills level is almost the same as the Finnish candidate, they will not hire you, but prefer to hire Finnish people. Our Finnish is certainly not as fluent as the natives. Even if I speak some Finnish, it is not as fluent to the extent that I could use it to teach a course. They would still prefer to hire a Finnish person, because most of their students are still Finnish, right? Unless you have something special in comparison to the Finnish people, for instance if you are better at conducting research. Otherwise why would they hire you and set up English courses for you to teach? Female, Computer Science)

4.2.3 Lack of English-Taught Courses

Although many Finnish higher education institutions have introduced bachelor's, master's and doctoral programmes taught in English, some of the degree programmes still do not have enough English-taught courses for the students to choose from, and some of the students were not satisfied with the variety of courses offered. One master's student interviewee who was studying computer science expressed his frustration with the limited range of choices of courses:

> I feel that the whole teaching system is not very developed, and the teachers' specialities are quite narrow. The teaching of computer science

> is much more focused on theories, such as project management, but not on practical things, such as programming. There were only two programming courses when I came, and one of them was not even a 'real programming course'. That is why I feel disappointed. However, among the Finnish-taught courses there are more course options available. (Male, Computer Science)

Another student also reported that the English-taught curriculum did not have enough courses to satisfy her academic interest, andh that she could only find those courses in the Finnish-taught curriculum.

> I am very interested in the operationalisation of 'play' in Finnish early childhood education. I also wonder how the teachers actually guide the pupils to play in kindergarten. I would like to take such courses, but those courses are not included in our study programme, but only in the Finnish-taught courses, unfortunately. I also found that the range of English-taught courses was much narrower than the Finnish-taught courses. (Female, Early Childhood Education)

4.2.4 Flexible Environment That Lacks Guidance for Students

Clearly, for the Chinese students who come from a study environment that gives them more guidance and structure in their studies, it is difficult to get used to the Finnish education environment, where students are often required to be decidedly independent and self-reliant. Here, the research shows how the interviewees understood the Finnish academic environment.

> I think this Finland is not like the U.S. or the U.K. that when they recruit you, you must produce the results immediately. They will give you the time to slowly produce the results. However, I think the overall environment is too relaxed and flexible. Doing research is a hard work, too flexible and relaxed environment requires individuals to be highly self-disciplined. Otherwise, it is easy for people to become lazy in such an environment. (Male, Computer Sciences)

Thus, to facilitate the integration of students from different cultural environments, it is better that the university should organise an orientation for the new students so that they have an expectation of what they need to do themselves, and how they can accomplish their study goals and tasks.

5 Discussion and Conclusion

At the beginning of this chapter, I drew attention to the strategy of the Finnish Ministry of Education and Culture (MinEd, 2019) "to promote a smoother integration of the foreign students, researchers and other staff into the Finnish higher education and research community". I reviewed the various ways in which integration can be interpreted and the importance of integration for higher education internationalisation. While attracting more international fee-paying students certainly fits the agenda of the need in Finnish higher education to generate revenue to compensate for the cuts in state funding, the data presented in this chapter clearly show that what is currently offered is not sufficient to achieve the Ministry's objectives. Although Chinese students may have distinctive socio-cultural characteristics that distinguish them from some other groups of international students, the lessons learned from their experiences may have more general implications for higher education reformers and policy makers. The various challenges experienced by Chinese students during their social and academic integration show that much work still needs to be done in order to achieve the integration of "all international students and scholars into the campus living and learning environment" (Hudzik, 2011, p. 35).

This chapter explored integration primarily from the personal (Chinese students) integration perspective. However, individuals are embedded in the social structures, as this can facilitate or hinder the former's agency. From the data analysis it is evident that the internationalisation of higher education, at least in some English-taught degree programmes in Finnish HEIs, is still in the early stages. More systematic efforts are needed to facilitate students' integration and personal growth into the university community. To advance into higher levels of internationalisation, there is not only a need for Finnish higher education to achieve 'compositional internationalisation' (Spencer-Oatey & Dauber, 2019a) where student and staff populations are more diverse, but also overall internationalisation, where the international students and staff members are welcomed and integrated into the Finnish academic environment. I recommend that HE internationalisation should not only be viewed in terms of numbers of international degree students recruited, or of the percentage of mobility of its students and academic staff, but also as building an academic community that is equal and genuinely open and multicultural so that international students and researchers feel welcome in the academic environment. Integration should be a bi-directional process, where both international students and local academic staff aim at a higher level of intercultural communication competence, and the university management aims at strategic goals to make the academic environment accommodate ethnic, cultural and linguistic diversity.

The strategy for the internationalisation of Finnish higher education also stresses the importance of retaining international students in its labour market as a potential supply of highly skilled labour (Li & Pitkänen, 2018). As Finland has only recently emerged as a new player in the competition for global talent and students, a range of stronger facilitation measures at the university level are urgently needed to integrate international graduates into both the university and the country's labour market. Better integration of international students in the academic environment can be an important prerequisite for their integration into the wider societal environment. Thus, Finnish higher education reformers need to put more emphasis on how to approach HE internationalisation holistically so that not only are international students or academics expected to integrate, but the Finnish universities and their local staff members should also learn to be more open and adaptive to the multicultural academic environment.

The scope of this study is limited to a specific number of interviewees participating in this qualitative research. I hope the experience of Chinese students' integration challenges will be helpful for university members, both students and staff, to start to think about the strategies for integration at the level that is relevant for them. The information provided by this chapter can, hopefully, be one element that helps Finnish HEIs and possibly HEIs in other countries to move forward on the challenging journey towards achieving a more holistic approach to internationalisation and greater intercultural competence.

Acknowledgements

The research reported in this chapter was conducted at the University of Tampere, Finland. It was funded by the Marie Curie TRANSMIC project coordinated by Maastricht University (see https://law.maastrichtuniversity.nl/transmic/) under the European Union's 7th Framework Programme, which the author gratefully acknowledges. The author would also like to thank all the interviewees who shared their experiences for this research.

References

Altbach, P. G. (2004). Globalisation and the university: Myths and realities in an unequal world. *Tertiary Education and Management, 10*(1), 3–25. doi:10.1080/13583883.2004.9967114

Beech, S. E. (2018). Adapting to change in the higher education system: International student mobility as a migration industry. *Journal of Ethnic and Migration Studies, 44*(4), 610–625. doi:10.1080/1369183X.2017.1315515

Cantwell, B. (2019). Are international students cash cows? Examining the relationship between new international undergraduate enrollments and institutional revenue at public colleges and universities in the US. *Journal of International Students, 512*, 512–525.

CIMO. (2018). *Statistics on foreign degree students in Finnish higher education institutions in 2016* (6B/2017). http://cimo.fi/instancedata/prime_product_julkaisu/cimo/embeds/cimowwwstructure/165112_FactsExpress6B_2017.pdf

de Wit, H. (2015). Is the international university the future for higher education? *International Higher Education, 80*, 7–7.

Hannan, A. (2007). *Interviews in education research*. http://cecs6200.pbworks.com/w/file/fetch/69409200/Using%20Interviews%20in%20Education%20Research.pdf

Hudzik, J. K. (2011). *Comprehensive internationalization: From concept to action*. NAFSA: Association of International Educators.

Kallunki, J., Koriseva, S., & Saarela, H. (2015). Suomalaista valtiollista yliopistopolitiikkaa ohjaavat perustelut tuloksellisuuden aikakaudella. *Kasvatus & Aika, 9*(3).

Kauko, J. (2014). Complexity in higher education politics: Bifurcations, choices and irreversibility. *Studies in Higher Education, 39*(9), 1683–1699.

Kauko, J., & Medvedeva, A. (2016). Internationalisation as marketisation? Tuition fees for international students in Finland. *Research in Comparative and International Education, 11*(1), 98–114.

Knight, J. (2004). Internationalization remodeled: Definition, approaches, and rationales. *Journal of Studies in International Education, 8*(1), 5–31.

Knight, J. (2007). Internationalization: Concepts, complexities and challenges. In J. J. F. Forest & P. G. Altbach (Eds.), *International handbook of higher education* (pp. 207–227). Springer.

Li, H. (2017). Academic integration of Mainland Chinese students in Germany. *Social Inclusion, 5*(1), 13. doi:10.17645/si.v5i1.824

Li, H. (2018). Aspiration and integration infrastructure: A study on Chinese students' integration in Finland and Germany. *Working Papers – Centre on Migration, Citizenship and Development, 160*.

Li, H., & Pitkänen, P. (2018). Understanding the integration of Mainland Chinese students: The case of Finland. *Nordic Journal of Migration Research, 8*(2), 107–115. doi:10.1515/njmr-2018-0008

MinEd. (2011). *Laadukas, kansainvälinen, profiloitunut ja vaikuttava yliopisto – ehdotus yliopistojen rahoitumalliksi vuodesta 2013 alkaen*. Opetus- ja kulttuuriministeriö.

MinEd. (2019). *International strategy for higher education and research 2017–2025*. https://minedu.fi/en/international-strategy-for-higher-education-and-research

Pitkänen, P., & Takala, T. (2012). Using transnational lenses to analyse interconnections between migration, education and development. *Migration and Development, 1*(2), 229–243.

Robertson, S. (2011). Cash cows, backdoor migrants, or activist citizens? International students, citizenship, and rights in Australia. *Ethnic and Racial Studies, 34*(12), 2192–2211.

Sawir, E., Marginson, S., Deumert, A., Nyland, C., & Ramia, G. (2008). Loneliness and international students: An Australian study. *Journal of Studies in International Education, 12*(2), 148–180.

Shumilova, Y., & Cai, Y. (2016). Three approaches to competing for global talent: Role of higher education. In B. Krishna & F. Charlotte (Eds.), *Global perspectives and local challenges surrounding international student mobility* (pp. 114–135). IGI Global.

Spencer-Oatey, H., & Dauber, D. (2019a). Internationalisation and student diversity: How far are the opportunity benefits being perceived and exploited? *Higher Education*, 1–24.

Spencer-Oatey, H., & Dauber, D. (2019b). What is integration and why is it important for internationalization? A multidisciplinary review. *Journal of Studies in International Education.* doi:10.1177/1028315319842346

Stensaker, B., Lee, J. J., Rhoades, G., Ghosh, S., Castiello-Gutiérrez, S., Vance, H., & Marei, M. S. (2019). Stratified university strategies: The shaping of institutional legitimacy in a global perspective. *The Journal of Higher Education, 90*(4), 539–562.

Tinto, V. (1975). Dropout from higher education: A theoretical synthesis of recent research. *Review of Educational Research, 45*(1), 89–125.

Tinto, V. (1997). Classrooms as communities: Exploring the educational character of student persistence. *Journal of Higher Education*, 599–623.

Tinto, V. (1998). Colleges as communities: Taking research on student persistence seriously. *The Review of Higher Education, 21*(2), 167–177.

Välimaa, J., & Weimer, L. (2014). The trends of internationalization in Finnish higher education. *Zeitschrift für Pädagogik, 60*(5), 696–709.

Wächter, B., & Maiworm, F. (2014). *English-taught programmes in European higher education: The state of play in 2014.* Lemmens Medien GmbH.

Welch, C., & Piekkari, R. (2006). Crossing language boundaries: Qualitative interviewing in international business. *Management International Review, 46*(4), 417–437.

Zepke, N., & Leach, L. (2005). Integration and adaptation: Approaches to the student retention and achievement puzzle. *Active Learning in Higher Education, 6*(1), 46–59.

Zheng, G., Shen, W., & Cai, Y. (2018). Institutional logics of Chinese doctoral education system. *Higher Education, 76*(5), 753–770.

Zheng, P. (2014). Antecedents to international student inflows to UK higher education: A comparative analysis. *Journal of Business Research, 67*(2), 136–143. https://doi.org/10.1016/j.jbusres.2012.11.003

CHAPTER 10

Seeds of Success in Russian-Dutch Collaboration: The Case of a Higher Education Capacity-Building Project

Olga Ustyuzhantseva, Olga Zvonareva, Klasien Horstman and Evgenia Popova

Abstract

On April 8th 2013 the President of Russia, Vladimir Putin, and Queen Beatrix of the Netherlands announced the Russia-Netherlands Year aimed at fostering bilateral relationships in various fields including education and science. A new Memorandum of Understanding on higher education and scientific collaboration was signed by the Dutch and Russian Ministers of Education and Science in the same year. According to official statements, there has been, as a result, an increase in cooperation in higher education between both countries with 97 existing cooperation agreements between them (Nuffic Neso Russia, 2013). A number of joint initiatives have taken place. Nonetheless, on-going active cooperative projects are rare and the case studies of these projects are even rarer. However, this chapter aims to make visible the day-to-day practices of one of the successfully delivered EU-Russia projects, demonstrating its inner workings, challenges and insights. The aforementioned project is 'Bridging Innovations, Health and Societies: Educational capacity building in the Eastern European Neighbouring Areas' (BIHSENA), funded by the Erasmus+ framework. This project was led by Maastricht University and involved a number of EU and non-EU universities. This case study explores the factors of success in building collaboration and analyses the problems and impediments the participants faced. The data used includes information provided by the participants and executives of the project; interviews with key participants of the BIHSENA project from Russia, the Netherlands, and Ukraine; and the self-reflection of the project teams of each participating country. The chapter provides an exploration of the controversies, motivation and drivers of such collaboration and helps in the understanding of whether the success or failure of cooperation is a matter of institutional practice or has deeper roots in the national strategies for the internationalisation of higher education in Russia and the Netherlands.

Keywords

internationalisation – higher education – EU-Russia collaboration

1   Introduction

The 20th century witnessed a major transformation in many scientific areas in the universities around the world. Organisational and cultural shifts in the practice of undertaking research indicate a transition from studies concentrated on a single area to extensive international interdisciplinary collaboration embracing, for example, molecular biology and ecology. The rise of large collaborative research studies explains the presence of multiple in-depth analyses of the processes and the implications of such collaboration between universities located on different continents.

Enhancement of large-scale collaboration between researchers from Europe and other continents has been made possible due to the availability of communication technologies, of funding schemes supporting international higher education cooperation and of the international compatibility of higher education systems, facilitated by the Bologna process since 1999. This international collaboration aims to improve the quality of education and science including the development of the content for new interdisciplinary degrees, and the adaptation of new teaching approaches to different organisational cultures, drawing on the joint capabilities and expertise of collaborating universities and academics. Successful collaboration can bring multiple and long-lasting benefits, primarily for new interdisciplinary knowledge for students and researchers. Therefore, it is essential to understand what underpins the successful collaborative work of partner universities from different regions of the world in the field of higher education. This chapter contributes to addressing this challenge, using the case of the EU-Russia international project 'Bridging health, innovations, and societies: Education capacity-building in Eastern European neighbouring areas' (BIHSENA).

BIHSENA was funded by the Erasmus+ Programme of the European Commission analysed in detail in Chapter 3 of this book; the project involved seven universities from both EU and non-EU countries: Maastricht University (the Netherlands); National Research Tomsk State University and Siberian State Medical University (Russia); National University of Kyiv-Mohyla Academy and National Pirogov Memorial Medical University, Vinnitsya (Ukraine); Plovdiv

University 'Paisii Hilendarski' (Bulgaria) and Andrzej Frycz Modrzewski Krakow University (Poland). Maastricht University coordinated their capacity-building efforts in close cooperation with two Russian universities located in Tomsk, a city in the Siberian Federal District. The research proposal for BIHSENA was made in 2014, received Erasmus+ funding in 2015, and began the implementation phase at the beginning of 2017, all in the context of international political turmoil and rapidly deteriorating relationships between both the EU and Russia and especially the three countries whose universities have participated in the project – the Netherlands, Ukraine and Russia. The continuous operation of BIHSENA in the face of these challenges makes this case particularly interesting and important for the exploration of EU-Russia collaboration and provides useful insights into how to sustain international university connections in times of political crisis.

Too often discussion of similar collaborative projects in higher education focuses on KPI achieved: numbers of courses and degree programmes designed, new models developed to deliver these programmes, and the number of domestic and international students enrolled etc. While these achievements are important for formal evaluation procedures, this chapter aims to make visible the day-to-day practices of collaboration within the BIHSENA project, demonstrating the centrality of such 'backstage' work for collaboration. For this purpose the authors used the results of an internal self-reflection survey, which was conducted at the final project meeting in Maastricht in 2018. In particular, the teams of every participating country were divided into mixed groups to exchange their reflections on the project, discuss results, outline good practice and note the pitfalls of project implementation.

Following that, the groups presented a resume of their discussions, which were recorded and used in the final report of the project. These records are used in this chapter too. The authors also conducted six interviews with the key BIHSENA project participants from EU (N = 2) and non-EU (N = 4) universities in 2018. The interviews were anonymised especially for this chapter to ensure interviewees' anonymity. All interviewees held academic positions in their universities but had also undertaken administrative functions in the project, and had contributed both to the project proposal and to its implementation. The interviews, which consisted of open-ended questions, allowed an in-depth exploration of how the arrangements and practices of university collaboration and personal collaboration developed from different perspectives. The responses were provided by participants who represented different areas of study, countries and universities. The interviews were transcribed and discussed by this chapter's authors who themselves were involved in BIHSENA. That provided a level of critical (self-)reflection on the significance and implications of project practices.

2 BIHSENA Project Initiation

2.1 *Bringing Together the Project Team*

Project BIHSENA was supported by Erasmus+ programme whose framework is considered by Nadine Burquel and Laura Ballesteros in Chapter 3 of this book. BIHSENA was financed in 2015 as one of 79 projects under Key Action 2 'Cooperation for innovation and the exchange of good practices'. However, the story of its success began before the successful application of the seven universities. It started from building an international team of like-minded people from EU and non-EU countries, who recognised the urgency of a new interdisciplinary field of study.

Maastricht University held a meeting with the researchers of Tomsk State University in 2013 under the auspices of the Netherland-Russia year declared by Beatrix, Queen of the Netherlands and Vladimir Putin, the President of the Russian Federation. It became apparent at the meeting that there was a common view on the intersection of health, medicine, and society as a new research field. The emergence of antimicrobial resistance, the rise of age-related diseases, and re-emergence of diseases that had been under control until recently, raised growing health concerns for society in the EU and outside it. These challenges are complex, multidimensional and often caused by irrelevant or collapsed health-care systems. Addressing these challenges required cooperation between university researchers specialising in biomedical sciences, and social sciences, and non-academic actors, such as governmental organisations, patient groups, and non-commercial organisations. Therefore, new kinds of experts were required, ones who would be able to develop and apply interdisciplinary approaches to collaborate and overcome these new threats for globalised societies.

Preliminary discussion on how best to use this opportunity provided friendly and productive relations between the researchers of the two divisions in Tomsk State University and Maastricht University. As a result, in March 2014, they decided to develop a new master's degree together.

> It was fortunate that we could not apply in 2014 … Within six months we had decided to definitely apply, but by ourselves. One of the Russian universities had decided to open a new master's programme which would

include medicine, one of the topics of the Maastricht team. It meant we would do it together. (Interviewee_non-EU_1)

In May 2014 these partner universities organised a conference in Tomsk, Russia. It became an occasion to discuss the opportunity to collaborate in the development of a master's degree with a Ukrainian university from Kyiv (Zvonareva & Melnikova, 2014) which had expressed an interest in joining the EU-Russia team to apply for the Erasmus+ call.

> I contacted people in Russia and other Eastern European countries. So, this idea came up – to do something with this topic and maybe in a larger research project or at least maybe in a kind of capacity development project. ... you have an idea to do something, and then you say: 'Ok, where can we get any funding?' And then there was Erasmus+ opportunity. [it] appeared to be a very good niche. (Interviewee_EU_2)

An application for the future BIHSENA was formulated under the guidance of colleagues from the Netherlands, with the participation of Ukrainian and Russian teams on the principles of integral partnership and horizontal interaction. In addition, they invited new partners to join the project on the grounds of their previous positive experience of collaboration. So, the consortium was gradually constituted as listed in the introduction of this chapter having Maastricht and Tomsk State as the core universities.

Academics from the EU and non-EU countries discussed ideas, priorities, and outcomes of the future project and agreed on them for mutual benefit. This application routine ensured the inclusion of the interests of every participant. As a result, the BIHSENA team established friendly personal relations, which would help to overcome any future challenges of the project.

2.2 Precarious International Collaboration in Times of Political Crisis

In 2014 the relationships between EU and Russia were cooling down due to the territorial conflict of Ukraine and Russia over the Crimean Peninsula in March 2014. Many world leaders considered it as an annexation of a part of Ukrainian territory; the EU put Russia under sanctions. In addition, two regions of Ukraine near the Russian border proclaimed themselves as independent republics; the Ukrainian government announced that they were occupied by the separatists suspected of being supported by Russia. Armed conflict broke out.

However, the Netherlands soon became involved in this conflict against their will. In July 2014, an international passenger flight Amsterdam-Kuala Lumpur (Malaysia Airlines Flight 17) was shot down, killing all 283 passengers who were mostly citizens of the Netherlands and other EU countries. The crash occurred about 50 km from the Ukraine–Russia border in an area controlled by the self-proclaimed republican troops. This incident led to the political fallout in relations between the Netherlands and Russia, already strained over developments in March 2014. The incident was seen as a national tragedy for all the citizens of the Netherlands. Almost every citizen of the Netherlands knew someone who lost neighbours or family members in the flight crash.

Dutch analysts stated that 'business as usual' was not possible anymore (Hartog, 2015). The crash provoked a wave of anti-Russian sentiment in the Netherlands. Dutch politicians expressed their attitude to the political crisis in measured tones. Foreign Minister Bert Koenders defined a new approach to Russia based on keeping sanctions on the one hand and maintaining a dialogue with Russia as equal partners aiming at the continuation of cooperation in areas such as education, science, and civil society (Government, 2015).

> There were difficulties on a different level. In particular, a local paper published an article with a question of how long would [EU university] maintain a relationship with [...] such regimes as Russia [...]. But somehow, we escaped it quietly, but there were such questions. In the midst of crisis, the head of the [EU university] Taskforce Russia called up the Ministry of International Affairs, and periodically asked whether everything was good ... We were not told 'no, do not do it', but university administration held the hand on the pulse – about not to do something that should not be done. (Interviewee_ EU_1)

Many people in Ukraine, also, held the personal view that the conflict in the self-proclaimed republics was a war.

In relation to preparing the international application for Erasmus+ funding, the situation became a source of uncertainty for all participants – the Dutch and Polish belonged to the EU, while the Ukrainians and Russians belonged to countries in conflict and outside the EU. It was not clear if the EU allowed Russians to participate in international collaboration under European funding programmes or not. It should be noted that these concerns related to Russian policy in relation to international foundations, because the Russian government had been restricting the activity of international foundations since the 2000s (Popova, 2015; Yusupova, 2019). Despite the escalation of the Russian-Ukrainian conflict, the heads of the national teams involved in the BIHSENA application decided to continue it, together with the participation of Russia and Ukraine.

... political tension is growing, and the plane fell. And here I sit and think, 'We have so many plans, we started to interact [with the international team to prepare an application to Erasmus+], we did the first exchange of students [...] We've just held the first conference and planned the second one, we have some plans for research collaboration, and now it's not clear how to react'. And you realise that you cannot keep silence about the situation. At the same time, we do not have rules and practices on how to behave in this situation. When it's a personal tragedy, it is clear that it is necessary to express condolences, but in case of interstate conflicts, it's unknown what you are supposed to do in such a situation, how to communicate, what to express ...

I gave it lengthy consideration, and wrote a letter to Dutch colleagues, to five people that were at the first conference at [a Russian university] ... [an EU colleague] wrote something like: 'Today we've received a letter from the Ministry that we stop scientific cooperation with Russian agencies at the official level for a while, but despite this, we continue our personal communications and our agenda does not change. Next month or two let them decide what to do with official relations, but we continue to interact and cooperate' ... it was the beginning of developing a certain style of communication in relation to complex political issues. We have identified that first of all, we are professionals, who maintain a working relationship in all situations. (Interviewee_non-EU_1)

The sustainability of established collaborative arrangements was tested again after the approval of BISHENA funding by Erasmus+. Ever-growing uncertainties of the political context raised concerns of the impossibility of project performance on the institutional level due to the fear of a diplomatic break between Russia and Ukraine.

Two main factors played a crucial role in the decision-making process for BISHENA. The first factor was the involvement of the third party, namely the Education, Audiovisual and Culture Executive Agency (EACEA), to mediate the negotiation process among the universities who participated. EACEA actively joined negotiations and searched for possible solutions. As the framework of the project was quite flexible, the solution was found in amending the terms of the project: not a single obligatory event of the project had to be conducted on the territory of Ukraine or Russia. Where events were to be held in these countries, the participants from Russia and Ukraine could attend them voluntarily. Every national team could focus on their own country but maintain professional interactions with participants from other countries.

The second factor, which ensured the success of the project despite political crisis, was a political tolerance and ability to place professional interests ahead of personal political preferences.

> I would note the basis [of BIHSENA] is openness and true desire to do something and change. This is very impressive and helps [...]. We have been working as a team, and more focused on our country than on the common product of the project, but in general it does not change the atmosphere of the project. (Interviewee_non-EU_2)

> We have a year of interaction with [EU university]. We hold the first conference at a time of all these political tensions in relations with Ukraine and later with the Netherlands. The conference ... was attended by our Ukrainian colleagues and we were acquainted ... but somehow we built communication because this is the level of political tolerance, it means we can talk. We start thinking about collaboration, and we understand that it does not influence personal demands and political positions because work is work. So, we see how we enrich ourselves, not in financial terms, but in terms of knowledge and resources, research that we get. (Interviewee_non-EU_1)

Political crisis generated an insecure institutional environment for collaboration between universities. But it was overcome through the determination of individuals – project participants, whose relations were based on friendship and sharing common goals.

> Institutional relationships might at some point be a kind of obstruction or might stimulate difficulties. Though people are reflexive about institutional difficulties, they are standing above it, they are able to see fruitfulness of an academic collaboration. Personal friendships ensured a kind of reflexive attitude, we were able to think about what's happening in different countries on the distance and to make a distinction between institutions and persons and to put things in perspective. I think it's very important. (Interviewee_EU_1)

However, this complicated political challenge also brought a few positive results for the BIHSENA. It helped to develop a balanced and goal-oriented approach to collaboration.

> They protect the project and control their own emotions or feelings, which might be there. The goal of the project is in the first place for most

people; it has priority. And this was how people dealt with things, like giving condolences, responding to death. It's a civilised way of keeping the relationships good. (Interviewee_EU_1)

Another positive outcome was also generated from communication issues, which inevitably appeared as the project listed the holding of joint meetings and training.

> At the first meeting in [the EU city] I was in group where there were two Russians and two Ukrainians, and we began to speak in Russian. One colleague from [a Ukrainian university] started to speak to us in Russian too. And colleague from [another Ukrainian university], who could speak the Russian language for sure, spoke only in Ukrainian: 'I do not mind you talk in Russian, but for me it's comfortable to talk in Ukrainian'. We said: 'No problem, you just speak more slowly, and we will improve our Ukrainian language'. This was the moment, I believe, of personal choice of each of us. If we understand each other, then, for God's sake why not [to speak any language]? (Interviewee_non-EU_1)

Therefore, it can be claimed that BIHSENA team constructed a kind of etiquette regarding behaviour in sensitive situations, that stabilised the project and taught the participants tolerance and 'emotion management'.

This situation revealed the strong interconnection between the political context and the uncertainty it generates for internationalisation activities. In an academic discourse on internationalisation, the political dimension is manifested mostly in two basic ways: the political rationale for internationalisation and internationalisation as 'soft power.' The political rationale includes issues of national security, stability, and peace as well as ideological influence, which is called the 'soft power' of diplomacy (Knight, 1997, 2004; de Wit, 1999, 2002). This positive side of political rationale appeared after the end of the cold war (de Wit, 1998), giving birth to such European programmes for cooperation as SOCRATES, COMET, and ERASMUS. Scholars emphasise the process of shifting internationalisation from interstate to interinstitutional level, followed by an overall shift in rationales from political to economic ones (Kälvemark & Van der Wende, 1997; Van der Wende, 2016; Luijten-Lub et al., 2005).

However, the political and military tensions of recent years have brought the politicisation of international higher education back on the agenda. As the BIHSENA case shows, these tensions generate high risks for international educational cooperation. One of the critical tasks for academic and political communities is to find a way of managing these risks. Altbach and de Wit (2015, 4) pose a query: 'Will the increasingly widespread global conflicts – based on religious fundamentalism, resurgent nationalism, and other challenges – harm the impressive strides that have been made in international higher education cooperation?' – They leave this question open. In the case of BIHSENA, this challenge raised the awareness of the importance of democratic norms and professionalism in collaborative activity at the levels of the university and personal collaboration. This recognition allowed the reconciliation of political and cultural differences and mitigated risks as much as it was possible.

3 Project Implementation

After the massive political and economic transformation on the Eurasian continent in the 1990s (dissolution of the USSR along with a large area of the Soviet bloc and the formation of the European Union) the discourse of internationalisation changed and at least two significant paradigms appeared: West-European (Knight, 1999; De Wit, 2010) and post-Soviet ones. Quite a large number of post-Soviet countries, including those located in Eastern Europe as well as in Russia were experiencing the evolving transition to new educational models, and sometimes the Soviet system was itself adapted to the new economic and political reality (Smolentseva et al., 2018; Ustyuzhantseva, 2017). Institutional structures and practices appeared as a result which were different from West-European ones, hence affecting collaborative activity. In the case of BIHSENA, this influence manifested itself, not in the process of project implementation, but in project outcomes, i.e., integration of a new degree programme in the existing higher education system at an institutional level. The challenges which faced participants were around differences in university organisational structures, national standards of degree programme implementation, bureaucratic clashes, and the financial sustainability of the newly developed master's programme.

3.1 *Institutional Challenges Outside and Inside the Universities*

A new master's programme: 'Innovation and Society: Science, Technology, and Health' was one of the BIHSENA planned results in Russia while Ukrainian participants modified their existing programme 'Healthcare Management'. These degrees combined knowledge from several field of studies: life sciences, medicine, technology, social studies, public health and innovation in all these fields. The interdisciplinarity of the programme was provided by the involvement of the universities with the wide spectrum of research. Historically, medical universities had implemented their degree programmes in medicine only: they had rigid divisions and had implemented their degrees in a very different manner from traditional universities since Soviet times. Traditionally, medical universities were outside the higher education sector, subordinate to the Ministries of Healthcare while most of the other universities were subordinate to the Ministries of Education and Science. Therefore, BISHENA provided a completely new 'product': an international, interdisciplinary, innovative, and intersectoral master's programme.

As Svetlana Shenderova proved in Chapter 6, the two-tier degree system is still in the process of integration into the Russian higher education system. In particular, degree system reforms are poorly adapted to national traditions and to the specifics of medical education in Russia and Ukraine. The BIHSENA experience confirmed that these complicated settings created a precarious basis for developing the master's programme, despite Russia's joining the Bologna process in 2003 and Ukraine in 2005.

> What I'm afraid of is instability, both in terms of regulation in higher education, and of what is happening in the country, because it definitely influences the content and design of our courses. (Interviewee_non-EU_2)

Moreover, after finishing the development of courses, the BIHSENA teams had to reconsider and adjust them owing to permanent changes in national legislation as well as its interpretation within the universities of Russia and Ukraine.

> [Changes] influence our courses' content and design much. For example, the course we are developing for [non-EU university] about the healthcare system of Ukraine. Ministry of Healthcare announced implementing medical insurance [new law]. All we did before, all discussions, course content, we have to reconsider in a year, when it should be launched. Every course is closely connected to the context. So, our context is not stable totally. That is why it will demand sufficient resources for adaptation. (Interviewee_non-EU_2)

State Educational Standards and their updates were announced by the governments of Ukraine and Russia as part of higher education system reforms, but they still did not cover interdisciplinary fields (Zajda, 2016) owing to the separation of degree programmes according to fields of study. That is why the incorporation of new interdisciplinary programmes into national educational standards was quite challenging.

On the one hand, leading Russian universities including Tomsk State which participated in BIHSENA were allowed to develop their own standards by the Government. On the other hand, a university may suggest the content and curriculum of a degree, which might be quite different (or too innovative) in comparison with existing degrees. But it is common for new interdisciplinary degrees not to match up to the demands of the State Educational Standard based on separate specific areas of study.

Therefore, there is a risk that such a degree might not be accredited by the Federal Service for Supervision in Education and Science. It means that such a degree would not to be recognised in Russia and abroad. In addition, as is indicated in Chapter 6, the State Educational Standards for any field of study are often differently interpreted by university and ministerial administrators. That is why even the leading universities in Russia are afraid to develop interdisciplinary degree programmes.

Moreover, all courses for master's degrees in public health should comply with the demands of the Educational Standards developed by two Ministries: Healthcare and Higher Education and Science. Neither Ministry was eager to align sectoral standards and become more sensitive to interdisciplinary studies. In addition, the interviewees mentioned rigid relationships between the universities which concentrated on medicine where there was little experience of the implementation of master's programmes and those partners which have already developed a wider range of such degrees.

> They [colleagues in non-EU university] try to stay away from [their partner in the same country]. It is also not helpful. At the same time the integration of degree programmes in graduate education is questionable too. I still do not understand. Everybody nods their heads, but I have not seen any specific proposals about where we can be helpful [for medical universities]. (Interviewee_ EU_2)

BIHSENA participants indicated that university administrators found it hard to resolve cross-sectoral bureaucratic clashes as one of the serious threats to successful degree accomplishment. There was no precise understanding about which office within any non-EU partner would be responsible for master's degree development among the following administrative departments: international relations office, research office, or academic affairs office. For example, degree programmes in a Russian university used to be based on faculty chairs. Later this university had started internal restructuring, and responsibilities for the degree programmes turned over to newly organised units, such as centres of excellence. But no one developed new internal regulations: accordingly federal legislation had become a source of many uncertainties.

> We have signed a contract, and no one opposed to the fact that money may come. But now ... I have a feeling that for example, in [non-EU university],

sometimes when I talk to some of the vice-rectors, they come to [the meeting], I do not see much enthusiasm. Well, they got the money – good, but we have an interdisciplinary programme, and it is the best way to use it for new field of study for [non-EU university], as [this university] implements the reform ... and I do not see any desire to think of how to incorporate our new interdisciplinary programme. Especially because the theme of innovation as a whole is occupied by some other people [in non-EU university]. So, it seems no one in particular is happy that someone else is doing this degree programme in innovation. And the fact of cooperation with [non-EU university] is generally such a terrible difficulty for management of [another non-EU university in the same country] – no one wants to hear about it there. (Interviewee_EU_2)

Russian and Ukrainian participants shared their experiences on how to solve these challenges to the impending BIHSENA implementation.

3.2 *Financial Sustainability*

Money had always been an issue since the beginning of the project. Developing courses for the master's programme is a resource-consuming process, which was challenging to cover with project funds. State funding of non-EU universities is mostly based on the number of state-funded places for domestic and international students. These places are distributed annually by the Ministries supervising the universities. The other available source of income is the contribution of self-paid students. Traditionally Russian universities calculate the number of academic positions for degree implementation based on the full-time student enrollment and number of contact hours required to study (e.g. about 600 contact hours per year for one academic position in a non-EU university).

Therefore, any existing degree depends on the numbers of the students enrolled for any field of study: no places taken up means no programme and the reduction of academic positions. In addition, the Presidential Decree (Ukaz Prezidenta Rossiyskoy Federacii ot 07.05.2012 No. 597, 2012) maintains that the average salary in public universities should not be less than the average salary in the region where a university is located. If someone is not able to provide contact hours for any reason, his/her workload and the academic position disappear simultaneously. Thus, the average university (but not personal) salary rises with the number of contact hours per academic. Under these conditions, heads of master's degrees find it challenging to develop a long-term strategy for their programmes.

If I had no money in the past and this year from another source of funding, this project would not exist, because the university is not co-financing anything. But [non-EU university] requires a lot of extra things: they are waiting for us to cover accommodation and travel costs. Project members have to perform their responsibilities, the main part of which includes a significant number of teaching workload. But ... the volume of work on the project is huge too. Employees cannot reduce their [contact] workload as their main responsibilities, because at the end of the project, they [non-EU university administration] cannot get back this load to us – State funding is constantly reducing.

I knew from the beginning that the project money in terms of salaries is not enough for project implementation. But if we would not have any additional external funding, we could complete the project by some formal indicators, but in reality, this project would not be done as it should be done. (Interviewee_non-EU_1)

Thus, the master's programme developed as the BIHSENA outcome is not the end. It is the beginning of implementation of the degree with a sustainable budget and student intake. However, during the development of the new programme in the interdisciplinary field of innovation, health and society, the Russian project team realised that there was no niche yet either in the Russian degree landscape, or in the socio-economic area of the country. The problems of innovative approaches in public health were (and are) not considered as an urgent need for healthcare practices and management. Initial assessment of existing demand for new kinds of experts in the field was well ahead of the real situation in Russia and Ukraine. Therefore, the demand for this programme and its graduates in the labour market is still a matter of concern for non-EU BIHSENA participants.

There are matters, which are good but are ahead of its time. We try to bring together these matters, but we are not at the point of its immediacy, therefore we will need more time for programme promotion, I guess, in order people to understand, why does it need, what they can do with it, what competences and skills they get, and specially how they can apply it at labour market. In Russia, I think, we are not ready for this ... after getting this education, people just cannot use it for a number of years. I suppose this is the highest risk, as the programme has to survive, and to have admission. (Interviewee_non-EU_ 3)

When a Russian university is lucky enough to receive a few state-funded places for a programme in a certain field of study, this university should provide at least the same numbers of student intake next year. If next year the Ministry does not provide the same numbers, the university should ensure the survival of the programme and of the academics involved by enrolling self-paid students, thus producing a sustainable budget for the next year. However, the BIHSENA team realised that they could not rely on self-funded students for the development of the master's degree, primarily owing to the level of uncertainty in terms of future job prospects for the graduates. It would be an almost impossible task to 'sell' this master's degree in Russia, especially outside the capital.

Nonetheless, it opened a window of opportunity by providing the master's programme 'Innovation and Society: Science, Technology, and Health' the needed period of time to be introduced and recognised in the higher education sector and by professional communities.

4   How Not to Be Lost in Translation in Interdisciplinary Projects

Interdisciplinarity is one of the most appreciated attributes of modern research and advanced study programmes. The BIHSENA team did not expect that doing an interdisciplinary project would be challenging. The participants managed to develop an interdisciplinary proposal and get funding for it; what else could go wrong?

> Interdisciplinarity is a problem at all stages [of the project]. In the beginning [...] it was obvious. Those participants, who worked already on the project, visited [...] events, worked in a team, and communicated by Skype – they accustomed to it. They have already defined common terms and concepts ... When a new participant joined, this was like going to outer space. And the situation repeated with every newcomer. We had fewer complications in the interaction between project members as national teams than between project members as professional teams ... We started the project, which unites professionals in medicine and humanities. Building this communication appeared to be more difficult than international one. Study programmes in Public Health are a big question in Russia. We do not even know how to translate it [in the Russian language]. (Interviewee_non-EU_1)

The work of the BIHSENA team exceeded the scope of just developing an interdisciplinary curriculum of the master's programme. The participants had to build consensus on the degree's basis and context. To what extent is sociology relevant to those taking medical studies as majors? How much is this programme of current interest for Russian and Ukrainian societies? These questions were an inherent part of almost all discussions concerned with the project and helped to formulate a common understanding.

> People from [non-EU medical university] call us spacemen, because of our ideas about interactive medicine, humanistic medicine ... for them, we look like spacemen, who cannot descend to reality. One colleague from [EU university] gave a brilliant lecture about patient-centered medicine ... she showed video, where ... a gigantic doctor stayed near a small patient. Gradually patient became the same size as doctor. This is a trend for them [EU countries]. And our [non-EU] sociologists started saying that this is not consistent with Russian reality. [...] In response to it our medical professionals said: 'Indeed! This is a matter of very important debates in medicine now! This is what we want to develop'. (Interviewee_non-EU_1)

The next challenge the BIHSENA team faced was the differences in concepts, terms, and ideas between medical professionals and sociologists, who participated in the project.

> We try to bridge different disciplines but different planets too: sociologists and medical professionals. This task is very good and important. In practice it's quite difficult to find a common language. Expressing our visions, we literally speak different professional languages ... we can have a similar vision, but express it very differently. (Interviewee_EU_ 2)

A very effective solution to this challenge were project sessions in small discussion groups, each of which included medical professionals and sociologists. These small interdisciplinary teams had the opportunity to develop a common language and a common conceptual base from different disciplinary perspectives. Cross-pollination of knowledge influenced professional transformation in some cases. As one of the medical doctors, who participated said:

> I will never be the same doctor anymore. Four years ago, I was absolutely sure that we have infection diseases, genetic diseases, any other types of disorders, but now I understand that each disease is socially placed ... interdisciplinary work turned upside down my understanding of the world and of my profession. (Participant reflection, non-EU group, 2018)

5 In Conclusion: Lessons Learned

'Bridging health, innovations, and societies: Education capacity-building in Eastern European neighbouring areas' (BIHSENA) incredibly enriched the experience for all participants. After the project finished, its team members are still engaged in joint research and education activity, as new ideas and fields of study appear, and possibilities open up.

In conclusion, there are three important questions to provide insights for possible improvement of practices in international interdisciplinary projects.

5.1 *What Lessons Have Been Learned?*
First, institutional practices do matter in an international project. In the cases of transition countries, administrative and institutional barriers for the implementation of collaborative degrees are high, but not insoluble. It should be considered and adjusted during planning. Next, it is better to recognise and try to address the challenge of resource allocation by developing courses, building on different activities in the workload of the participants. Most of the non-EU academics responsible for the courses' developments have to fulfil a teaching workload as their main duties. This fact should be taken account of in project implementation. And finally, an interdisciplinary programme urges the development of communication language, and the co-creation of intelligible conceptual apparatus and approaches. This time-consuming and laborious work within an interdisciplinary team cannot be avoided, as it determines the effectiveness of further teamwork.

5.2 *What Made This Project Work?*
The basic reasons for success included preliminary meetings and knowing each other even before writing a proposal. Joint determination to achieve the project goal created an effective working environment as well as the sharing and discussion of challenging issues in an open and democratic manner. And personal ability to put professionalism ahead of personal emotions and political preferences was crucial in the current political tensions between EU and Russia. These all created a good resilient team and the ability to deal with institutional and political risks and uncertainties.

5.3 *How Could the Practices of an International and Interdisciplinary Project Be Improved?*
What was missing but demanded by an interdisciplinary collaborative degree was the participation of the administrative staff of the universities in project activity. Introducing a new degree programme, adapting to the national

educational standards, and providing innovative teaching methods could not be successfully undertaken without certain institutional transformation, accompanied by changes in routines and practices. The administrative staff of the universities should be involved in the project with relevant and clearly understandable responsibilities. They should participate in workshops on good practice to administer innovative degrees as complex international projects, implemented in a permanently changed institutional environment. This would ensure the transformative impact of collaborative international EU-Russian degree programmes at the institutional level.

References

Altbach, P. G., & de Wit, H. (2015). Internationalization and global tension: Lessons from history. *Journal of Studies in International Education, 19*(1), 4–10. https://doi.org/10.1177/1028315314564734

de Wit, H. (1998). Rationales for internationalization of higher education. *Millemium, 3*(11), 11–19.

de Wit, H. (1999). Changing rationales for internationalization. *International Higher Education, 15*, 2–3.

de Wit, H. (2002). *Internationalization of higher education in the United States of America and Europe: A historical, comparative, and conceptual analysis.* Greenwood Press.

de Wit, H. (2010). *Internationalisation of higher education in Europe and its assessment, trends and issues.* NVAO Nederlands-Vlaamse Accreditatieorganisatie.

Government of the Netherlands. (2015). *Koenders: Need for new international balance with Russia.* News item. Retrieved July 20, 2019, from https://www.government.nl/latest/news/2015/05/13/koenders-need-for-new-international-balance-with-russia

Hartog, E. (2015, October 12). MH17 report to put Dutch-Russian relations in spotlight. *The Moscow Times.* https://www.themoscowtimes.com

Kalvemark, T., & van der Wende, M. (1997). *National policies for the internationalization of higher education in Europe.* National Agency for Higher Education.

Knight, J. (1997). Internationalization of higher education: A conceptual framework. In J. Knight & H. de Wit (Eds.), *Internationalization of higher education in Asia Pacific countries.* European Association for International Education Publications.

Knight, J. (1999). Issues and trends in internationalization: A comparative perspective. In S. L. Bond & J. P. Lemasson (Eds.), *A new world of knowledge. Canadian Universities and Globalization* (pp. 201–238). International Development Research Centre.

Knight, J. (2004). Internationalization remodelled: Definition, approaches, and rationales. *Journal of Studies in International Education, 8*(1), 5–31. https://doi.org/10.1177/1028315303260832

Luijten-Lub, A., Van der Wende, M., & Huisman, J. (2005). On cooperation and competition: A comparative analysis of national policies for internationalisation of higher education in seven Western European countries. *Journal of Studies in International Education, 9*(2), 147–163. https://doi.org/10.1177/1028315305276092

Matei, L., & Iwinska, J. (2015). National strategies and practices in internationalisation of higher education: Lessons from a cross-country comparison. In A. Curaj, L. Deca, E. Egron-Polak, & J. Salmi (Eds.), *Higher education reforms in Romania*. Springer.

Popova, E. (2015). Russian Universities: Between internationalization and technonationalism. *Sociology of Power, 3*.

Smolentseva, A, Froumin, I., & Huisman, J. (2018). *25 years of transformations of higher education systems in post-soviet countries*. Palgrave Macmillan. https://doi.org/10.1007/978-3-319-52980-6_1

Ukaz Prezidenta Rossiyskoy Federacii ot 07.05.2012 No. 597. (2012). O merakh po realizacii gosudarstvennoy social'noy politiki (Ct. 1 a). Paragraph V [Decree of the President of Russia from 07.05.2012 No. 597, On measures of implementation of the state social policy]. Retrieved January 10, 2020, from http://base.garant.ru/70170950/

Ustyuzhanseva, O. (2017). Internationalisation in a non-market environment: The case of Russia. In H. de Wit, J. Gacel-Ávila, E. Jones, & J. Jooste (Eds.), *The globalisation of internationalisation: Emerging voices and perspectives* (pp. 121–130). Routledge.

Yusupova, G. (2019). Exploring sensitive topics in an authoritarian context: An insider perspective. *Social Science Quarterly 100*(4), 1459–1478.

Zajda, J. (2016). Globalisation, ideology and politics of education reforms. In J. Zajda & V. Rust (Eds.), *Globalisation and higher education reforms*. Springer.

Zvonareva, O., & Melnikova, O. (2014). Crossing boundaries: Medicine, innovations and society. Report on the international conference "social sciences and medical innovations". *Journal of Technology Assessment in Theory and Practice, 2*(23), 94–97.

CHAPTER 11

South Africa: The Role of Cross-Continental Research Initiatives: Case Studies of the EU and Others

Patrício V. Langa and Charl Wolhuter

Abstract

This chapter examines the presence and significance of South African research institutions and universities in collaborative endeavours with their counterparts in the EU and BRIC (Brazil, Russia, India, and China) countries. The European Union (EU), is a political and economic union of 28 member states that are geopolitically located primarily in Europe (European Commission, 2018). BRICS is a transnational community which includes Brazil, Russia, India, China and South Africa, often referred to as the emerging political and economic bloc formed in 2009 and which South Africa joined in 2010. Both the EU and the BRICS form two continental and transcontinental blocs operating on the basis of regional and international frameworks and platforms to enhance strategic cooperation, and integration at both economic, geo-political, research and cultural levels.

Keywords

South Africa – South African higher education – South African academic co-operation policy – academic cooperation between South Africa and EU – academic cooperation between South Africa and the BRIC countries – South African science, technology and innovation policies

1   Introduction

Research collaboration measurement is part of a discourse associated with research productivity measured through co-authorship. Globally, research collaboration has been a significant part of emerging research communities as, by 2016, 60% of total academic publications were internationally co-authored

(UNESCO, 2010; NSB, 2016). Higher education institutions and scholars are urged to collaborate, particularly in respect of research activities, and in obtaining research funding. The internationalisation of academic activities, particularly through research collaboration, is an important topic which stands at the crossroads of the sociology of science, the history of academic institutions, scientometrics, bibliometrics, the study of research policies and the geography of innovation, along with the contribution of various other specialties (Grossetti et al., 2014).

This chapter examines the presence and significance of South African research institutions and universities in collaborative endeavours with their counterparts in the EU and BRIC (Brazil, Russia, India, and China) countries. The European Union (EU), is a political and economic union of 28 member states that are geopolitically located primarily in Europe (European Commission, 2018). BRICS is a transnational community which includes Brazil, Russia, India, China and South Africa, often referred to as the emerging political and economic bloc formed in 2009 and which South Africa joined in 2010. Both the EU and the BRICS form two continental and transcontinental blocs operating on the basis of regional and international frameworks and platforms to enhance strategic cooperation, and integration at both economic, geopolitical, research and cultural levels.

To construct the chapter, we relied mostly on two sources: first, we used existing literature on South African scholars and institutions, which described collaborations with the EU and BRIC. Secondly, we relied on a comprehensive 2019 report on the "State of South African Research Enterprise" produced by Johann Mouton and his research team at the DST-NRF Centre of Excellence in Scientometrics and Science, Technology and Innovation Policy, Stellenbosch University. The chapter also covers the period between 2010 and 2019, since South African formally joined the BRIC in 2010. Apart from providing new data, the chapter explores the significance of the patterns of research collaboration by South African scholars and institutions, particularly with the EU and BRIC counterparts.

Globally, scientific research is increasingly undertaken collaboratively in teams of individual scholars, institutions and countries. Collaboration enhances the competency, skills and knowledge of partners while ensuring the quality of research. It strengthens research activities and capabilities; and failure in collaboration weakens science and technical enterprise (Sooryamoorthy, 2013; Sooryamoorthy & Shrum, 2007; Sonnenwald, 2007). One of the advantages of research collaboration is the visibility it brings to the individual scientist as well as to their institutions and countries. Wide dissemination of the researchers, scientific products, publications and the institutions of a country or region in the face of the global scientific community translates into more recognition and prestige. Research communities strive to achieve impact beyond national and regional borders, and collaboration provides a pathway to global impact.

This chapter is divided into three parts: First, we provide an overview and reflect on the state of scientific (in)visibility of (South) Africa in the context of knowledge production. Secondly, we address the issue of research funding as a key factor that enables scientific collaboration and leads to more visibility. Third, we examine the South African patterns of scientific collaboration; fourth, we also look closely into the issue of dissemination of scientific activity; and fifth, the relationship between scientific collaboration and citation impact. Finally, the chapter ends with a reflection on the significance of collaboration between South Africa, the EU, and BRIC, before drawing the conclusions.

2 The Scientific (In)visibility of (South) Africa

African scientists and scholars are understated in global science, and within African countries, access to science is often difficult and uneven. Science in Africa is mostly visible in the northern and southern extremities of the continent. There is a clear division in scientific productivity between the northern African states and the sub-Saharan states. Egypt, Algeria, Mauritania, Libya, Morocco and Tunisia are prominent among the northern African countries for their growing scientific outputs. South Africa in Southern Africa is another powerhouse of science production on the continent.

According to Mouton et al. (2019) publication output in individual African countries shows the continued dominance of South Africa with 28.2% share of all African papers, followed by strong contributions from Egypt (19.6%), Tunisia (9.2%) and other Maghreb countries such as Algeria and Morocco. Other African countries like Nigeria in Western Africa, but also Kenya, Uganda and Tanzania have a smaller but significant contribution to scientific production and productivity on the African continent.

An analysis of research publication production on the African continent shows that it is skewed. The combined publication output of the northern African countries and South Africa constitutes more than two thirds (69.2%) of the entire continent's publications. The longitudinal trends show that South Africa, Egypt and Tunisia, and to a lesser extent Kenya, increased their relative world shares over the past 15 years quite substantially. For the remainder of countries, the world shares increased minimally (Mouton et al., 2019).

Egalitarian and even-handed collaborations are very often mutually beneficial. In Africa, where a large proportion of published research is from collaborative undertakings, collaboration helps to enhance the quality and the general output of African scientists. Often underappreciated, however, is that Northern scientists collaborating with Africans perform higher-impact research than their peers who do not (Blom et al., 2016).

Funding (schemes) and incentives to promote scientific collaboration are amongst the most important factors that contribute to scientific productivity and visibility of national and regional science systems. Our assumption, in this study, is that South Africa's bilateral and multilateral cooperation with both the EU and BRIC would create the conditions for more support and financial resources allocated to scientific collaboration, leading to more productivity and visibility.

3 South (Africa) Funding of Research from EU and BRIC

In 2019, the President of the European Research Council (ERC), Professor Jean-Pierre Bourguignon, visited Kenya, to meet with African and European representatives from the research and innovation field to review and promote cooperation between the two continents. Setting the platform for new EU-African partnerships in the science and technology areas, Bourguignon recognised that most African Scholars do not apply and receive funding from the European Research Council (ERC) (European Commission, 2019). The EU invested a total amount of €123 million in African Union partners and it has already funded 310 projects under the programme that is aligned with the African Academy of Sciences' (AAS) strategic vision of 'transforming lives through science' (EC, 2019).

South Africa constitutes the African country that has benefited the most from Horizon 2020, one of the EU-flagship funding projects, in a total 126 projects funded. It is followed by Morocco, with a total amount of 50 projects supported by the EU and Kenya, with 47 projects.

Horizon 2020 is the largest EU Research and Innovation programme with approximately €80 billion of funding offered over a period of seven (7) years, 2014 to 2020. These funds were in addition to the private investment generated through research. The key areas of EU-African cooperation under Horizon 2020 are environment, food, ICT and health. The projects that have been financed in Africa under the initiative include the establishment of a resilience platform to assist communities in crisis situations, the research on rare diseases that affect children, the design of the world's largest radio telescope and the investigation of biodiversity in the Serengeti-Mara ecosystem (EC, 2019).

In the BRICS countries governments are mainly responsible for most of the research and development funding. China is an exception, where the industry sector is also a major source of R&D funding. In South Africa the National Research Fund (NRF) is one of the Government funding agencies. Between 2002 and 2015, NRF has provided funds across all fields at an average growth rate of 10.5%, in terms of the total value of individual grants. The field of social sciences and health sciences were the ones that benefited most from the increase. At the other end, a relatively low average growth rate of 2.4% grant was allocated to the engineering sciences (Mouton et al., 2019).

In the policy section of this book, Langa and Wolhuter (Chapter 7, this volume) indicated that there are two main frameworks governing EU relations with Africa. On the one hand, the Cotonou agreement which established a legal basis for relations with Sub-Saharan African countries including the Caribbean and Pacific countries, but without South Africa: on the other hand, the second framework, the Joint Africa-EU Strategy (JAES) adopted by the African and European Heads of State at the Lisbon Summit in 2007, which included South Africa.

Many countries in Africa, as in the case of South Africa, have signed bilateral Science and Technology Cooperation Agreements with the European Union. In 1996 (came into force in 1997) South Africa was welcomed into the group of nations benefiting from EU funds in the transition into a democratic dispensation following the fall of Apartheid in 1994. Other countries such as Egypt (2005, came into force 2008), Tunisia (2003, came into force 2004), Morocco (2004, came into force 2005) and Algeria (signed 2012, came into force 2013) also signed bilateral agreements with EU (EC, 2019). It is quite obvious that EU funding has a significant impact on the positioning of most Northern African countries and South Africa as the African powerhouses in research and development. In the following sections, we try to visualise the influence these funding and policy frameworks have on institutional and individual research collaborations.

4 South African Scientific International Collaboration

By and large, South African scientists and scholars are increasingly collaborating with the rest of the world and specifically with countries outside Africa. Generally "international collaboration has increased from 34% in 2000 to 52% in 2016" (Mouton et al., 2019, p. 3). Associated with this rise, the country has seen a decline in national collaboration and single-authored journal articles. Mouton's report shows that "the average proportion of multi-country authored papers for the comparator countries increased slightly from 40% in 2001 to 46% in 2015" (op. cit., p. 3). However, these averages disguise some significant country differences. Mouton's research team argues that "Turkey consistently recorded the lowest proportions over this period: from 19% in 2001 to 21% in 2015 (most likely a function of the effect of language on international collaboration). The highest proportions of internationally co-authored papers were recorded for Chile (from 51% in 2001 to 63% in 2015) and Portugal (from 51% in 2001 to 57% in 2015)" (Mouton, 2019, p. 3).

While Chile is part of the Merco-Sul community in Latin America, and does not seem to directly benefit from any trans-continental policies by belonging to an economic and political block to promote scientific collaboration, Portugal, as an EU member may be collaborating more with South Africa despite the fact that the Portuguese language may constitute a barrier for most scientists in Portugal. Overall, South Africa's share of internationally collaborative papers increased significantly from 34% in 2001 to 52% in 2015.

5 The Extraversion Effect on Scientific International Collaboration

If compared to other African countries, South African knowledge production and publication is less dependant on collaboration with foreign partners. In other words, the South African share of scientific publication is more self-reliant than that of most of the African countries which produce publications with high proportions of foreign authors.

While international scientific collaboration can be a sign of the strength of a research system and institution in a particular country, overreliance on foreign collaboration is a sign of weakness. Most African countries rely on external funds and co-authors from the north to be visible on the global knowledge and scientific radar. If it were not for international collaboration through either bilateral or multilateral funded (capacity building) research projects from donor countries, the research from these countries would not be visible.

The extreme reliance on foreign research collaborators is often a sign of weakness in a research system that depends on the research agenda set by foreign scholars, what the Beninan Philosopher, Paulin Hountondji (1988a, 1988b, 1990), called the extraversion of African scientific activity in Africa. According to Hountondji (2009, p. 8) extraversion, in this sense, means that African scientific activity is extraverted, i.e. externally oriented, intended to meet the theoretical needs of the Western counterparts and answer the questions they pose.

The exclusive use of European languages as a means of scientific expression reinforces this alienation. The majority of African country people are de facto excluded from any kind of discussion about the research outcome, given that they don't even understand the languages used. The small minority who understands knows, however, that they are not the first addressees but only, if anything, occasional witnesses of a scientific discourse meant primarily for others.

The average proportion of internationally collaborative papers for the African countries is 74%. For the most part these proportions have been consistently high over the past 15 years. The three countries that have shown the largest increases in international collaboration are Egypt (from 27% in 2000 to 57% in 2015), South Africa (from 34% in 2000 to 52% in 2015) and Botswana (from 32% in 2000 to 77% in 2015) (Mouton, 2019).

As suggested earlier in this chapter, South Africa is a powerhouse on the continent in terms of research collaborations with partners within the continent and with non-African partners. A study by Kozma and Calero-Medina (2019, pp. 1293–1294) "on the role of South African researchers in intercontinental collaboration, used centrality measures of the network to calculate and establish the frequency of involvement regarding different countries, with a focus on South Africa, in the collaboration process. Moreover, the study examines first and last authorship positions of the publications to highlight the influence of the selected authors on the direction of and resources provided to the publications".

South African researchers play a significant role in inter-continental scientific collaboration, particularly in the fields of Zoology, Ecology, Water Resources, and Plant Sciences (Kozma & Calero-Medina, 2019). Additionally, the quantity of co-publications in more technical fields feature more prominently across the African continent. The high level of collaboration of (South) African researchers particularly with the more developed countries, including EU member states, shows a twofold logic of research extraversion in international collaboration.

On the one hand, the intensity of collaborations does not necessarily always reflect the strength of the local research systems and its capacity. It may actually reveal a certain kind of weakness, particularly if we consider the position (South) Africans take in the publications as secondary co-authors. A study by Cloete et al. (2015) shows that some African researchers, particularly in technical fields, such as medicine, tend to have high levels of collaboration because

African researchers only have access to funding in those fields and often the Western partners lead the research projects and take the role of principal investigator in the publication outputs.

On the other hand, South Africa is also seen by many Western partners as a gateway to the rest of the African countries. Funding, for instance, plays a key role in this phenomenon. While in most African countries, especially those with National Research Funding agencies, the funding is typically designated for local researchers. The South African National Research Fund from time to time makes calls for research funding applications that include regional and continental collaboration from the continent.

The rise of the emerging economies, including BRICS, may change the dynamics of international scientific collaboration, particularly given the growing influence of China in Africa's knowledge landscape. However, in general, international collaboration patterns for the four BRIC countries have remained mostly unchanged between 2001 and 2015: India being the lowest at an average of 20%, followed by China (23%), Brazil (29%) and Russia (34%).

The EU and China, working together, have established a particular policy framework for their bilateral relations with South Africa, distinct from that with the other sub-Sahara African countries. This somewhat reflects the position of South Africa as an emerging economy. Similar to that with China, India and Brazil, the EU established a "Strategic Partnership" with South Africa in 2007 (Council of the EU, 2007). For South Africa this treatment indicates the elevation from a development-oriented relationship to that of a geopolitical dialogue (Grevi & Khandekar, 2011). For instance, with the EU this strategic partnership involves specific annual summits, and systematic exchange between the EU and South Africa at a technical level through working groups in various policy fields.

6   Scientific Collaboration and Citation Impact

Globally, research shows a significant correlation between the degree of international research collaboration and citation impact. The more engaged in international collaboration the scholar and research institution are, the more they tend to see high citation impact. According to Mouton et al., (2019) the citation impact of South African-authored papers, as measured by the Mean Normalised Citation Score (MNCS), has steadily increased from 0.8 in 2000 to 1.1 in 2016. South African-authored papers in 2016 are slightly above the world average impact for the fields in which they publish. The South African research system performs relatively well in comparison with selected African (Egypt, Ethiopia, Senegal, Botswana, Kenya & Uganda) and BRIC countries (1.01 compared to 0.97). The higher citation impact for South African research is mostly related to the well-established correlation between citation impact and the intensity of international collaboration. Various bibliometric studies have shown that citation impact increases as international collaboration increases. This is also the case in Mouton's (2019) study of international collaboration and citation impact for South Africa.

7 The Significance of Scientific Collaboration between SA, EU and BRIC

The framework of Africa–Europe collaboration in science, technology and innovation (STI) is becoming increasingly complex (Kraemer-Mbula, Vaitsas, & Essegbe, 2018). The production of research outputs in South Africa as well as in other African countries is significantly influenced by international funders, particularly the European Union, and American Philanthropic Organisations, such as the Carnegie Foundation, A. W. Mellon, Rockefeller (Jaumont, 2016).

7.1 South Africa Participation in EU Framework Programmes

When the EU Framework Programmes (FP) were launched in the mid-1980s for research, they aimed at strengthening the scientific and economic development of the European Community, while promoting international cooperation. South Africa was then under international sanctions due to Apartheid. In 2007, in its seventh edition, the EU FP7 focused on promotion of the EU's strategic goals on research and development (R&D) through partnerships with third countries including African states. The FP addressed specific challenges that third countries faced or which had a global impact such as climate change and sustainable development.

Sub-Saharan African participation in the FP7 increased significantly from previous programmes. According to Barugahara and Tostensen (2018, p. 21) "1315 participants from organisations in 45 African countries took part in 565 EU-funded projects, with a total budget of 178 million euros. In comparison, FP6 counted, in 2006, 882 African participants for 322 research projects, for an allocated budget of 95 million euros from the EU". Under FP7 South Africa, followed by Ghana, Uganda and Kenya, were the leading partnerships in terms of project participation in EU (Barugahara & Tostensen, 2018; EU-eCorda, 2016).

South African higher education institutions and research centres, including the universities of Cape Town, KwaZulu-Natal and Pretoria, along with the Council for Scientific and Industrial Research, the Agricultural Research Council, the Institute of Natural Research Association and the National Research Foundation, were amongst the beneficiaries of FP7 funded projects. Barugahara and Tostensen (2018) shows that South African small- and medium-sized enterprises (SMES) were also involved in FP7. Nevertheless, SME participation has remained limited, a trend that applies to most African countries (Barugahara & Tostensen, 2018; EU-eCorda, 2016).

South Africa was highly engaged in FP7 with 12 projects, ahead of most African countries. As argued by Kraemer-Mbula et al. (2018) South Africa's achievement under the FP7 was mainly a result of a resolute effort to promote cooperation, undertaken by the European South African Science and Technology Advancement programme, an advisory, information and support platform for researchers, funded under FP7 and implemented by the South African Department of Science and Technology, together with South Africa's FP7 Network of National Contact Points (NCPS) (op. cit., 2018).

7.2   South Africa in UE-Horizon 2020 and BRICS Collaborations

Horizon 2020 replaced FP7 in 2014 and became the 8th EU Framework programme on research and innovation (R&I) programme to date. In its framework it was projected to draw on additional private investment funds based on the appraised results produced when engaging with the market, particularly through SME ventures. Horizon 2020 was based on three pillars: (i) Excellence of science to reinforce and extend the EU science base; (ii) Industrial leadership focusing on speeding up the R&D process behind new technologies and innovations that enable SMEs to grow; and (iii) which was concerned with societal challenges reflecting the policy priorities of the EU strategy for 2020 and addressing major issues raised by citizens in the EU and elsewhere (such as health and demographic change, food security, clean energy, transport, climate change and security)(EU-eCorda, 2016).

The H2020 is particularly geared towards acquiring additional financing through increasing the number of topics explicitly flagging "international collaboration", which increased from 12% for topics in FP7 to over 27% in the 2014–2017 round of funding calls. It also strives to simplify and eliminate red-tape (bureaucracy) to enable global participation with a focus on the substance of their R&I undertakings.

Notwithstanding the efforts to facilitate a smooth implementation of H2020 projects, the proportion of participation of partners from third countries in grant agreements for collaborative projects and actions plummeted from 4.9% in the FP7 to 2.4% (Kraemer-Mbula et al., 2019). South Africa was ahead of most African participation in Horizon 2020 projects, as under FP7, followed by Ghana, Kenya and Uganda, often with the same organisations that participated in FP7 either extending their projects or engaging in new partnerships.

Overall, when compared to other African countries, South Africa has performed relatively better in international collaborative projects both through engaging directly with the EU, BRICS or other partners or by playing the gateway role to Africa by leading regional (SADC) or continental higher education, research, development and innovation projects.

A comparison across the BRICS countries confirms that South Africa has a reasonably 'well-rounded' science system with agricultural sciences, social sciences and the humanities as the strongest fields especially over the most recent period. All other countries have little to no activity in the humanities, at least on a globally accessible scale. China and Russia place a high priority on the natural sciences and engineering and applied sciences. India shows this to a lesser degree, placing more emphasis on agricultural sciences. Brazil is very strong in agricultural sciences and average in health and natural sciences (Mouton et al., 2019).

8   Conclusion

This chapter argued that collaboration is an essential element of the scientific and academic enterprise. We examined the presence and significance of South African scientific institutions including universities in collaborative endeavours with their counterparts in the EU and BRIC countries. South Africa's research performance and that of South African scientists and scholars are increasingly collaborating with the rest of the world and specifically with countries outside Africa. South African knowledge institutions and scholars are becoming more visible on the worldwide scientific radar, both as leading partners in African projects and as the most internationally collaborative partners with their counterparts in EU and BRIC.

By and large, South African international collaboration has increased from 34% in 2000 to 55% in 2016. Concomitant with this increase, there has been a decline in national collaboration as well as in single-authored articles (Mouton et al., 2019). However, South African collaborative patterns, that is, co-authorship, vary significantly by field. Research has established that single-authored publications are more prevalent in the humanities, whereas multi-authorship is the norm in various natural science disciplines and fields. As argued by Mouton et al. (2019) "The high collaboration proportions for the natural and health sciences are functions of very large international projects in high-energy physics and astronomy and large clinical trials and other big studies under the auspices of the Global Health Network".

South Africa leads most EU funded projects, while African participation particularly within Horizon 2020 appears to have decreased in comparison to FP7. This trend shows the significance of South Africa as a flagship country in higher education, science and innovation and the role it can play as a bridge between EU and BRIC with the rest of the continent. Through multiple cross-national and trans-continental networks of collaboration South Africa can provide an excellent platform to strengthen the collaboration among companies and research organisations between Africa and the rest of the world.

Cross-national, trans-continental, and bi-regional higher education, science, technology and innovation collaborations are often more reflective of the political will and aspiration towards co-ownership and equal partnership for mutual interest and shared benefit. However, more remains to be done in terms of co-financing to prevent the scientific extraversion effect, well delineated by Hountondji (1988a, 1988b, 2009). Once again, South Africa has taken the lead by extending some aspects of the NRF call to other African countries promoting intra-continental collaborations. Such funding programmes could eventually be co-funded and owned by African countries. Similar approaches would apply to cooperation with international partners, including the EU, and BRIC and provide a stronger and more diverse basis for bi-regional scientific cooperation.

References

Barugahara, I., & Tostensen, A. (2018). Policy frameworks supporting Africa–Europe STI cooperation: Past achievements and future responsibilities. In A. Cherry, J. Haselip, G. Ralphs, & I. Wagner (Eds.), *Africa-Europe research and innovation cooperation*. Palgrave Macmillan.

Blom, A., Lan, G., & Adil, M. (2016). *Sub-Saharan African science, technology, engineering, and mathematics research: A decade of development*. World Bank Publications.

Council of the EU. (2007, May 15). *The South Africa-European Union strategic partnership joint action plan*. Brussels, 9650/07 (Presse 105).

European Commission. (2016, November). *eCORDA and Cordis*. Retrieved November 12, 2019, from http://www.ncpacademy.eu/wp-content/uploads/2016/11/20161103_eCORDA-and-CORDIS.pdf

European Commission (2018). *The European Union – What is it, what it does*. Retrieved November 20, 2019, from https://op.europa.eu/en/publication-detail/-/publication/9ab2da22-14da-11ea-8c1f-01aa75ed71a1

European Commission (2019). *The Africa-Europe innovation partnership as emerging valley*. Retrieved January, 2020, from https://ec.europa.eu/research/iscp/index.cfm?pg=africa

Grevi, G. (Ed.). (2011). *Mapping EU strategic partnerships* (with G. Khandekar). FRIDE.

Grossetti, M., Eckert, D., Gingras Y., Jégou, L., Larivièrev, V., & Milard B., (2014), Cities and the geographical deconcentration of scientific activity: A multilevel analysis of publications (1987–2007). *Urban Studies, 51*(10), 2219–2234.

Hountondji, P. (1988a). Situation de l'anthropologue africain: note critique sur une forme d'extraversion scientifique. In G. Gosselin (Ed.), *Les nouveaux enjeux de l'anthropologie. Autour de Georges Balandier. Special issue of Revue de l'Institut de sociologie (Bruxelles), 3–4*, 99–108.

Hountondji, P. (1988b). L'appropriation collective du savoir: tâches nouvelles pour une politique scientifique. *Genève-Afrique, 26*(1), 49–61.

Hountondji, P. (1990) Scientific dependence in Africa today. *Research in African Literatures, 21*(3), 5–15.

Hountondji, P. (2009). Knowledge of Africa, knowledge by Africans: Two perspectives on African Studies. *RCCS Annual Review, 1*. Retrieved November, 2019, from https://www.ces.uc.pt/publicacoes/annualreview/media/2009%20issue%20n.%201/AR1_6.PHountondji_RCCS80.pdf

Jaumont, F. (2016). *Unequal partners: American foundations and higher education development in Africa*. Palgrave Macmillan.

Kozma, C., & Calero-Medina, C. (2019). The role of South African researchers in intercontinental collaboration. *Scientometrics, 121*, 1293–1321. https://doi.org/10.1007/s11192-019-03230-9

Kraemer-Mbula, E., Vaitsas, C., & Essegbey, G. O. (2018). The dynamics of EU–Africa research and innovation cooperation programmes. In A. Cherry, J. Haselip, G. Ralphs, & I. Wagner (Eds.), *Africa-Europe research and innovation cooperation*. Palgrave Macmillan.

Mouton, J., Basson, I., Blanckenberg, J., Boshoff, N., Prozesky, H., Redelinghuys, H., Treptow, R., van Lill, M., & van Niekerk, M. (2019). *The state of South African research enterprise. DST-NRF centre of excellence in scientometrics and science*. Technology and Innovation Policy Stellenbosch University.

Sonnenwald, D. H. (2007). Scientific collaboration. In B. Cronin (Ed.), *Annual review of information science and technology* (Vol. 41, pp. 643–681). Information Today.

Sooryamoorthy, R. (2013a). Publication productivity and collaboration of researchers in South Africa: New empirical evidence. *Scientometrics, 98*(1), 531–545. https://doi.org/10.1007/s11192-013-0990-z

Sooryamoorthy R. (2013b). Scientific collaboration in South Africa. *South Africa Journal of Science, 109*(5–6), 1–5. http://dx.doi. org/10.1590/sajs.2013/a0016

Sooryamoorthy, R., & Shrum, W. (2007). Does the internet promote collaboration and productivity? Evidence from the scientific community in South Africa. *Journal of Computer-Mediated Communication, 12*(2), 733–751. https://doi.org/10.1111/j.1083-6101.2007.00347.x

PART 5

Conclusion

CHAPTER 12

Opportunities and Challenges in Higher Education Cooperation between the EU and Four Continents: Towards a Typology of the Internationalisation of Higher Education

Elizabeth Balbachevsky, Yuzhuo Cai, Heather Eggins and Svetlana Shenderova

Abstract

In this concluding chapter, we draw lessons from the higher education cooperation between the EU and the four countries of Brazil, China, Russia and South Africa. Each of the previous chapters in this book provided a variety of good practices, challenges and suggestions. We aim to bring together these insights and reflect on these experiences through building a new typology for the internationalisation of higher education from the perspective of policy logics. The typology helps in understanding the dynamics and tensions between the global, national and institutional levels of higher education cooperation between the EU and the third countries.

Keywords

internationalisation of higher education – university cooperation – typology of the internationalisation of higher education – higher education cooperation – EU – Brazil – China – Russia – South Africa

1 Introduction

In this concluding chapter, we try to draw lessons from studies of higher education cooperation between the EU and the four countries of Brazil, China, Russia and South Africa. Each of the previous chapters in this book provided a variety of practices, challenges and suggestions. In this conclusion, we aim to bring together these insights and reflect on these experiences. In doing so, we propose a new framework to enable us to understand the interplay between the university and the logics of higher education regarding the new developments in internationalisation. In order to achieve this goal, we also propose a new typology of supra-(EU) and national policies related to the internationalisation of higher education. Our typology explores the consistency between the policies for the internationalisation of higher education with, respectively, national strategies in economics and politics. In doing so, the typology helps us to understand the dynamics and tensions between global, national and institutional levels in higher education cooperation between the EU and the countries with the most developed higher education systems in their continents.

2 Revisiting Internationalisation of Higher Education from a Policy Logics Perspective

The modern university was born under the sign of internationalisation, typically reflected in the mobility of scholars, travelling from one centre of learning to another, from one kingdom to another, connecting the north of Africa, Middle-East and Europe. This academic mobility comprises one of the building blocks of the history of universities (Perkin, 2007). Since the Humboldtian revolution, when science became an integral part of the university's institutional fabric, international cooperation and academic mobility have become significant parts of the contemporary university. It can be argued that the science emanating from the global web of knowledge production (Balbachevsky & Kohtamäki, 2020) indicates that internationalisation is always present. It is an integral part of the inner dynamics of the contemporary university which provides global knowledge as a public good in cooperation with international partners.

This bottom-up movement towards internationalisation is a kaleidoscope of separate entities, formed and reformed within each department, laboratory or division. It answers to the priorities posed by disciplines and research areas and responds to the particular agendas of collaboration developed by individual academics. As such, its dynamics follow the garbage-can model of organisational choice, as proposed by Cohen et al. (1972).

Since the end of the twentieth century, governments and international organisations have added a new layer of policies trying to guide and steer the internationalisation of higher education – for their own purposes (Mäkinen, 2016). In the new environment, knowledge diplomacy is becoming increasingly essential and external economic and political interests become a major driver of the processes of university internationalisation. Knight and de Wit

(2018) claim that since the 1990s, the meanings, rationales, and approaches to internationalisation have evolved to respond to the new pressures that are coming from governments, international institutions and society in general.

In the past 20 years, there have been various attempts to categorise the internationalisation of higher education according to its drivers, functions, and activities. (e.g., Cheng, Cheung, & Ng, 2016; de Wit et al., 2015; Edelstein & Douglass, 2012; Knight, 2004; Zha, 2003). Nevertheless, most of these approaches are from the perspective of the higher education sector itself.

To address this situation, Brandenburg, de Wit, Jones, Leask, and Drobner (2020) have developed the concept of 'internationalisation in higher education for society'. The authors explicitly use this concept when referring to policies guided by the goal of bringing benefits to the wider community, at home or abroad, through international or intercultural education, research, service and engagement.

Is it possible to use the perspective of 'internationalisation in higher education for society' to compare the experiences of higher education cooperation between the EU and other countries? We believe it has the potential to do so, especially when the focus is the future development of internationalisation. However, in comparing the experiences and building synergies among them, it is necessary to explore this concept in depth and develop a typology for understanding the main drivers that shape the national policies sustaining the internationalisation of higher education. Thus, inspired by the insights of these book contributors, we propose a two-dimensional typology for the internationalisation of higher education (see Table 12.1).

In this typology, the first dimension refers to the degree of alignment between policies for the internationalisation of higher education and the national drivers for international political cooperation. The second dimension is the alignment between policies supporting the internationalisation of higher education with the country's drivers for international economic cooperation.

Thus, when policies supporting the internationalisation of higher education are aligned with both the national drivers for international political cooperation and economic cooperation, we have a process of *higher education internationalisation for broad societal engagement*. When these processes are mainly guided by the country's drivers for economic cooperation but loosely linked with the country's drivers for international political cooperation, the internationalisation of higher education is mostly designed to *attract global talent and advanced knowledge*. On the other hand, when the country's goals for international political cooperation are the main driver shaping the policies for the internationalisation of higher education, we have the *internationalisation of higher education for expanding soft power* (Nye, 1990). Finally, our

TABLE 12.1 Typology for the internationalisation of higher education: political economy drivers

		Alignment between internationalisation of higher education policies and the country's drive for international political cooperation	
		High	Low
Alignment between the internationalisation of higher education policies and the country's drive for international economic cooperation	High	Internationalisation of higher education for broad societal engagement	Internationalisation of higher education for global talent and advanced knowledge
	Low	Internationalisation of higher education for expanding soft power	Internationalisation of higher education for enhancing the global reputation of higher education institutions and systems

typology allows us to identify a fourth, quite common situation, when the policies for the internationalisation of higher education are not aligned with the country's strategies for international economic or political cooperation. In this situation, internationalisation only serves the country's higher education institutions, thereby promoting *the system's higher education global reputation.*

Our typology produces a new perspective to re-examine the four rationalities commonly acknowledged in the literature (e.g., Knight, 2004; Zha, 2003) for policies supporting the internationalisation of higher education, namely academic rationale, cultural/social rationale, economic rationale, and political rationale. While the current studies often juxtapose these rationales when analysing the internationalisation of higher education, our typology enables us to analyse the consistency and/or tensions between different rationales or policy logics, which refer to institutional logics underlying public policies (Cai, Normann, Pinheiro, & Sotarauta, 2018).

The two dimensions in the typology entail three kinds of policy logics suggested by Zha (2003). The policies for the internationalisation of higher education are underlined by the academic and cultural/social logics, 'reflected in measures like the mobility of students and staff, the improvement of the quality of education, a greater compatibility of study programmes and degrees, and enhanced knowledge of other languages and cultures, seem all to be derived from the overarching economic rationale of strengthening human resources for international competitiveness' (Zha, 2003, p. 254). The political logics of internationalisation policies are related to 'issues concerning the country's position and role as a nation in the world, e.g. security, stability and peace, ideological influence, etc.' (Zha, 2003, p. 252). The economic logics refer 'to objectives related to either the long-term economic effects, where the internationalisation of higher education is seen as a contribution to the skilled human resources needed for international competitiveness of the nation, and where foreign graduates are seen as keys to the country's trade relations, or to direct economic benefits, e.g. institutional income and net economic effect of foreign students, etc.' (Zha, 2003, pp. 252–253).

The literature usually implies that the overarching economic goals at the national level drive the institutional level activities (Knight, 2004; Zha, 2003). However, there is little research to scrutinise these links. The suggested typology serves as a lens to make a more comprehensive analysis of the experiences of the EU and the four countries in their international higher education cooperation (Figure 12.1).

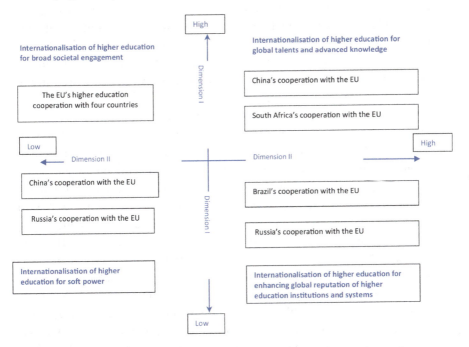

Dimension I: Alignment between internationalisation of higher education and national drives for economic cooperation
Dimension II: Alignment between internationalisation of higher education and national drives for political cooperation

FIGURE 12.1 Policy logics of internationalisation of higher education: The EU and four countries

3 Policy Logics of internationalisation of Higher Education: The EU and Four Countries

The topic of this volume, a study of collaboration between the European Union and countries within the four continents of Africa, South America, Europe and Asia, enables us to examine in detail the range of higher education cooperative initiatives seen there. The centrality of the EU is paramount, and the goals of the EU are a key element in the particular expression of internationalisation displayed in those relationships.

The founding treaty of the European Union, entitled the Treaty on the Functioning of the European Union, was signed in Rome on March 25th, 1957. The goals of the European Union are to promote peace, disseminate its values, promote the well-being of its citizens, and to proffer freedom, security and justice without internal borders. It is noteworthy that the original underlying political objective was to strengthen Franco-German cooperation and banish the risk of war. It offered a single market for goods, labour, services and capital. Although it was originally established as the European Economic Community, as it developed it moved to becoming, in 1992, the European Union, with the Maastricht Treaty. Among other goals were those to combat social exclusion and discrimination, promote scientific and technological progress, and respect cultural and linguistic diversity. These goals and related values of human dignity, freedom, democracy, equality, the rule of law and human rights have formed the basis of the EU and are laid out in the Lisbon Treaty and the EU Charter of fundamental rights. Indeed, the EU was awarded the Nobel Peace Prize in 2012 for advancing these causes within Europe.

Part Five, The Union's External Action, establishes in Article 205 that EU foreign policy must be in accordance with the general principles laid down in Chapter 1 of Title Five. Title III, Cooperation with Third Countries and Humanitarian Aid, states in Article 208 'Union development cooperation policy shall have, as its primary objective, the reduction and, in the long term, the eradication of poverty'. Article 209 states that "the Union may conclude with third countries and competent international organisations any agreement helping to achieve the objectives referred to in Article 208 of this Treaty. Thus, one can argue that the major drive for EU internationalisation policies in higher education with third countries is that of promoting social goals. The establishment of the Bologna Process in 1999 explored the relevance of pursuing the aim of social cohesion in higher education; the Erasmus Mundus programme 2003 established a prestigious international study programme which marked a concern for quality and the rise of international cooperation in higher education and 'A Strategy for the External Dimension of the Bologna Process' in 2007 underlined the concern for quality and the rise of international cooperation in higher education. This was emphasised by the Modernisation Agenda of 2006 with the theme of the 'internationalisation of higher education'. As Burquel and Ballesteros, the authors of Chapter 3, point out 'the EU as a global player ... has long underpinned interventions in education and training as a vehicle for peace and stability'.

This is not to say that this is the only driver of the EU's interests in international collaboration with higher education, but it is of major importance. Our thesis is that the chosen countries examined in this volume exhibit other drivers, which may take precedence in particular countries. Our typology takes account of this and offers a new approach to understanding the nuances of international collaboration between the EU and the third countries considered here. Thus, although the EU clearly has interests in the other quadrants of the typology, the positioning of the EU itself in the quadrant relating to the internationalisation of higher education for broad societal engagement has to be recognised as a key driver (Figure 12.1).

As discussed in Chapter 4 by Sá and Martinez, the primary rationale guiding Brazilian policies supporting internationalisation is related to increasing the exposure of the internal environment of the universities to new dynamics present in global higher education (Figure 12.1). The main instruments supporting this approach are fellowships focused mostly on young academics with the aim of providing these academics with some international experience and opportunities for networking. Even when the country took on board new policy instruments – such as the PrInt programme, which tried to support universities' efforts to establish internationalisation, the main focus was left to the universities to design, and its primary goal was to connect domestic academics (and domestic students) with the global web of science and foreign universities.

China is a compelling case, in that its experiences are located in two quadrants, as shown in Figure 12.1. As indicated by Cai and Zheng in Chapter 5, as well as some other recent studies (Cai, 2019), China's international cooperation with the EU is changing. Two decades ago, its main goal was the exchange of students and academics. Today, the country's policies focus on a deeper level of education and research collaboration, representing a new feature of the cooperation. First, one can identify the traditional policies supporting the mobility of Chinese students and scholars in the EU, the efforts for developing joint degree programmes in cooperation with universities from the EU, and programmes for attracting researchers from the EU to work in China. These efforts can be classified as ' the internationalisation of higher education for global talents and advanced knowledge'.

However, China's ambitious endeavour to host a large number of international students reflects another dimension in the policies supporting the internationalisation of Chinese higher education – internationalisation of higher education for soft power. After ten years implementing China's plan for hosting 500,000 international students, the country has not only achieved the goal but also become the host of the second-largest international student population, after the USA. This move is more closely associated with China's soft power strategy; as noted by Cai (2020), 'China's illusion of its international students is based on the idea that they return to their home countries after graduation and become the "ambassadors" to convey the image of China'.

Russia, being the only EU neighbour amongst our cases, supports cooperation with the EU to such extent as it deems necessary for enhancing the global reputation of national higher education institutions and the higher education system (Figure 12.1). In Chapter 6 of this book Shenderova points out that Russia uses the internationalisation of higher education in order to compete with Europe globally for international students from the third countries. In particular, Russian universities increase their attractiveness and reliability by cooperating with partners from the EU in collaborative degree programmes, by providing an option for students to earn two degrees, one in Russia and one in the EU member state. Russia tries to revive the soft power which USSR had, and restore its regional priorities by turning to the global East and South. Students from these regions are primarily considered as future 'ambassadors' for Russia in their countries; they provide sources of income for Russian higher education institutions and global talent for the Russian economy.

The South African study, explored in Chapter 11, makes a strong case for that country's inclusion in the quadrant relating to the internationalisation of higher education for global talent and advanced knowledge (Figure 12.1). Bilateral Science and Technology Cooperation Agreements have been concluded with the EU since 1996. The opportunity for research collaboration is seen as 'a significant part of emerging research communities' (Grossetti et al., 2014). The report by Mouton et al. (2019) on 'The State of South African Research Enterprise' makes it clear that South Africa, which is already the leading African nation in terms of research, wishes to establish itself as a global player, and sees international research collaboration with the EU as a means to gaining more visibility. As the authors indicate 'collaboration provides a pathway to global impact'.

4   Connections between Policy Logics and Institutional Practices

While the new layer of policy initiatives has become more salient in recent years, it is unclear if there is real alignment between the drivers that move the academics, and the drivers coming from political, social/cultural and economic motivation. Of course, a well-aligned policy, supported by enough links with the inner academic drivers for internationalisation, should have leverage to pull the internal dynamics towards the priorities specified by the policy, as an expression of the overall social expectations for the university. However, the case studies presented in this volume show that building the links between the policy and the academic logics should not be taken for granted. This intersection is crucial, even if usually disregarded by the literature. Without a clear connection between the dynamics inside the academic community and the signals coming from the policy system, the impact of the policy initiatives on university life could be at the very least ineffective or even disruptive.

As explored by Sá and Martinez in this book (Chapter 4), in the Brazilian experience the bottom-up initiatives coming from academics (and now, more and more, also from students) represent a relevant part of the country's entire efforts for internationalisation. As discussed above, these choices reflect more on the individual research agenda and personal interests than on the policy rationale behind the public support for academic and student mobility. This situation blurs the central rationality of these policies in the eyes of the external stakeholders and makes them particularly vulnerable every time the country faces an economic downturn. On the other hand, as explored by Granja and Carneiro in Chapter 8, also relating to the Brazilian experience, a government programme with a top-down design, without building enough links with the university's inner drivers, can be disruptive. It could not only be ineffective in cost-benefit terms but could even break down prior initiatives taken at the university level.

Russian experience, as shown by Ustyuzhantseva, Zvonareva, Hortsman, and Popova in Chapter 10, describes the reality of the tradition of top-bottom management, combined with the lack of academic freedom in Russian higher education institutions, which hampers the sustainability of internationalisation activities. As Shenderova mentions in Chapter 6, the multiplication of authorities responsible for internationalisation and the misunderstanding of national traditions of academic affairs distort the picture for national policy makers, negatively affecting the reliability of Russian higher education institutions, and undermines their opportunities to develop the internationalisation of higher education in cooperation with the EU partners.

China has stronger governmental steering of Chinese higher education institutions, and, therefore, is likely to have tighter connections between Chinese higher education policies and implementation at institutional level. As discussed in Chapter 5, the practices of internationalisation in Chinese higher education institutions basically echo the national policies of the internationalisation of higher education. The Chinese students' study experience in Chapter 9 is a good example of implementation of the Chinese policies of encouraging Chinese students to study abroad. Nevertheless, a discrepancy between the national policy and institutional practice can appear.

South African policy and interests lie particularly in building up research collaboration between its research institutions and universities and those of the EU, thus enhancing the status of its higher education system. It has also found the Erasmus scheme valuable, as a means of exchanging global talent, and enabling its scholars to contribute to global research. South Africa is the leading hub in Africa for the mobility of staff and students: its links with the EU enhance that position.

5 Opportunities and Challenges in Higher Education Cooperation between the EU and the Chosen Countries

When analysing the opportunities and challenges in the EU and China in relation to higher education cooperation, Cai (2013) proposed using the alignment between the EU's expectations and China's interests in the internationalisation of higher education as an analytical framework. We now suggest modifying the approach to fit it into the framework of policy logics for the internationalisation of higher education. In particular, our opportunity-challenge analysis will be based primarily on the following two issues. First, to what extent is one country's policy logics for the internationalisation of higher education compatible with those of the EU? According to our argument, the higher the level of compatibility of the policy logics of both sides, the more opportunities for cooperation there will be. Second, to what extent can the compatibilities at the policy level be realised at higher education institutions? Both loose and tight coupling between the national policies and institutional practices pose different challenges in international higher education cooperation.

In Table 12.2, the policy logics of the internationalisation of higher education between the EU and the four countries are juxtaposed and the compatibility of the logics between both sides are discussed. Although the logics compatibilities are generally high in each of the dimensions of academic, economic and political as indicated in Table 12.2, one of the challenges in the internationalisation of higher education in the four countries is that the three policy logics are not well integrated at the national level. This is exemplified in the case of China in Chapter 5, and in the case of Russia in Chapter 6.

For example, misunderstanding of the peculiarities of the Russian higher education system during the Bologna reforms combined with current political

TABLE 12.2 Compatibility of policy logics of the internationalisation of higher education between the EU and the four countries

Policy logics	Policies in the EU	Policies in the four countries	Compatibility analysis and extent of cooperation opportunities with the EU
Academic and cultural/social logics	Recruiting more international students to study in European universities (all four countries) Exporting educational programmes and services to other countries (China, Russia) Enhancing education and research cooperation with foreign universities (Brazil, China, and South Africa) Sending more EU students to study in foreign higher education (Brazil, China, and South Africa)	Encouraging students to study abroad (all four countries) Meeting growing demands for higher education by importing high quality education resources from advanced higher education systems (China, Russia, and South Africa) Increasing international reputation and competitiveness through cooperation with (prestigious) EU universities (China, Russia, South Africa) Attracting EU students (China) Development of complicated internationalisation activities such as collaborative degree programmes (China, Russia) Invitation of the EU researchers to enhance national reputation in the world (China, Russia, South Africa)	High (the activities of both sides supplementing each other): China Low (the activities of both countries meet serious resistance of external institutional environment): Russia Low: South Africa hampered by economic challenges and historic cultural inequalities

(*cont.*)

TABLE 12.2 Compatibility of policy logics of the internationalisation of higher education between the EU and the four countries (cont.)

Policy logics	Policies in the EU	Policies in the four countries	Compatibility analysis and extent of cooperation opportunities with the EU
	EU and Russia: Supporting internationalisation activities as the tools of people-to-people contacts, but cutting the general support measures due to political EU-Russia tensions	Increasing connections between domestic science community and the international community (all four countries) Increasing visibility and reputation of domestic higher education institutions due to cooperation with the EU universities (all four countries)	
Economic logics	The EU member states welcome international students as global talents from four countries to areas that are affected by a potential labour shortage.	Developing/supporting collaborative research networks targeting global and/or local needs (all four countries) Invitation to the EU students and researchers as global talent to areas that are affected by a national labour shortage (China, Russia)	High (Although both sides are competing for global talent, the people to be targeted are different): China Low: (non-EU priorities in global talent search due to economic reasons) Russia, South Africa
Political logics	Promoting mutual understanding	Education export for distributing influence, values and ideologies to other states (China, Russia) Student mobility and exchange programmes targeting the promotion of other countries' goodwill toward the promoting country (Brazil, Russia)	High: (both partners are focused in promoting mutual understanding): Brazil, South Africa Low: China (competing ideologies), Russia (foreign policy tensions)

tensions have negatively influenced higher education cooperation (Shenderova, 2020). Despite the low EU-Russia alignment in our Typology, the coexistence of Russia and the EU within the Bologna Process, and the reassessment of the significance of geographical neighbourliness after the Corona crisis, combined with the ability of individual researchers to interact on a friendly basis (Ustyuzantseva et al., Chapter 10, this volume), still offer hope of increasing Russia's cooperation with the EU in the future.

Most challenges in higher education cooperation between the EU and the four countries are at the level of higher education institutions. This can be due to the fact that the practices of internationalisation associated with higher education institutions are loosely coupled with the national policy drivers of international cooperation with respect to higher education. In other words, it is difficult to realise national policy logics at the institutional level. For instance, in Brazil and in Russia, the lack of connection and understanding between the Federal policy supporting internationalisation and practices at the institutional level ended up in disrupting some local successful experiences and limited the number of opportunities for deepening the cooperation. Russia and Brazil demonstrated a low level of readiness in the authorities and national policy makers to discuss internationalisation policies and support measures within the national academic community until these measures become obligatory. This trend, which is based in national top to bottom traditions of sector governance, increases the transaction costs of national policy implementation: it impedes and depreciates multiple efforts of higher education institutions both in the chosen countries and in their EU partners. In the systems where higher education institutions tend to closely follow national policies, the challenge could be that the centralised policy finds it difficult to accommodate and support over one thousand higher education institutions with various characteristics and diverse needs in delivering international higher education cooperation. As a result, participation in internationalisation activities can become more of a personal benefit than a public good which allows the global academic community to produce new knowledge-based research.

With the help of our typology it is possible to systematise the rationales guiding the efforts of both European and third countries. These rationales guide both the kind of commitments and the expectations both partners have when engaging in an agreement for advancing internationalisation. Awareness of the main drivers sustaining each partner's policies for higher education internationalisation is crucial for the success of any initiative. And our typology helps to map some relevant dimensions which guide the preferences of both partners. In order to succeed, a partnership does not necessarily have to share similar goals. As our book shows, it is possible to build up collaborative efforts in situations where each partner sustains a different agenda. However, a clear understanding of these differences helps each partner to have a more realistic expectation of what will be the main results of the initiative. This realism is necessary for building sound and lasting collaboration agreements.

6   Concluding Remarks

This study has examined the interconnections between the European Union and the chosen countries on two levels, those of the particular national policies and those of the institutions in four continents. The objectives of the EU have remained constant since its inception: the interpretation and delivery of these objectives are seen to vary country by country and institution by institution. The ability to deliver those international objectives can depend on many factors: the economic health of the country, the particular system of higher education provision in the country, the political will of individual governments, and the level of autonomy of institutions. Where the objectives of the EU are in accord with national and institutional interests, with a high level of alignment of international policies, then one can find internationalisation of higher education for broad societal engagement, for global talent and advanced knowledge, for economic cooperation and the expansion of soft power, and for the enhancement of the global reputation of both the higher education systems and individual institutions.

The balance of interests can change over time, with changes of national government, and changes in institutional focus, but the proposed typology holds. This nuanced approach to a fuller understanding of the complex relationships between the European Union and the countries of the four continents will, we hope, enhance our understanding of the phenomenon of internationalisation in higher education.

We, the editors, are finalising our book in the midst of the Coronavirus pandemic. Located in distant cities, on different continents, being divided by oceans and closed national borders, we nevertheless were able to work together online in cooperation. Our book itself, and the comprehensive insights provided by our valued contributors, confirm that the internationalisation of higher education has lasting effects when based on research cooperation. The pandemic situation created by the global spread of COVID-19 poses a difficult challenge for the internationalisation of higher education. Everywhere universities have been forced to close down face-to-face teaching, and to move learning activities to online mode with different degrees of success. International mobility is facing a worse situation, with international students no longer able to travel abroad, and confined to their home countries.

However, our experience highlights a core fact of internationalisation: the importance of building global academic networks based on research collaboration. The efforts and insights of individual academics and research groups, who are working globally to undertake research and share their results with colleagues, students and the public, is well illustrated by the worldwide research currently being undertaken to seek a vaccine. Expanded online communication is also enabling academics from all disciplines to join in global webinars, online conferences and public talks to share research findings relating to all areas of academic life.

COVID-19 has brought global changes to internationalisation; it is expected to reallocate the flows of international students and academics, to increase distance and blended learning and to boost intraregional study (Johnson, 2020). Although there are losses, the current crisis provides new opportunities. The European Higher Education Area still acts as a major means of connection which unites the countries of Europe and provides bridges that support transcontinental cooperation, thus offering a focus for continuing forms of internationalisation in higher education.

References

Adelman, C. (2009). *The Bologna process for U.S. eyes: Re-learning higher education in the age of convergence.* Institute for Higher Education Policy. https://files.eric.ed.gov/fulltext/ED504904.pdf

Balbachevsky, E., & Kohtamäki, V. (2020). University, science and the new (and old) academic roles: Inner sources of institutional resilience. *Sociologias 22*(54), 64–86. http://doi.org/10.1590/15174522-99512

Brandenburg, U., Wit, H. d., Jones, E., Leask, B., & Drobner, A. (2020). *Internationalisation in Higher Education for Society (IHES). Concept good practice.* DAAD.

Cai, Y. (2013). Erasmus Mundus joint programme and EU's strategy on higher education cooperation with China – Lessons from the MARIHE programme. *Journal of European Higher Education Area, 2,* 95–112.

Cai, Y., Normann, R., Pinheiro, R., & Sotarauta, M. (2018). Economic specialization and diversification at the country and regional level: Introducing a conceptual framework to study innovation policy logics. *European Planning Studies, 26*(12), 2407–2426. doi:10.1080/09654313.2018.1529142

Cheng, Y. C., Cheung, A. C. K., & Ng, S. W. (2016). Internationalisation of higher education: Conceptualization, typology and issues. In Y. C. Cheng, A. C. K. Cheung, & S. W. Ng (Eds.), *Internationalization of higher education: The case of Hong Kong* (pp. 1–18). Springer Singapore.

Cohen, M. D., March, J. G., & Olsen, J. P. (1972). A garbage can model of organizational choice. *Administrative Science Quarterly*, 1–25. http://www.jstor.org/stable/2392088

de Wit, H., Hunter, F., & Coelen, R. (2015). Internationalisation of higher education in Europe: Future directions. In H. de Wit, F. Hunter, L. Howard, & E. Egron-Polak (Eds.), *Internationalisation of higher education* (pp. 273–280). European Union.

Edelstein, R. J., & Douglass, J. A. (2012, December 19). *Comprehending the international initiatives of universities: A taxonomy of modes of engagement and institutional logics*. CSHE Research and Occasional Papers.

Grossetti, M., Eckert, D., Gingras Y., Iégoul., Larivièrev., & Milard, B. (2014). Cities and the geographical deconcentration of scientific activity: A multilevel analysis of publications (1987–2007). *Urban Studies*, *51*(10), 2219–2234.

Johnson, J. (2020, April 20). Competition for overseas students is going to be fierce. *Financial Times*. https://www.ft.com/content/4912f032-74da-11ea-90ce-5fb6c07a27f2

Knight, J. (2004). Internationalization remodeled: Definition, approaches, and rationales. *Journal of Studies in International Education*, *8*(1), 5–31. doi:10.1177/1028315303260832

Knight, J., & de Wit, H. (2018). Internationalization of higher education: Past and future. *Internationalization of Higher Education: Past and Future*, *2018*(Fall). https://doi.org/10.6017/ihe.2018.95.10715

Mäkinen, S. (2016). In search of the status of an educational great power? Analysis of Russia's educational diplomacy discourse. *Problems of Post-Communism*, 1–14. https://doi.org/10.1080/10758216.2016.1172489

Mouton, J., Basson, I., Blanckenberg, J., Boshoff, N., Prozesky, H., Redelinghuys, H., Treptow, R., van Lill, M., & van Niekerk, M. (2019). *The state of South African research enterprise*. DST-NRF Centre of Excellence in Scientometrics and Science, Technology and Innovation Policy Stellenbosch University.

Nye, J. S. (1990). Soft power. *Foreign Policy*, *80*, 153–171.

Perkin, H. (2007). History of universities. In J. J. F. Forest & P. G. Altbach (Eds.), *International handbook of higher education* (pp. 159–205). Springer.

Shenderova, S. (2020). Finnish-Russian double degree programmes: When partner's responsibilities become a challenge for internationalisation. In B. Broucker, V. Borden, T. Kallenberg, & C. Milsom (Eds.), *Responsibility of higher education systems: What? Why? How?* (pp. 185–203). Brill | Sense. https://doi.org/10.1163/9789004436558_011

Zha, Q. (2003). Internationalization of higher education: Towards a conceptual framework. *Policy Futures in Education*, *1*(2), 248–270. doi:10.2304/pfie.2003.1.2.5

Index

Alliance of the New Silk Road   79

Bologna Process   x, 37, 40–42, 45, 47, 87, 93, 164, 173, 204, 211
Brazilian Coordination for the Improvement of Higher Education Personnel Foundation (CAPES)   30, 33, 55–58, 61–63, 131–134, 136
BRIC countries   183–185, 189, 190, 192, 193
Bridging Health, Innovations, and Societies: Education Capacity-Building in Eastern European Neighbouring Areas (BIHSENA)   164–168, 170–179

China   XI, 5, 10, 21, 25, 31, 42, 68–81, 87, 115, 131, 154, 156, 183, 186, 189, 192, 199, 205–209
China Scholarship Council (CSC)   17, 77
Cotonou agreement   118, 186
COVID-19 pandemia   212, 213

drives for internationalisation or higher education   19

ERASMUS Program   x, 22, 37, 38, 40, 42, 47, 70, 108,
ERASMUS+ Program   20, 29, 48, 74, 118–120, 164, 166
EU-China Higher Education Platform for Cooperation and Exchange (HEPCE)   76
Europe   x, xi, 4, 5, 8–10, 22, 24, 29, 30, 36–38, 40–45, 47, 53–55, 57–62, 73, 75–81, 86–88, 91, 108–111, 118–120, 134, 148, 155, 164, 172, 183, 190, 200, 204, 206, 213
European Higher Education Area (EHEA)   38–40, 42, 45, 46, 79, 87, 90–92, 110
European Research Area (ERA)   44, 46, 79
European Union   4, 11, 16, 20, 22, 28, 36, 37, 54, 63, 69, 73, 108, 109, 118, 130, 134–137, 140, 160, 183, 186, 190, 204, 212
EU-South Africa collaborative framework in higher education   120

global talents   4, 78, 160, 201, 202, 206, 208, 210, 212

higher education and research   15–19, 21, 23, 24, 26–29, 31, 32, 44, 108, 192
Horizon 2020 Program   38, 45, 77, 119, 185, 191–193

interdisciplinary projects   177, 179
international students   x, 21, 88, 131, 147, 206
internationalisation in higher education for society   4, 7, 201
internationalisation of higher education   x, xi, 3–11, 21, 70–72, 75, 86, 87, 90, 96, 121, 129, 147–149, 159, 199, 200–210, 212, 213

joint academic degree programmes   73

policy drivers   211
policy logics   200, 202–204, 206, 208–211
policy rationale   x, 207

Russia   XI, 5, 10, 38, 39, 87–100, 164–169, 172–174, 176, 177, 179, 183, 189, 192, 199, 206, 208, 210, 211
Russian Academic Excellence Project 5–100   94

Science without Borders programme   11, 57, 129–131, 134
Silk Road policy   78
societal engagement   201, 202, 205, 212
soft power   17, 20, 23, 63, 88, 91, 171, 201, 202, 206, 212
South Africa   XI, 5, 10, 25, 42, 87, 107–109, 111–122, 182–193, 199, 204, 206, 208–210

TEMPUS-TACIS programme   93
transaction costs of internationalisation   92, 93, 98, 100, 211
typology of internationalisation of higher education   7, 199, 201–203, 205, 211

University of Campinas (UNICAMP)   130, 137–139

Printed in the United States
By Bookmasters